Coats & Clark's
SEWING BOOK
Newest methods from A to Z

Coats & Clark's
SEWING BOOK

Newest Methods from A to Z

Published by the
EDUCATIONAL BUREAU
of Coats & Clark Inc.
430 Park Avenue,
New York, N.Y. 10022

Contents

Dear Home-Sewer,
  Dear Reader   7
Following Through—
  Picture Story   8
Alterations 11
Assembling a Garment 15
Backing or Underlining 18
Basting 19
Belt Buckles 21
Belt Loops 22
Belts 23
Bias 25
Buttonholes 32
Button Loops 40
Buttons 42
Casings 45
Collars 46
Corners 49

Cuffs 49
Cutting 50
Darts 55
Decoration 57
Easing 63
Equipment 64
Fabrics 68
Facings 80
Fasteners 88
Fitting a Garment 89
Gathers and Shirring 91
Grain in Fabric 92
Gussets 93
Hand-Sewing 96
Hems 98
Interfacing 108
Lining 112
Machine-Stitching 114

Marking 120
Notions 124
Patterns 127
Plackets 146
Pleats 149
Pockets 154
Pressing 157
Seams and Seam Finishes 158
Sleeves 162
Stitch in Time 164
  (Mending)
Tailoring 171
Threads and Needles 194
Thread Loops 197
Tucks 199
Waistbands 200
Zippers 202
Index 217

DEAR HOME-SEWER, DEAR READER

We know a man—no sissy—who made a dress for his wife. He had never tangled with needle and thread before except, in his bachelor days, to sew on a button. But, sitting just a few desks from here, he got curious as to what all this sewing fuss was about. So, asking for no help, he puzzled through a pattern primer and a sewing machine manual. We haven't seen the dress— we can't tell you about fit and finish—but we have his word for it that his wife wore it at a party. So how did he do it?

Why, as we were saying, he read the directions:
. . . in the pattern layout
. . . in the pattern primer
. . . in the sewing machine manual.
Step by step, he followed them.
He took no shortcuts.
He didn't say: "I can't be bothered with those notches," or ". . . that marking," or ". . . that pressing."
He followed through.
Now, *anybody* can do that.
Anybody can read and follow directions.
Anybody can work step by step.
Anybody can shun shortcuts. (Professionals don't take them—why should you?)
Anybody can follow through.
But, alas, not everybody does. We can only hope, dear reader, that *you* will.

This book is meant to supplement, not take the place of, your pattern primer.

The methods given are the most up-to-date, chosen in every case because they work, save time and error, and give beautiful results. Paying attention to the details we bring out (we have simplified where we could)—measurements, alterations, marking, proper choice and sequence throughout—may slow you up at first, but how much time and annoyance it will save you later! Besides, a sewing job that is carefully prepared is finished when it looks least about to be so. Suddenly, it's done. And done correctly.

The book is arranged according to subject, in alphabetical order. Throughout, you will see references to subjects found elsewhere in the book. We have used different type to distinguish these references—SMALL CAPITALS indicate titles of chapters; **boldface** type indicates headings within chapters. Since every subject contains dozens of references to details that do not have headings of their own, there is an exhaustive Index at the back of the book. We have also, in every case, tried to give you the *why* of what you do, so you can understand and use the principle when you need it.

In general, just **follow through,** and you will be all right.

Educational Bureau
COATS & CLARK INC.

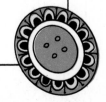

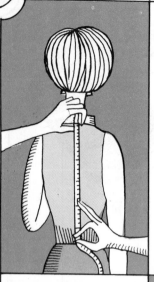

1 Take your measure-ments—you will need help for that. Then decide on the size and type of pattern that is right for you. See PATTERNS, p. 132.

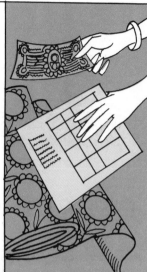

2 Buy pattern—fabric —notions. The pattern envelope tells you how much fabric and which notions you will need. Buy everything at the same time so you won't be held up. See FABRICS, THREAD AND NEEDLES, INTERFACING.

6 Mark garment sections—this is ex-tremely important and must always be done with great care. Try out on a scrap. See MARKING.

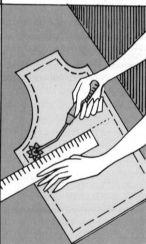

7 Look at the pattern primer to see how your garment will be put together. See ASSEMBLING A GARMENT.

8 Get the s machine ready— out time to te stitch length sion, pressur balance on the you are using MACHINE-STITCH

11 Try on the garment —with side seams and waist seam (if any) basted. There should be very few altera-tions, if any. Do not overfit! See FITTING A GARMENT.

12 Finish all machine-stitching and put in the zipper if you haven't done so before. See ZIPPERS.

PICTURE STORY

...t organized—
...re a cutting
...e, set up the
...g board and get
... necessary
...ment out. See
...MENT.

4 Study the pattern primer—pick out the pattern pieces you will use. Press pattern pieces, check for fit and make any necessary alterations. See PATTERNS, p. 133.

5 Cut out the garment—prepare the fabric, if necessary, straightening ends and grain. See FABRICS, p. 71. Pin pattern in place, following the cutting layout, and cut out. See CUTTING.

9 To baste or not to baste—let your judgment and experience be your guide; with an easy fabric and a simple pattern you may do very little basting but with a slippery silk or velveteen it may be better to baste. See BASTING.

10 Press as you sew—the pressing of seams as you finish each section is very important. You will hardly have any pressing to do at the end. See PRESSING and the various sewing techniques under individual headings.

Have someone ...
your hemline—in
... cases this is the
...way. See HEMS.

14 Do all the hand-sewing for the finishing touches—see HAND-SEWING, BUTTONS, BUTTONHOLES, HEMS, FACINGS.

15 A final pressing and you can wear it.

ALTERATIONS ON FINISHED GARMENTS

An alteration, not to be confused with a make-over, is an adjustment made in one detail of a garment that is otherwise satisfactory (though more than one alteration may, of course, be needed).

Except in the matter of hemlines, which are dictated by style, alterations are made for fit. They are often necessary in ready-to-wear (which does *not* mean that, if a model you like is not available in your size, you can alter an entirely wrong size to fit!). Alterations may also become necessary in your existing wardrobe, either because you have gained or lost weight, or because of a change in style—meaning usually hemlines.

WHAT CAN AND WHAT CANNOT BE ALTERED

The general principle here is that you can almost always *take in,* i.e., make smaller; *letting out* a garment in order to make it wider or longer may present serious problems.

For instance, you can always
. . . raise a hemline,
. . . raise a waistline,
. . . take in waist and hips,
. . . shorten sleeves,
. . . take in a plain faced neck,
. . . let out seams or hems *if* there is enough fabric *and* it is not marked, clipped or faded.

But you cannot
. . . lower a waistline (there isn't enough seam allowance),
. . . add width to shoulders or sleeve-caps, or to a back in one piece,
. . . let out seams or darts in fabrics that *mark,* because original seamlines will always show (wash-and-wear, tricot, taffeta, pile fabrics, etc.),
. . . let out seams where allowance is not wide enough or has been clipped through; or darts that are slashed, or punctured at the point,
. . . let down a hem when outside fabric has faded or hemline fold has left a permanent mark.

Certain alterations, while possible, are inadvisable. You would find it extremely involved to
. . . change an armhole with a sleeve,
. . . change shoulders and neck where there is a collar.

WHEN YOU ARE READY TO ALTER

If you have no one to help you with pinning and marking, you *can* do the job alone by pinning as seems necessary and trying on repeatedly. But it is both easier and safer with a bit of help.

If the zipper is not in a seam you are altering, so much the better. The presence of a zipper, however, should not discourage you. It is easy to take out (see **Ripping Out** at end of chapter on MACHINE-STITCHING); after this, you press the opening allowances smooth. When your new seamline is established, machine-baste opening together and proceed as directed in ZIPPERS. After a let-out, widen seam allowance with seam binding (p. 204).

The alterations that follow are the ones most often needed. When more than one is necessary (for instance, changing both hemline and side seams), study the steps in the instructions and combine them.

GENERAL ALTERATION IN WIDTH

An armhole-through-hips alteration in the width of a dress is simple, especially if the dress is one-piece, with zipper at center back (if there is a waistline seam, you remove waistline stay and open waist seam at points of alteration). If you take in or let out a fraction of an inch at each side seam and each dart or in-between seam (ignoring center front and back), it will add up to a sizeable change. For carrying through, see this alteration on a skirt on pages 13 and 14.

CHANGING A HEMLINE

This is the simplest and most common alteration. It can be made to **straighten,** to **raise,** or to **lower** the hemline. When you buy a garment, an alteration in the hem will often be marked for you at the store. For any change in the hemline:

• Take out old hem. In a manufactured garment, this may be chainstitched: Cut through stitching (1), free one loop and pull—in the right direction! Removing seam binding may or may not be necessary. Press hem open. Follow directions in HEMS. When lowering a hemline, it is sometimes necessary to make a **Faced Hem** (p. 104).

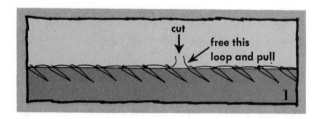

RAISING A WAISTLINE

(all around or in part)

• Put on dress. Tie a string around waist. Have someone mark correct waistline with pins along string.

• Take off dress. Even out pinned line; replace it with a line of baste-marking. If any points on skirt (center front and back, side seams, darts, etc.) do not automatically match corresponding points on bodice, be sure to thread-mark position of such points.

• Remove zipper, if any, or just bottom half, to clear waistline. Rip out waistline seam or that part of it to be altered. Press open.

• With skirt and bodice right sides together, match old waistline on skirt to new waistline on bodice and pin together (2), first at center front and center back;

then work toward side seams, matching marked points between. Because of the tapering of seams and darts, bodice may now be wider than skirt. Depending on fabric and design, you may be able to ease or gather bodice to skirt, or you may have to take in darts and side seams.

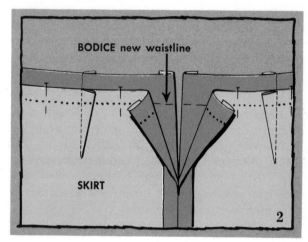

• After adjusting bodice to fit, pin again as described, baste and try on. Then stitch new waistline seam and trim away excess bodice fabric even with skirt seam allowance. Replace waistline stay; press. Replace all construction details (zipper, facing, hooks and eyes, buttons, etc.) as they were before.

DEEPENING BUST DARTS

(to correct underarm bagginess)

This alteration shortens side seams and gives greater fullness in bust.

• Try on garment. Tie a string around waist. Have someone check if back needs shortening; if so, mark correct waistline with pins. Pin bust darts deeper to take in excess fullness, tapering to nothing at point (don't worry about open tuck at wide end of darts— this will disappear later). Take off garment.

• Open waistline seam across back to about 2″ beyond side seams. Open side seams of bodice to within 1″ of armhole seam. Take out zipper, if any. Press opened seams.

• Transfer pin-markings on darts to wrong side. Mark new stitching line with ruler and chalk. Remove pins.

• Re-stitch darts and press. Re-stitch side seams, except any zipper opening (front will now be shorter than back), and press open.

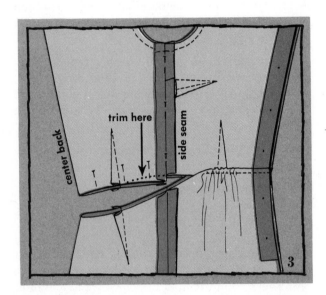

• Still wrong side out, fold bodice in half along center back line and pin side seams and bottom edge together, as shown. Cutting through both thicknesses, trim off excess fabric in back, either tapering as shown, or across back if back needs shortening (3).

• Pin and re-stitch waistline seam. Replace waistline stay, zipper, etc. Press.

TAKING IN NECKLINE

Unless you are an expert, and know how to re-cut a collar to fit, we do not advise this alteration except for a plain, faced neck. In this case, remove facing and turn to **The Gaping Neckline,** p. 90 in the chapter FITTING A GARMENT.

TAKING IN A SKIRT

This is normally done at side seams alone.

• Put on skirt. Have someone pin side seams deeper (taking in zipper, if any) from waist down, so that skirt fits comfortably and smoothly and hangs straight. Then sit down to make sure there is enough ease. Check on fit of waistband.

• Take off skirt. Transfer pin-markings to one thickness of fabric on wrong side. Remove stitching in hem for a few inches at each side seam. Remove zipper if it is in side seam. Waistband does not always need to be removed in its entirety; if it fits, remove stitching as needed to free side seams so that altered seamlines can taper to it. Press seam allowances together. Using chalk and yardstick, mark new seamlines parallel to old ones from hip down through hem.

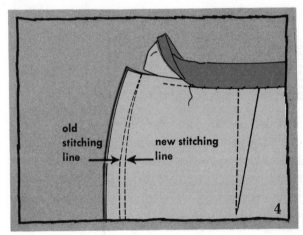

• Stitch new seams (4). Take out old stitching. Trim seams, finish as needed, and press open.

• Replace zipper and refinish hem. When replacing waistband, change position of closing as necessary.

WIDENING A SKIRT BY LETTING OUT

If fabric and seam allowances permit (see p. 11), this method is suitable for any skirt, and it is the only possible one for a straight skirt. It is usually done at side seams alone, but if there are more seams, it may be advisable to distribute the amount to be let out equally among them.

• Measure your hips (7″ below waist); add 2″ for ease. Measure your waist, adding nothing.

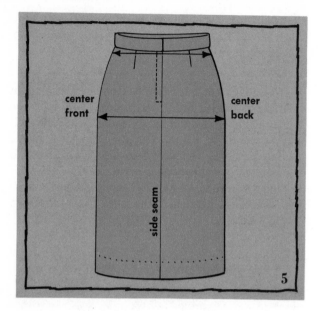

center front

center back

side seam

5

• To measure skirt, fold it lengthwise with side seams together, as shown. Measure from center front to back at waist and hips (5); double these amounts. The difference between skirt measurements and your own will be total amount of alteration.

• If alteration extends to waist, remove waistband. Remove zipper if it is in a seam to be altered. Remove stitching in hem for a few inches at seams to be let out.

• Do not take out seams. Press seam allowances together (as stitched).

• Using chalk and yardstick, mark new seamlines, going all the way through hem and either tapering to waistline if waistline is not altered, or carrying the alteration through as necessary. Amount to add at each seam will be:
. . . One-fourth of total alteration if only side seams are involved.
. . . Otherwise, one half of total alteration divided by number of seams.

• Stitch new seamlines. Remove old stitching. Press seams open.

• Replace zipper, adding seam binding to widen seam allowance (see ZIPPERS, p. 204). Refinish hem. If

waistband is included in alteration, lengthen it by adding a piece of fabric at end that will lap under. Replace and press.

WIDENING A SKIRT BY RAISING AT WAIST

A gored, flared, or A-line skirt that is long enough can be widened at waist and hips by raising it at the waistline (6).

• Put on skirt. Raise around waistline (opening zipper as necessary) until hips are fitted comfortably. Tie string snugly around waist and adjust skirt evenly. Have someone mark new waistline with pins along string.

• Take off skirt. Even out pin-marked line; replace it with line of baste-marking.

• Remove waistband and zipper. Press.

• Trim away top of skirt ⅝″ above new waistline marking.

• Replace zipper, opening seam at bottom to fit. If waistband fits "as is," it will be necessary either to ease new waistline to it, or to deepen seams and re-fit darts at top to fit. If waistband is too snug, lengthen it with a piece of fabric at end that will lap under. Replace and press.

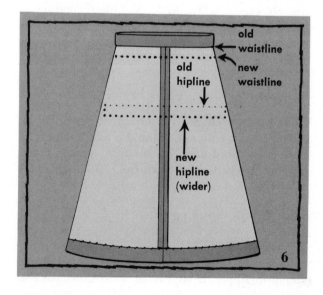

old waistline

old hipline

new waistline

new hipline (wider)

6

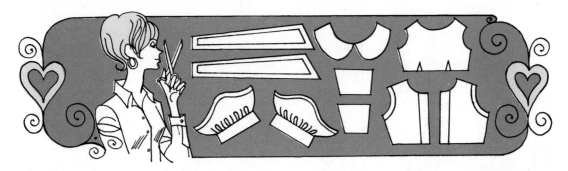

ASSEMBLING A GARMENT

Assembling a garment should be a simple, efficient procedure based on intelligent organization of work. All instruction sheets (primers) accompanying patterns follow to some degree a system called *unit construction,* the purpose of which is to eliminate waste motion and unnecessary handling.

You will find that in the two illustrated systems of unit construction that follow, the sequence is slightly different from that given in most pattern primers. This is, however, the simplest and most streamlined way of assembling a garment, **Unit Construction I** being used on most garments, **Unit Construction II** (sleeves sewn in before side seams are stitched) on children's and sports clothes. In both cases, we have applied the principle to a basic dress with bodice, collar, and set-in sleeves. Adapt the idea to your needs, which may be simpler—a one-piece dress, with kimono sleeves or none, will be but a single unit!

And remember that these picture stories just give you the sequence, the "When to." For the "How to" of sewing your garment, continue to consult your pattern primer, and this book.

UNIT CONSTRUCTION

The principle of unit construction is to do as much work as possible on one garment unit (garment part) before attaching it to another unit—in fact, to complete it when possible; and to complete all the small units (sleeves, collar, belt, patch pockets) first, so that work on the large ones (bodice, jacket, or other) can proceed without interruption.

Before cutting, you have, of course, made any basic alterations necessary, on the pattern. Small alterations after that can be made before attaching the small units to the large ones (see FITTING A GARMENT, p. 89). A skirt and bodice can be pin- or thread-basted together to be tried on, then separated before you proceed.

Practical Procedure

• After cutting and marking, sort the cut pieces into a pile, with the pieces to be used first on top (see picture sequence). Put all the small units together. The skirt is usually prepared first, to have it out of the way (when the skirt is separate, it can be finished completely). If, however, small units (such as patch pockets) are to be attached to it, these are completed first, and then are applied to the skirt before it is put together.

• Do all you can to one garment part (unit) before attaching it to another. See the picture sequences—in a bodice you not only put in the darts before stitching shoulder seams, but attach interfacing, make bound buttonholes, etc.

• Keep garment fresh and unwrinkled by hanging up each unit as it is completed: pin skirt to hanger, hang up top when shoulder seams are stitched. A coat box is handy to store pieces, finished and unfinished, that cannot be hung.

• The final steps (zipper insertion, hem, etc.) are done after garment is assembled, as indicated in the picture sequences on pp. 16–17.

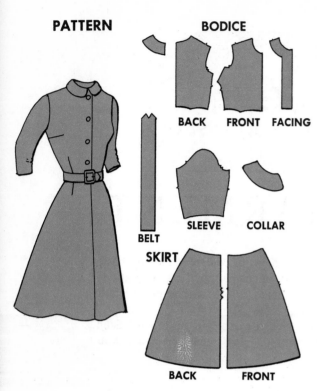

PATTERN

BODICE

BACK   FRONT   FACING

SLEEVE   COLLAR

BELT

SKIRT

BACK   FRONT

UNIT CONSTRUCTION I

1 Complete the skirt front.
2 Complete the skirt back.
3 Join skirt front and back, leaving zipper opening open.
4 Finish belt.
5 Finish sleeves, including hem or cuff.
6 Prepare facing.
7 Finish collar.
8 Complete bodice front. Make buttonholes if bound.
9 Complete bodice back.
10 Stitch shoulder seams.
11 Attach collar and facing. Tack facing to shoulder seams.
12 Stitch side seams, leaving zipper opening open.
13 Set in sleeves.
14 Stitch bodice to skirt. Apply zipper. Finish bound buttonholes or make worked buttonholes. Make hem. Make belt carriers (if any). Sew on buttons.

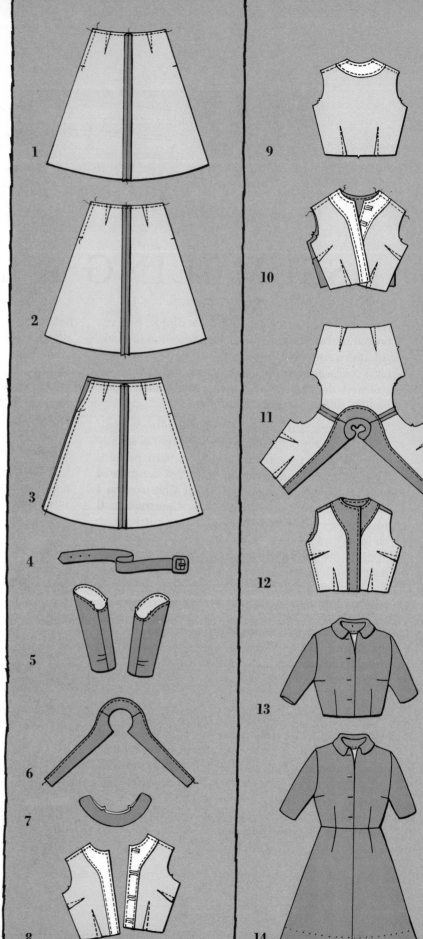

PATTERN

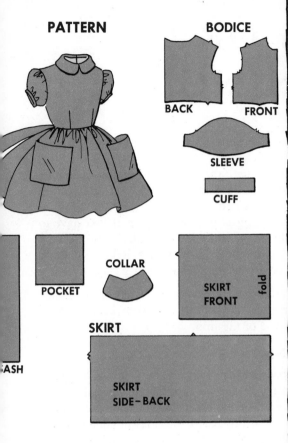

BODICE

BACK   FRONT

SLEEVE

CUFF

COLLAR

POCKET

SKIRT
FRONT

fold

SKIRT

SKIRT
SIDE-BACK

SASH

UNIT CONSTRUCTION II

1   Finish sash.
2   Make sleeves, leaving cuffs (hems) and underarm seams open.
3   Finish collar.
4   Finish pockets.
5   Complete bodice front.
6   Complete bodice back.
7   Stitch shoulder seams.
8   Attach collar.
9   Sew in sleeves. Attach sash-ends.
10   Stitch underarm seams. Turn up and finish cuffs (or sleeve hems).
11   Complete skirt.
12   Stitch bodice to skirt. Make machine buttonholes, and sew on buttons. Then make hem.

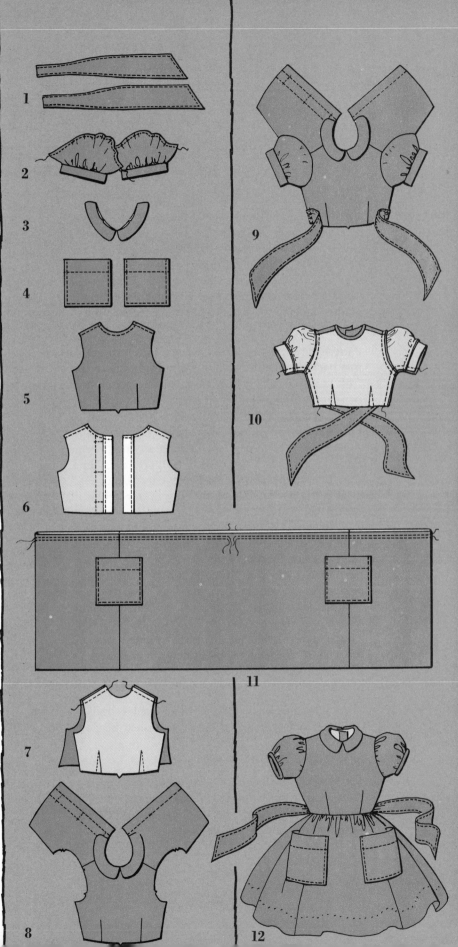

1

2

3

4

5

6

7

8

9

10

11

12

BACKING OR UNDERLINING

Backing, or underlining, which is stitched to the wrong side of an outer section before any seams are joined (the two layers then being handled as one), must not be confused with lining. Lining sections are seamed together separately, then sewed into an otherwise completed garment as an inside finish covering the seams. Backing serves a number of purposes, but is never a finish.

Pattern directions generally do not specify or mention backing. The decision to use it rests more or less with you, and whether the garment fabric you have bought requires it (knits and stretch fabrics are never backed except to reinforce certain points, such as buttonholes and belts). A garment may be backed in its entirety or in part, the backing serving to reinforce, lend body and/or opacity, and preserve shape.
. . . In a straight skirt, backing prevents "sitting out," even if the backing is present only in upper half of skirt back.
. . . In certain designs, such as A-line or bell-shaped, or in a bodice shell, backing preserves the silhouette when outside fabric does not have enough body.
. . . With some silks and soft wools, backing will prevent pulling out at the seams.
. . . Lace and sheer fabrics can be made opaque with a backing.
. . . In general, backing gives body where it may be missing. It does not give stiffness or crispness, as interfacing does; and it does not cover raw seams on the inside.

A garment may be both backed and lined, especially if, like a coat or jacket, it must be finished inside.

A WORD OF CAUTION

The whole performance of a backed garment rests on the fact that the two fabrics must react as one. The backing must enhance, not interfere with, the outer fabric. Make sure, therefore, that:

. . . where the pattern calls for gathers or draping, the backing is soft;
. . . if the outer fabric is either a) dry-cleanable, b) washable, c) wash-and-wear, the backing has the same properties and calls for the same handling;
. . . the backing is preshrunk, even if you have to do the shrinking yourself. A slightly loose backing does no harm, but one that has tightened up in washing or dry-cleaning can ruin a garment.

If, even after these precautions, a slight discrepancy develops after use, it can be taken care of by a judicious use of the iron.

BACKING FABRICS

There are a number of fabrics, both woven and non-woven, in a variety of weights, that are specially made for backing. You can also use many of the regular fabrics, such as organza, batiste, lawn, China silk, or taffeta. The important thing is to be sure that the backing is of the right weight—generally lighter than the outer fabric—and that it requires the same handling. A washable backing not guaranteed to be preshrunk must *always* be shrunk before using.

BACKING A GARMENT

• After cutting out a garment, remove pattern pieces from sections to be backed *before* transferring any marks. Cut backing from the same pattern pieces, then transfer marks to backing.

• Place unmarked side of backing to wrong side of corresponding outer section; smooth out. Match edges carefully and pin together, leaving seam allowances clear. Place on machine with backing side up. Stitch together on all edges, ½" from edge, but *with the grain* (see **Directional Stitching,** p.118), which means that you will have to start from the same edge to stitch along two opposite sides, even if on the second trip the bulk of work will have to go to the right.

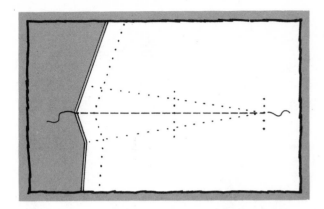

• If there are darts, baste the two layers together along center of dart before stitching, as shown here.

• Construct garment as usual, handling backing and outer fabric as one.

• After marking a hemline, hand-baste the two layers together all around, ¼″ above hemline. Leave this basting in until hem is finished. If backing is of heavy or stiff fabric, cut it off at hemline to reduce bulk. While sewing down hem, catch hem to backing only, but every few inches catch outer fabric with a stitch invisible on outside.

BASTING

Essentially, basting means temporary sewing, done with long, loose stitches, and removed after a job is completed. Nowadays it is often done by machine. (It is sometimes used for MARKING—see that chapter). Its usual purpose is to hold two or more layers of fabric together preparatory to stitching. In modern sewing, this is done whenever possible with pins only (pin-basting).

When basting is part of the construction process, it is indicated in the directions. Otherwise, depending on the degree of your expertness, you will want to either pin- or thread-baste (to be safe, first pin-, then thread-baste) in the following instances:
. . . where there are more than two layers of fabric, as in applying collars and cuffs,
. . . in seams containing fullness, such as ease, gathers, or pleats,
. . . when setting in sleeves,
. . . when matching plaids and stripes,
. . . with slippery fabrics, such as satin, velvet, etc.,
. . . when a garment is to be tried on.

PIN-BASTING

Pin-basting may serve by itself or it may be a preliminary to thread-basting. The position of the pins depends on whether your basting is a preparation for sewing or for fitting.

Pinning for thread-basting or for stitching—Place pins at *right angles* to fabric edge (in fabrics that mark, within seam allowance), so they are on top for stitching. Match and pin notches and seam-ends (1), then place pins between, as close as necessary to hold seam securely (2). Remove pins as you stitch. Even a hinged foot will not prevent the needle from striking a pin.

Pinning for fitting—On right side of garment (to allow pins to be moved while trying on), place pins *parallel* to fabric edges (3), on seamline. After fitting, if seamline has been altered, mark new seamline on wrong side; remove pins and baste on wrong side.

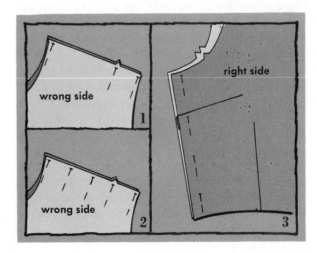

THREAD-BASTING BY HAND OR MACHINE

Machine-basting is quicker than hand-basting, of course, but it requires greater expertness. Choose whichever method you prefer; instructions for both follow.

Thread-basting for fitting is done on wrong side. Clip threads as necessary for changes.

Basting of seams is done just outside seamline, to keep clear of final stitching.

To remove basting, clip thread every few stitches before drawing out. This will avoid pulling fabric out of shape.

Hand-Basting

Use a good needle, suitable for your fabric (see THREAD AND NEEDLE CHART, p. 196). There is special basting thread, but any light-colored sewing thread will do.

Even basting is done with stitches about ¼″ long and ¼″ apart (4). Generally, it is done flat, on the table, as shown (5). When one layer of fabric is to be eased to the other, basting is done over the hand (6), with layer to be eased on top.

Uneven basting—long stitches on top, short stitches through fabric (7)—is used for marking, and for holding fabric together only where there is no strain, as in a hem.

Slip-basting is done on right side of fabric to match a fabric design at a seam. Use matching thread—you may not be able to remove all of it after stitching because it will be exactly on seamline. Turn seam allowance under on one edge and place fold along seamline on right side of corresponding section. Pin in place, matching design. At right-hand end of seam, bring needle and thread out through fold of upper section. Put needle into seamline of under section, at point precisely opposite where it came out of fold, and bring it out ¼″ ahead. Take a ¼″ stitch along fold, again putting needle in exactly opposite where it came out and running needle along inside of fold. Repeat. This actually makes a plain seam with even basting (8).

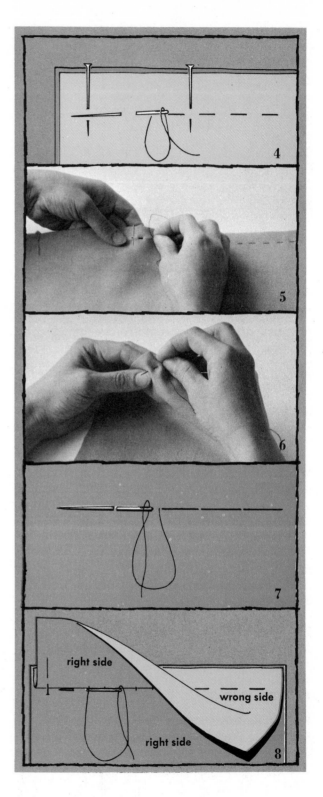

right side

wrong side

right side

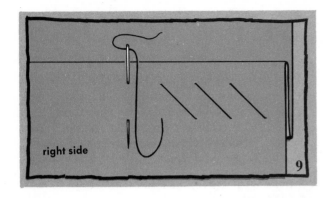

right side

Diagonal basting is used to hold two or more layers of fabric together; it prevents shifting. It is used in the preparation of pleats and in tailoring. Working on right side of garment, take vertical stitches through all layers, as shown (9), thus forming the diagonal basting.

Machine-Basting

This requires some preliminary pin-basting. Then set machine at longest stitch and use matching thread. Where seams are not to be pressed open, machine-basting may be left in.

BELT BUCKLES

The usual fastening for a belt is a buckle. When the belt closure is a simulated tie or a simulated button closure (with sewed-on bow or decorative buttons, etc.), it is fastened with large snaps or strong hooks and eyes.

Belt buckles are available at notion stores and counters in a variety of materials—wood, metal, plastic, etc. The most frequently used belt buckle, however, is one covered with the garment fabric.

The covered buckle is made (covered) with your own fabric. You may:
[a] order it from a notion store or counter;
[b] make it yourself, with a kit sold for the purpose (directions come with kit);

[c] re-cover an old buckle. If you have a wire-type buckle from an old belt (1), proceed as follows:

Using pliers, carefully remove prong and metal clip. Remove old fabric. Measure around buckle for length of strip needed. Cut strip on straight grain 1⅛″ to 1½″ wide (depending on thickness of fabric). Fold both long edges in about ¼″; fold strip in half lengthwise and topstitch edges together, close to edge (2). Slip cover over buckle. Then replace the prong and metal clip.

SEWING BUCKLE TO BELT

Buckle without prong (3)—Fold straight belt-end over bar and sew down (4).

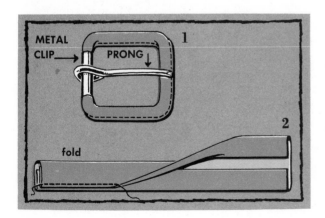

METAL CLIP → PRONG ↓

fold

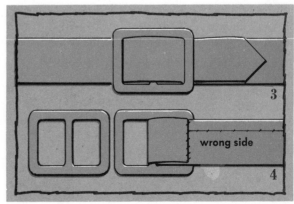

wrong side

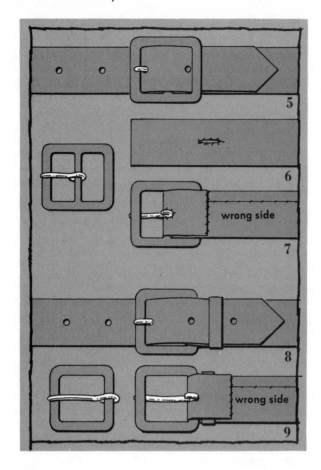

BELT LOOPS

Belt loops, or belt carriers, are necessary for any belt that is not at the natural waistline; or for keeping a narrow belt in place over a wider waistband. They also serve to keep belts from getting separated from garments, particularly coats, bathrobes, etc. The number of loops needed depends on design and function.

For belt loops made of thread, used on most dresses, see THREAD LOOPS.

Fabric Loops

A belt must slide easily through loops. When attaching loops, make sure there is enough slack.

• Prepare the number of loops desired in a single strip. The length needed for one loop is equal to width of belt plus 1″ (plus a little extra if belt is very thick).

• Cut the strip along fabric selvage. Unless your pattern calls for a specific, different width, make strip ¾″ to 1″ wide (the greater width for the heavier fabric or belt) and the total length of loops.

• Fold long raw edge one-third to inside; press (1). Fold selvage over it; press. Topstitch along both edges. Cut strip into single loop lengths.

• Mark placement—width of belt centered over belt line, one half above, one half below. Fold under ¼″ at each end of strip and sew folded ends to garment, by hand (2) or machine (3).

Buckle with prong (5)—Cut a ½″ slot 1½″ from straight end of belt. Overcast edges of slot (6).

• For a **whole buckle,** fold belt-end over bar with prong through slot; sew down (7).

• For a **half-buckle** (8), make a fabric-loop (see next column), long enough to be folded over belt and overlap ¼″. Sew ends together on wrong side of belt without catching them to belt. Fold belt-end over buckle bar with prong through slot. Slide fabric-loop close to buckle and sew belt-end down, turning raw edges under (9).

Try on belt. Mark point where prong should come through, and two more points 1″ to each side of first. Make three eyelets, using either a metal eyelet kit or by first punching holes, and then finishing them with buttonhole stitch.

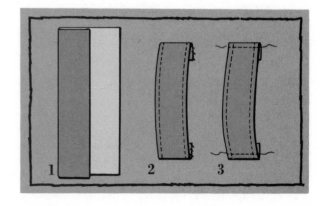

BELTS

Belts of leather, suede, plastic, satin, and other materials are bought ready-made. Belts made from the same fabric as the garment, however, are the ones most in demand and are an integral part of the garment. These may be:

[a] ordered from a notion store or counter,
[b] made yourself with the help of a kit sold for the purpose (directions come with kit),
[c] made yourself without a kit. Following are instructions for making a **Covered Belt,** suitable for any fabric; a **Belt Stiffened with Iron-on Fabric,** suitable for linen, cotton, and other washable garments (but *not* recommended for sheer, napped, or pile fabrics), and a **Corded Belt.**

COVERED BELT

This can be made from any fabric, over a strip of belting. Belting, which is washable, is sold by the yard, in widths ranging from ½″ to 3″. Buy it the width of finished belt.

• Cut belting to your waist measurement plus 6″.

• Cut fabric along selvage edge to twice the width of belting plus ½″; length equal to your waist measurement plus 6¾″.

• At one end of belting, carefully measure and cut a point, as shown (1).

• Fold one end of fabric strip in half lengthwise, wrong side out. Stitch as shown. Trim seam to ⅛″ (2); press open.

• Turn stitched end to right side, opening out strip to form a point. Push point out carefully; place pointed end of belting inside point of fabric; press. Fold long cut edge of fabric over belting, following line of grain; press (3).

• Fold and press selvage edge over belting. Pin this edge over the other so fabric is snug over belting (4).

• Slipstitch selvage edge down (5). At straight end of belt, trim away fabric ¼″ beyond end of belting.

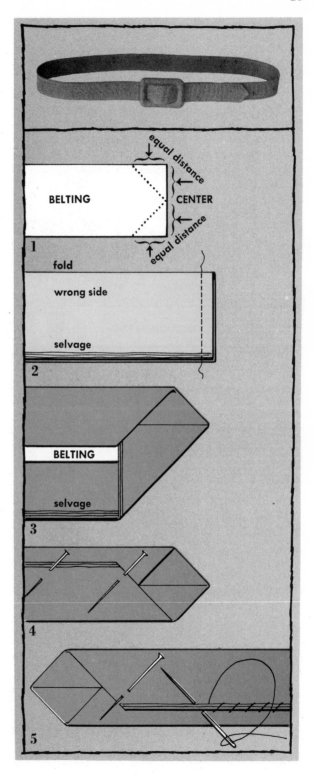

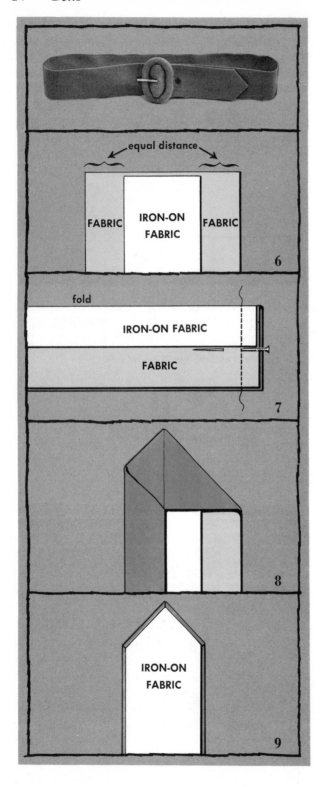

• If desired, finish by topstitching around belt. Begin at straight end and keep a scant ⅛″ from edge.

To attach buckle, see BELT BUCKLES.

NOTE: If fabric strip for belt cannot be cut along selvage, cut it on lengthwise grain, adding ¼″ to width. On one long edge, turn ¼″ under and stitch. Use this edge as "selvage edge."

BELT STIFFENED WITH IRON-ON FABRIC

A belt interfaced and backed with iron-on fabric is supple and well-suited for washable garments.

Iron-on fabric may be bought in 1¼″ strips, 32″ or 80″ long. Select a color as close to garment color as possible. You will need two lengths (one for interfacing, one for backing), each as long as your waist measurement plus 5½″. If each length needs to be made up of more than one piece, which is permissible, make sure that the joinings do not fall in the same place. If you wish a belt narrower than 1¼″, trim the strips accordingly, but be sure to measure, mark, and cut evenly.

• Cut a strip of garment fabric twice the width of finished belt and as long as your waist measurement plus 6″.

• Center one iron-on strip on wrong side of garment-fabric strip, matching edges at one end, as shown (6). Press in place, following directions in package. If iron-on strip consists of more than one piece, have ends just touch, not overlap.

• At even end, fold strip in half lengthwise, as shown, wrong side out. Pin together carefully, with iron-on edges exactly even. Stitch across end (7). Trim seam to ⅛″. Press seam open with thumbnail.

• Turn stitched end to right side, opening out strip to form point. Push out point carefully; press with seam in center. Fold and press fabric toward center, exactly along edge of tape (8). If fabric does not press flat, hold edges together at center with catchstitch.

• On remaining length of iron-on-fabric, cut one end to a point, as shown (9). Place over raw side of belt, matching edges. Starting at point, press down, following directions in package. At straight end, trim away outer fabric ¼″ beyond end of iron-on fabric.

• If desired, finish by topstitching around belt.

To attach buckle, see BELT BUCKLES.

CORDED BELT

You will need covered cord, or corded tubing, of a length equal to twice your waist measurement plus 1½ yards. Buy fluffy upholstery cord of desired thickness and follow instructions in BIAS, p. 30.

• Fold covered cord in half, with seam facing you. Keep seam on same side (inside) throughout. About 2″ from fold, tack together, forming a loop. Sew a hook on end of loop, as shown (10).

• Try on belt, pulling both ends through loop. Place a pin (for eye) at point opposite hook. Mark desired length of hanging cord-ends with pins. Take off belt. At pin-mark for eye, tack cords together on inside. On outside, make a thread loop, or attach a straight eye. To finish cord-ends, you can either knot each end into a Chinese ball button (see BUTTONS, p. 44), or attach a tassel, or make a simple knot.

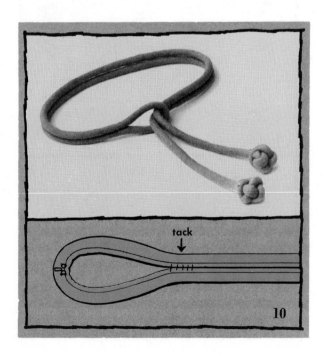

tack

10

BIAS

Bias is any diagonal direction in fabric. *True bias* is the true (45 degree) diagonal across a square of fabric, cutting exactly in half the right angle formed by the lengthwise and the crosswise grains (1). The fabric along this true bias line is the direction in which fabric has the greatest "give" and flexibility. A close-fitting garment with the center line on the true bias will mold the body. A narrow strip of bias-cut fabric can be stitched to the edge of a curve without a wrinkle—hence the wide use of bias strips (see next page) in trimming and finishing.

GARMENTS CUT ON THE BIAS

Fabric cut on the bias allows for certain effects—often very elegant—of fitting and draping; and handsome designs can be made with bias-cut stripes and plaids. Pattern instructions as to grain must be carefully followed: arrows indicating straight grain automatically make the true bias fall where it should.

A bias seam (two bias edges stitched together), whether or not it is on the true bias, may have a tendency to stretch or sag, especially in loose-woven fabrics. To stabilize a seam, use a short stitch—about 20 to the inch—or place straight seam-binding over seamline and stitch through all layers.

BIAS STRIPS

Bias strips are used for binding, tubing, piping (see these headings in the present chapter) and facing (see FACINGS, p. 80).

Bias strips may be hand-cut or ready-made. **The Hand-Cut Bias Strip** (see below for preparation) allows you to choose your fabric—matching or contrasting—and your width, and is suitable for any garment. The ready-made or **Packaged Bias Strip** (bias tape and piping) provides timesaving finishes for casual clothes.

The **length and width** of a bias strip are determined by the use for which it is intended.

For the **length** required of a bias strip (edge-finish or flat trimming), measure length at place of application with a tape measure; when cutting strips, add 1″ for every joining necessary, and at least 4″ for a final joining (beginning and end joined after application, as in a neckline). For separate pieces of trimming, such as frogs, make a sample out of tape or cord, then open it out and measure.

For the **width** of a bias strip, see instructions under the heading describing its intended use. "Cut width" refers to actual width of strip from raw edge to raw edge. "Finished width" is width that will show on garment (right side or wrong side) being finished or trimmed; it is also the diameter of round tubing. "Packaged width" is the width of a packaged bias strip (edges folded in), ready for application.

THE PACKAGED BIAS STRIP

The packaged bias strip, available in a wide range of colors, comes in lengths of from 3 to 5 yards. The folded-in edges may be pressed open when necessary. On p. 124 you will find a chart of the various packaged bias strips sold at notion counters.

THE HAND-CUT BIAS STRIP

The length of a single bias strip is limited by the width of the fabric available. The bias cut is about one-third longer than the straight grain, as shown (4). When a long strip is needed, shorter strips may be joined end-to-end, each strip having been cut as long as possible. However, when it is important that joinings should not show, it is best to figure and measure each length so that joinings will fall in inconspicuous places, such as center back, side seams, under belt, etc.

Locating the True Bias

This may be done in two ways. For either of these methods, lay out a fabric-end and work with a straight edge on the lengthwise grain (a selvage or an edge cut parallel to selvage).

METHOD I . . . Fold the straight edge so that it lies at right angles to itself, along the crosswise grain (2). The fold formed will be on the true bias. Mark fold by pressing; open out.

METHOD II . . . Straighten the adjoining crosswise edge. On the two sides of the right angle thus formed, mark off equal distances with yardstick and chalk. The line between the two marks will be on the true bias (3). Mark line with chalk.

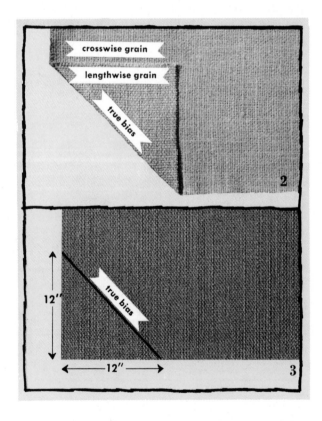

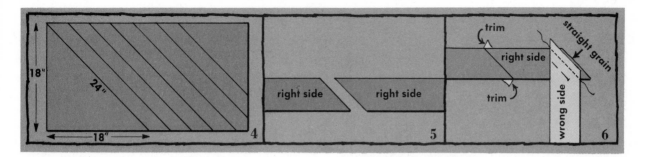

Marking and Cutting Bias Strips

Mark a true-bias line on your fabric as shown above. Measuring from the true-bias line, mark the desired width of strip at a few points, then use yardstick to draw a continuous line (4). Repeat for as many strips as you need. Cut along marked lines.

Joining Bias Strips

IMPORTANT: The ends of bias strips to be joined must be on the straight grain and parallel to each other. If they are not parallel, trim one end to match the other (5).

Place strips right sides together as shown (6): at right angles to each other, with straight-grain edges even but with points extending so that edges cross at *seamline,* forming small angles. Stitch on straight grain, beginning and ending at angle centers. Press seam open and trim to a scant ¼″. Trim off extending points.

Stretching or Swirling

You will find it helpful to stretch a hand-cut bias strip before using. This is particularly true when making tubing, on which the stitching may break when you turn it. To stretch strip, press firmly while stretching it with the other hand.

Swirling means pressing or steaming strip into a curve, as needed (7).

Final Joining of a Bias Strip (Seam or Lap)

Start application at an inconspicuous spot.

METHOD I (seamed joining) . . . When starting, leave 2″ of bias strip free *beyond* point at which you wish joining to be. When, after stitching, you are about to reach that point again, stop just short of it. Cut off strip 2″ beyond point. Fold garment (8) so that strips are at right angles as for any joining (when using packaged bias strip, open out folds). Seam ends together on the straight grain, close to fold of garment (8). Trim seam; press open. Complete stitching to garment, across joining.

METHOD II (lapped joining) . . . Before beginning to stitch, fold that end of bias strip ½″ to wrong side on the straight grain. When completing stitching, cut second end on the straight grain to lap over first for about ½″ (9). Stitch across.

Basting

A bias strip should be pinned in place before stitching, especially around curves. On a close curve, basting is definitely necessary.

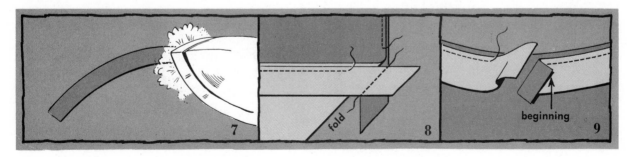

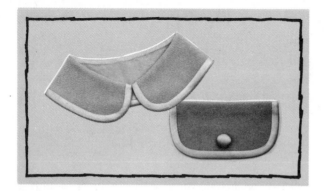

BIAS BINDING

A bias binding is a decorative finish which encases an edge. Its finished width varies, but is seldom less than ¼″ or more than. ½″.

Trim away the entire ⅝″ seam allowance (since bias strip covers garment edge, no allowance is needed). *Before* doing this, stay-stitch ¾″ from raw edge. To bring any binding around a corner see p. 29.

Regular Binding

For either hand-cut or packaged bias strips.

Hand-Cut Bias Strip

• Cut strips 3 times as wide as desired finished width plus ¼″. Example: For a ½″ binding, strips are 1½″ plus ¼″, or 1¾″ wide.

• Pin or baste right side of strip to right side of garment, with raw edges even; if ends are to be joined, see p. 27 before starting. Stitch at a distance from edge exactly equal to finished width (10). Press strip up; fold to wrong side over cut fabric edges. Turn in raw edge of strip even with stitching line. Slipstitch to stitching line (11).

Packaged Single-Fold Bias Strip

For a ¼″ binding, use standard ½″ bias tape. For a ½″ binding, use 1″ tape (Wide Bias Tape).

Applying ¼″ binding: Open out one fold of bias tape and apply to garment edge, following directions for applying hand-cut bias strip.

Applying ½″ binding: Mark a line on right side of garment, ¼″ from raw edge. Open out one fold of bias tape and pin or baste right side of tape to garment, matching raw edge of strip to marked line. Stitch along crease. Fold to wrong side over fabric edges and slipstitch second fold to stitching line.

French Binding

Suitable only for hand-cut bias strips in sheer or lightweight fabrics.

• Cut strips 6 times as wide as finished width. Fold strip in half lengthwise, right side out. Press. Pin or baste raw edges of folded strip to right side of garment, all edges even. (If ends of strip are to be joined, see p. 27 before starting, but leave 3″ free at beginning and, when joining, open out strip completely). Stitch at a distance from edge exactly equal to finished width. Press strip up; fold to wrong side over cut fabric edges. Slipstitch to stitching line (12).

Machine-Finished Binding

Packaged Double Fold Bias Tape is used for all-machine application in one of three ways:

Quick-topstitched: With garment right side up, insert edge between edges of tape, narrower fold of tape on top. Topstitch; you will automatically stitch through the wider bottom fold (13). If ends must be joined, lap them (14).

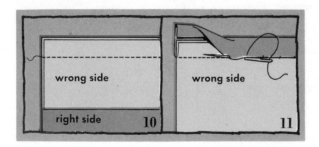

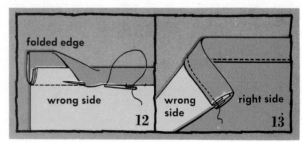

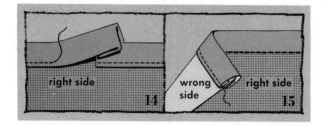

Topstitched finish: (If tape-ends are to be joined, see p. 27 before starting.) Open out seam allowance on *narrower* fold of tape; place right side of tape along garment-edge on *wrong* side, raw edges even; stitch along crease. Fold tape up and over garment edge to right side; topstitch.

Concealed machine-finish: (If tape-ends are to be joined, see p. 27 before starting.) Open out seam allowance on *narrower* fold; place tape along garment-edge right sides together, raw edges even. Stitch along crease. Fold tape up and over garment edge to wrong side. Machine-stitch on right side, on garment fabric but as close as possible to edge of binding, to catch wider fold underneath (15).

Sewing Machine Attachment

A binder can be used for a topstitched application of both packaged Single Fold Bias Tape or hand-cut bias strips. Follow the directions in your sewing machine manual.

Corners in Binding

Outside Corner (as in pointed collars, pockets)

Regular and French Binding: When stitching toward corner, stop at width of seam allowance from corner. Cut thread; secure ends. Folding strip as shown, bring it around corner (16). Starting at very edge of corner, stitch as shown across fold and along edge. When finishing binding on wrong side, form miter at corner.

Quick-topstitched binding: Stitch to edge of fabric, as shown (17). Cut off thread, form miter and start stitching again from point of miter (18). Bring thread-ends to wrong side and fasten.

Inside Corner (as in a square neck)

Regular and French Bindings: Stitch to width of seam allowance beyond corner. Pivot on needle to turn; bring strip around corner, stretching it around needle; continue stitching (19). When finishing binding on wrong side, form miter at corner.

Quick-topstitched binding: Clip carefully about 1/8″ into corner. When applying binding, stitch to width of seam allowance beyond corner. Pivot on needle to turn. Forming miter, bring tape around corner and continue stitching (20). Fasten miter in place with a few stitches on wrong side.

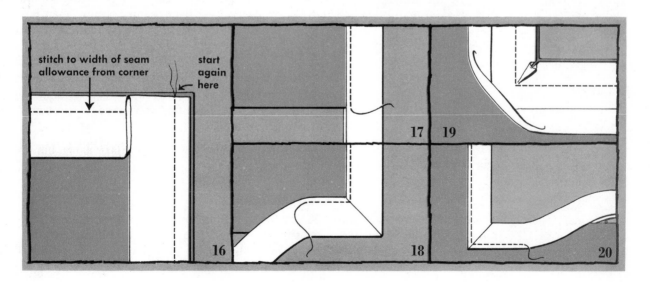

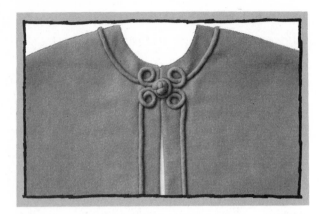

BIAS TUBING

Tubing is made by stitching the edges of a bias strip together to form a tube which is then turned inside out. It is used either flat or round; flat tubing is suitable for ties and appliquéd decorations, round tubing (filled with its own seam allowance or with cord) for loops, buttons, ties, belts, frogs, decorations. Tubing is generally made from hand-cut bias strips. Packaged bias tape (see chart on p. 124) can also be used if the width from raw edge to raw edge is right. Whenever possible, make tubing without joinings. For turning tubing, use a loop turner (21), a bodkin, or a heavy tapestry needle.

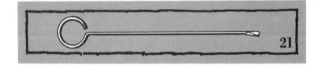

Flat Tubing

• Cut bias strips twice as wide as finished width plus ½″.

• Fold strip in half lengthwise, wrong side out. For ease in turning later, begin (and end) stitching in a funnel shape, as shown (22); then make a scant ¼″ seam, stretching strip as you stitch.

• Press seam open lightly with tip of iron (if necessary, insert a pencil or rod into tube to avoid creasing). Trim funnel-ends diagonally, as shown, slanting in from the seam (23).

Turning with loop turner: Insert loop turner into tubing, gathering up fabric until hook comes out at other end. Catch hook securely to point of funnel (seam). Pull turner back through tube, turning tube inside out. Keep seam allowances open. Press tubing flat with seam at center.

Turning with bodkin or tapestry needle: Thread a bodkin or heavy tapestry needle with about 4″ of extra-heavy thread (crochet thread or Button & Carpet thread), and knot the two ends together. Using a sewing needle and "Heavy Duty" Mercerized thread, sew this knot of heavy thread securely to point of funnel (23). Insert bodkin or tapestry needle into tube. Push it through, turning tube inside out. Keep seam allowances open. Press tubing flat with seam at center.

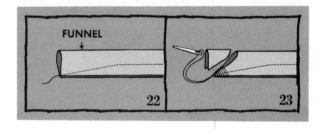

Self-Filled Tubing

The diameter of self-filled tubing depends on the bulk of the fabric used—finished organdy tubing should be no more than ⅛″ wide; satin no more than ¼″; other fabrics in proportion to their weight.

• Cut bias strips 5 times as wide as finished width.

• Fold strip in half lengthwise, wrong side out. Starting (and ending) with funnel shape—see above (22)—stitch midway between fold and cut edges, stretching strip as you stitch.

• For turning, see directions for **Flat Tubing,** but do not press.

Corded Tubing

Cable cord for filling comes in thicknesses from thread-like to ½″ plus. Select by eye (size designations vary). Remember that tubing may compress a large, fluffy cord to a smaller size.

• To determine width of bias strip, fold a corner of fabric over cord to be used; with a pin, fasten the two layers of fabric together so that cord is tightly enclosed. Cut ¼″ beyond pin (24). Open out piece— the width between the two parallel edges will be width of strip needed.

• For stitching see directions for **Flat Tubing,** but do not press.

Turning tubing and inserting cord (one operation): Thread needle with a short length of "Heavy Duty" thread, doubled. Wind tightly around cord-end and take a stitch through cord. Do not cut thread.

Follow instructions for turning flat tubing.
. . . If you use a loop turner (21), catch cord-end securely to hook, together with point of funnel, before pulling turner back through tubing.
. . . If you are working with a bodkin or a tapestry needle, sew cord-end to bodkin or needle before turning tubing (25).
Keep seam allowances open.

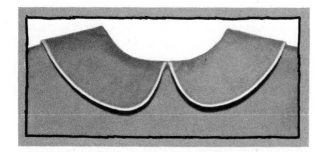

PIPING

Piping is made of a folded bias strip, either plain or corded (for packaged corded piping, see chart for NOTIONS on p. 124). Whether piping is placed on an edge or in the body of a garment, it is always caught in a seam.

Corded Piping

To Make Corded Piping

To determine width of bias strip, see **Corded Tubing,** but cut fabric ⅝″ below pin, for seam allowance.

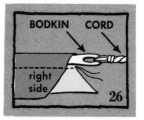

• Fold strip in half lengthwise, right side out. Stitch, leaving a ⅝″ seam allowance.

• Draw cord through piping with a loop turner or a bodkin (26).

• Piping is stitched to a single garment section before the two garment sections are seamed together. Pin or baste piping to right side of section, raw edges even. Clip seam allowance of piping if necessary (27).

Stitch with cording foot over stitching on piping. Pin or baste the two garment sections together, wrong sides out and raw edges even. With cording foot, stitch alongside former stitching, closer to cord (28). Finish seam in usual manner.

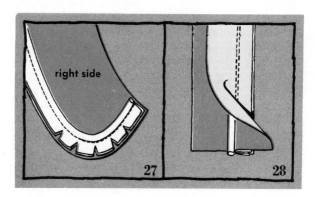

Packaged Corded Piping

Packaged corded piping comes in only one width and has a seam allowance of about ⅛″.

• On right side of one of the two garment sections to be seamed together, measure and mark a line ½″ from raw edge. Pin or baste piping along this line, raw edges even with line. Then follow directions for applying **Corded Piping** (27, 28).

Plain Piping (uncorded)

This is always hand-cut.

Cutting: To determine width, add ⅝″ to desired finished width. Cut strips double the width of that measurement.

Stitching: Fold strip in half lengthwise, right side out. Press. Stitch at finished width from fold.

Applying: Follow directions in last paragraph on p. 31, but use regular presser foot.

Final Joining of Piping

Start application in an inconspicuous place, leaving ½″ of piping free. When stitching piping in place, stop ½″ from end. (If piping is corded, pull out ½″ of cord at end and cut cord). Rip back a few stitches; fold raw end in and lap over beginning. (See 15, in **Machine-Finished Binding,** p. 29. Follow the illustration and instructions exactly as given on this page for a concealed machine-finish.)

BUTTONHOLES

Buttonholes are basically slits cut through the fabric. What interests us is the finish of their edges, which may be bound with fabric, or worked over with thread, either by hand or machine.

The Bound, or Piped, Buttonhole, almost always finished with self-fabric (the possible exception being trimming fabric), is the one most in vogue today. It is good in all garments except when fabric is unsuitable, i.e. . . .

. . . sheer, embroidered, or nubby,

. . . ravelly (though this can be corrected by backing with iron-on interfacing (see p. 33, top),

. . . untreated cotton, where inside layers may wrinkle when washed.

The Hand-Worked Buttonhole is best in lightweight and sheer fabrics, especially on blouses; also in the difficult fabrics mentioned above.

The Machine-Worked Buttonhole is always suitable in casual and children's clothes, which are subject to frequent washings. A carefully-made machine buttonhole, however, can be used in other garments as well.

Buttonholes are most often horizontal; less often vertical; now and then, to carry out a design, diagonal. The making of either bound or hand-worked buttonholes undeniably requires care and precision; it also requires that the grain of your fabric, if it is plain to the eye, be straight. Otherwise, if you do not want machine buttonholes, select a pattern that does not call for buttonholes at all. There are, incidentally, several gadgets sold in department stores at notions counters for making bound buttonholes; they come with their own directions, which must be followed precisely.

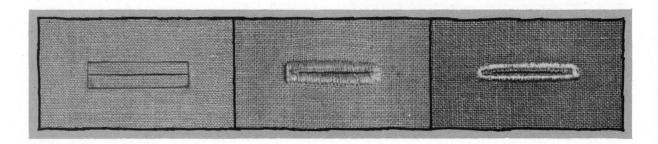

FOR SUCCESSFUL
BUTTONHOLE-MAKING . . .

. . . Have, first and foremost, a pair of good scissors with *very sharp* blades and points. Also a 6″ ruler, a longer ruler or yardstick, and a contrast-colored pencil, not too hard and very sharp.

. . . Have on hand, before you even start marking your pattern, the *actual buttons* you are going to use.

. . . If you are inexpert, try out the directions, *skipping no details,* with a few practice buttonholes on scraps of closely-woven cotton, properly backed (interfaced).

. . . Never fail to reinforce with *interfacing* any edge that is to have buttonholes, whether the pattern specifies it or not. That edge will always have wear and tear. Avoid loose-woven or ravelly interfacing fabrics, especially for bound buttonholes.

. . . When garment fabric itself is ravelly, or has "give" (knit and stretch fabrics), stabilize the buttonhole area by backing it with a piece of *lightweight iron-on interfacing,* 1″ wide and 1″ longer than buttonhole. Apply these patches to wrong side of fabric before attaching regular interfacing.

. . . In every case, before making buttonholes in a garment, make a *test buttonhole* to see how this particular fabric handles. Cut a 4″ x 4″ piece each of fabric and interfacing, on straight grain. Mark interfacing with position line and end-lines duplicating the ones made in **Marking The Garment Section** (p. 34), and baste to fabric as instructed. For a worked buttonhole, baste a second piece of fabric under interfacing. For a bound buttonhole, make test buttonhole after **Preparing the Buttonhole Strip** (p. 35). Follow directions as for actual buttonhole.

MARKING THE PATTERN

Possible Re-spacing—If you have altered the length of your pattern the buttonholes may need re-spacing. As a general principle, top and bottom buttonholes should be placed at same distance from top and bottom edges of garment as they were originally; and the ones between re-spaced to be at equal distance from each other.

Length of Buttonhole—Buttonhole markings printed on pattern indicate position of buttonhole, not necessarily exact length. To determine the correct length, measure your button, as follows:

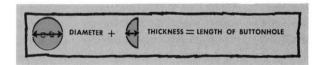

Diameter and thickness added together generally equal necessary length of buttonhole. For instance, a round button, 1″ in diameter and ⅛″ thick, requires a 1⅛″ buttonhole. Buttons that are fabric-covered, dome-shaped, ball-shaped, or odd-shaped, often need extra length. For such buttons, cut a slit in fabric, measured as above. Try button in slit and lengthen slit until button slides through easily. Length arrived at should be marked on pattern.

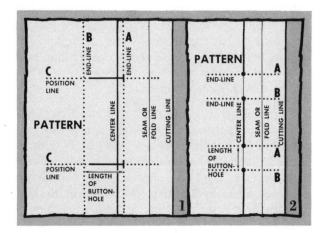

Marking—In diagrams 1 and 2 here, the solid lines represent markings printed on most patterns. Dotted lines represent markings to add for correct and uniform buttonhole length. Use pencil and yardstick.

For **Horizontal Buttonholes** (1) draw in lines A, B, C. At top and bottom of pattern, extend end-lines [A and B] at least 1″ beyond existing markings. Extend position lines [C] 1″ beyond end-lines.

For **Vertical Buttonholes** (2), draw in lines A and B (end-lines). Extend these lines 1″ beyond center line, which is also position line.

MARKING THE GARMENT SECTION

Here we need accuracy. Lines must not only be correct as to placement, but also absolutely on grain if grain is clearly visible. Markings for buttonholes must be on outside of garment, since that is where the greater part of the buttonhole is made. Since dressmaker's carbon paper would leave permanent and visible marks, the marking is done in two steps, the second one by basting through to right side.

Step 1. From pattern to interfacings (3). Place pattern with buttonhole markings over interfacings for both sides of opening; match edges carefully; if interfacing is woven, make sure center-line is on grain. Pin together through seam allowance along opening edge. Transfer all lines, printed and pencil, to interfacings with dressmaker's carbon paper, using a ruler. Pin interfacings to wrong side of corresponding garment sections, matching edges exactly.

Step 2. From interfacings to garment sections (4). Many fabrics can be marked with machine-basting. Others (taffeta, polished cotton, certain treated fabrics), which show needle-marks, must be hand-basted with a fine needle. On women's clothes, buttonholes are on right hand side of opening. On left (button) side, baste-mark *center line only*. On buttonhole side, disregard center line, unless buttonholes are vertical. If garment fabric has a noticeable grain, put a pin through from interfacing to outside at ends of all marked lines. Machine- or hand-baste on garment side between pin markers, following a thread in grain. If fabric grain is not noticeable, baste-mark by going over lines from interfacing side through to outside.

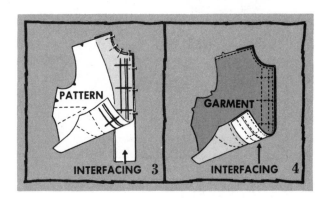

THE BOUND BUTTONHOLE

Bound buttonholes are made first thing after **Marking the Garment Section,** with interfacing attached as described, *before* the section is seamed to any others. The buttonholes can be made in various ways; two most satisfactory types follow—a **One-Piece Folded Buttonhole** and a **Patch Buttonhole** (both begin with **Preparing the Buttonhole Strip,** p. 35). In both, the finished buttonhole has lips either on the bias or the straight grain, of even width and meeting in the center; and the outer shape is usually rectangular and must be exactly on grain, especially when fabric

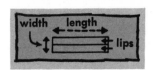

grain is noticeable. Width is about ¼″ overall, a little less if fabric is thin, a little more if fabric is heavy.

Either buttonhole can be **corded** to give body to the lips—which in this case *must* be on the bias. At what point and how this is done is indicated in the directions. Soft cord of suitable thickness, soft twine (single or doubled) or doubled knitting worsted (for wool fabrics), can be used for cording.

. . . If you are planning an elegant buttonhole only 3/16″ wide, you will find the half-width measurement for lips hard to locate on a ruler. Instead, mark the 3/16″ on a paper-edge, then fold this in half to mark width of lips (see buttonhole directions).

. . . Do not, unless you are an expert, try to make a bound buttonhole less than ⅞″ long. To fit a smaller button, buttonhole may be shortened after it is finished, by slipstitching lips together invisibly on wrong side, at far end from garment edge.

. . . When buttonhole is finished, press with steam iron or dampened press cloth—lightly, as the added thickness may mark outer fabric.

PREPARING THE BUTTONHOLE STRIP

With this long strip, you prepare the lip-fabric for all your buttonholes at once. The strip may be cut on straight grain, but it is far easier to achieve professional-looking buttonholes when the lips are on the bias; with corded buttonholes this is a *must*.

Measure, mark and cut strips as follows:

WIDTH: 1″ for One-Piece Folded Buttonhole. Add ⅛″ if fabric is heavy;
2″ for Patch Buttonhole.

LENGTH: Add 1″ to length of your buttonhole. Multiply this figure by number of buttonholes, including test buttonhole.

On wrong side of fabric, mark lengthwise center of strip *accurately* (5). Baste-marking is most exact.

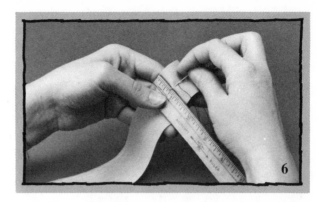

. . . To baste-mark, start at one end of strip, with ruler held across it (6). Keep end of ruler (or zero mark) even with edge of strip and your needle pointed to half-width mark on ruler. Take short stitches, moving ruler down the strip about ¼″ at a time.

. . . To mark with colored pencil, place strip on hard, flat surface. Use yardstick, and mark with dashes rather than with a continuous line.

ONE-PIECE FOLDED BUTTONHOLE

Fold both edges of buttonhole strip (5) to center-line and press (7). Baste-mark ⅛″ from each fold (i.e., halfway between fold and center), going through both thicknesses (8). The two basted lines must be ¼″ apart. Now cut strip into individual sections (length of buttonhole plus 1″) for each buttonhole. Make test buttonhole, following directions on p. 36. When making buttonholes on garment, do not complete each separately. Do one step on all, then the next step on all, etc.

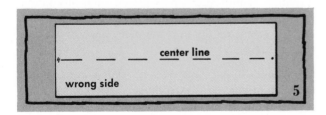

center line

wrong side

5

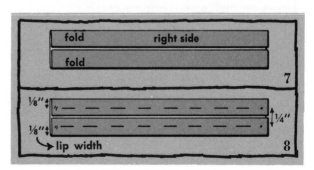

fold   right side

fold

7

⅛″   ¼″

⅛″

lip width

8

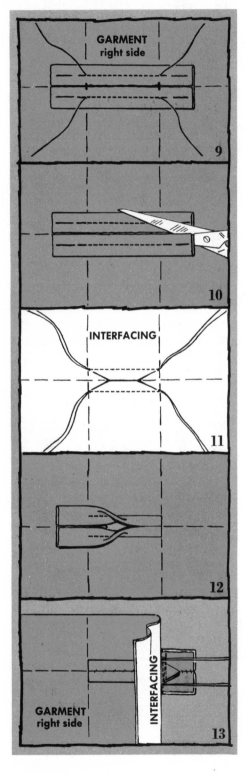

- Pin a buttonhole strip over a buttonhole position on outside of garment section, center line of strip over position line, ends extending ½″ beyond end-lines, as shown (9). Baste in place along center line. Re-connect end-lines, marking across strip.

- Starting and finishing at end-lines, stitch (20 stitches to inch) over basting lines on either side of center, as shown (9); leave 3″ thread-ends. Check: On both right side and interfacing side, stitching lines must be on grain, ¼″ apart, extending exactly to end-lines (if necessary, pull out a stitch or two, or put thread-end into a needle and make an extra stitch). If stitching is not perfect, remove carefully and stitch again.

- Pull thread-ends to interfacing side. Knot close to fabric, but do not trim off. Remove baste-marking from strip.

- Cut strip in two through entire length of center line (10). Be careful not to cut garment.

If you want a corded buttonhole, draw short lengths of cord through lips with tubing turner or tapestry needle. Cut cord-end off even with fabric.

- Cut buttonhole opening from interfacing side, through interfacing and garment fabric only: Start cutting at center and stop ¼″ from each end-line; then clip into each corner as far as possible without clipping stitches (11). *Be careful* not to cut into strips on other side.

- Put strips gently through opening to interfacing side (12). Flatten strips and see that lips meet. Secure lips on wrong side with diagonal basting (remove only after garment is finished). Beyond ends of opening, overcast folds of strips together.

- Place garment section on machine right side up. Fold one edge back as far as end of buttonhole, exposing strip-ends with tiny triangle lying on top. Holding thread-ends taut, stitch back and forth across base of triangle at end-line (13). Repeat on other end of buttonhole. Trim off thread-ends.

- Remove all baste-markings on garment section. Press buttonholes.

PATCH BUTTONHOLE

- Cut buttonhole strip (prepared as directed on p. 35) into individual patches (length of buttonhole plus 1″) for each buttonhole. Make test buttonhole, following directions on p. 37. When making buttonholes on garment, do not complete each separately. Do one step on all, then next step on all, etc.

- Pin patch to outside of garment section, right sides together, center line over position line, ends extending ½″ beyond each end-line. Baste in place along center line as shown (14).

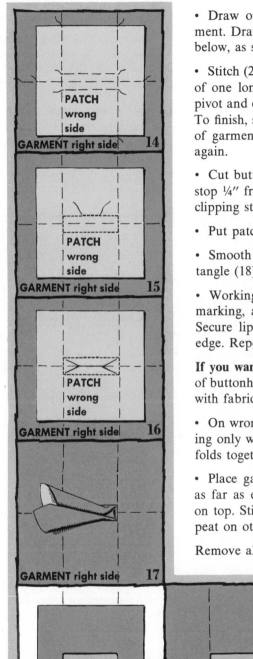

• Draw or baste-mark end-lines across patch, connecting lines on garment. Draw or baste-mark two lines parallel to center line, ⅛″ above and below, as shown (14). The rectangle formed outlines the buttonhole.

• Stitch (20 stitches to inch) slowly over outlined rectangle: Start at center of one long side; at corner, pivot on needle; count stitches across end; pivot and continue, counting off same number of stitches across other end. To finish, stitch over beginning stitches (15). Check stitching on right side of garment. If it is not perfectly on grain, remove carefully and stitch again.

• Cut buttonhole through all thicknesses (16): Start cutting at center and stop ¼″ from ends. Then clip into each corner as far as possible without clipping stitching. Remove basting on patch.

• Put patch gently through opening to interfacing side (17).

• Smooth out patch (especially corners); opening should be a perfect rectangle (18). Press lightly to flatten edges.

• Working from right side (19), bring a fold of patch even with center marking, as shown, forming a ⅛″ lip (keep seam allowance out of lip). Secure lip in position with hand-backstitching hidden in seam on long edge. Repeat to form second lip.

If you want a corded buttonhole, draw short lengths of cord through lips of buttonhole with tubing turner or tapestry needle. Cut cord-ends off even with fabric.

• On wrong side (20), secure lips with diagonal basting (remove this basting only when garment is finished). Beyond ends of opening, overcast the folds together.

• Place garment section on machine right side up. Fold one edge back as far as end of buttonhole, exposing strip-ends with tiny triangle lying on top. Stitch back and forth across base of triangle at end-line (21). Repeat on other end of buttonhole.

Remove all baste-markings on garment section. Press buttonholes.

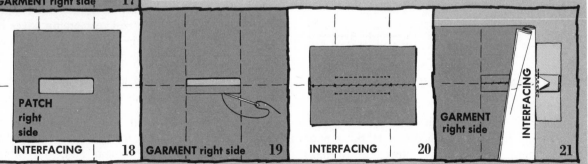

FACING THE BUTTONHOLES

The under or facing side of buttonholes may be finished by one of the three methods below.

• The **first two** are done after facing has been applied and pressed. If you have backed buttonhole area of outer fabric with iron-on interfacing to prevent fraying (p. 33), do the same on facing. Secure facing in place with pins near sides and ends of buttonholes.

. . . **Two-cornered finish** (22). Good for springy and ravelly fabrics. From outside of garment, stick a pin through *each end* of buttonhole. On facing side, cut between pins, following grain. Remove pins and cut ⅛″ more at each end. Turn both raw edges under and hem in place, as shown.

. . . **Rectangular finish** (23). Good for garments that may be worn open. From outside of garment, stick a pin through *each corner* of buttonhole. On facing, cut through center of buttonhole and into corners (as for buttonhole itself). Turn in raw edges; hem in place.

. . . **Rectangular with lightweight facing added,** described in TAILORING. Easy to do, very neat and durable. Best finish for garments that may be worn open and for heavy fabrics. Done *before facing is entirely applied*. See p. 188.

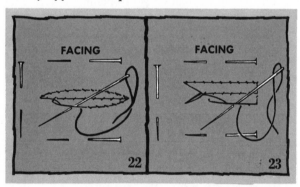

THE WORKED BUTTONHOLE

Worked buttonholes, whether made by hand or by machine, are worked on the outside of a garment after facing has been applied (for marking pattern and garment, see pp. 33–34). Never fail to make a test buttonhole first (see p. 33).

HAND-WORKED BUTTONHOLE

Depending on fabric, use regular sewing thread, "Heavy Duty" thread, or buttonhole twist. The first two may be used single (about 18″ long) or double (24″ before doubling).

Horizontal hand-worked buttonholes have a rounded fan end near garment opening (where button rests); the other end is finished with a bar tack (24). **Vertical** buttonholes have the same finish at both ends—either bar tacks or fans (25).

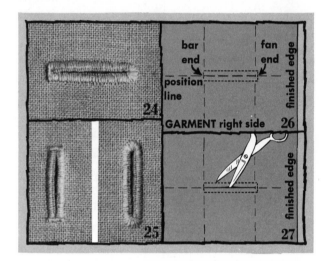

• Before cutting slit, outline and reinforce buttonhole edges with a row of fine machine-stitching (20 stitches per inch) 1/16″ to either side of position line (26). Starting at an end-line, stitch carefully to next end-line; pivot on needle; count stitches across end; pivot and continue around, counting off same number of stitches across other end. Another way of outlining and reinforcing edges before hand-working is to make a narrow machine-worked buttonhole.

• Cut slit between end-lines, starting at center and cutting toward each end-line (27).

• Make a knot in your thread-end. Have garment edge to your left (28). Insert needle into right side of fabric about ½″ from bar end, and bring out through slit at that end. Knot will be removed later.

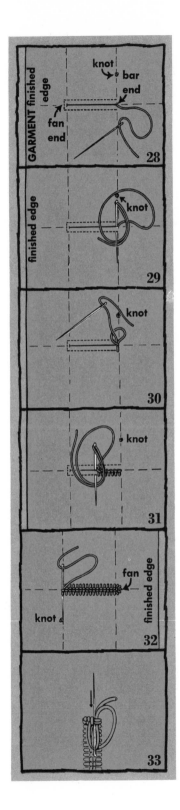

The Buttonhole Stitch is done from right to left, needle pointing toward you. Use machine-stitching as a guide for stitch depth (except at fan end).

• Insert needle into slit and bring out just below stitching. Bring thread hanging from eye of needle from right to left under point of needle (29).

• Draw up needle away from you (30), so that purl (knot) comes at edge of slit. Do not draw thread tight when you do this.

• Repeat this stitch (31), placing stitches close together so that purls cover edge. Work to other end-line.

• Where there is a fan, work around fan end as shown (32), keeping stitch depth the same and turning work gradually; make 5 to 7 stitches in fan, pushing purls to underside except on center stitch, in line with slit. Where there is no fan, turn work after reaching end-line.

• Cover second edge with buttonhole stitch. When last purl is completed, put needle through purl of first stitch; bring out just below last stitch (32).

To make bar tack, take one or more stitches across end of buttonhole, spanning width of both rows. Then work over this thread with blanket stitch without catching fabric. Use needle eye-first, as shown (33).

• Put needle through to wrong side. On a **horizontal buttonhole,** run thread under a few stitches and cut. On a **vertical buttonhole,** which has two bar tacks, run thread under stitches to other end of buttonhole and make a second bar tack like the first one.

• Cut off extra ½″ of thread used for starting, and pull out knot.

To start a new thread while working, run thread under a few finished stitches on wrong side; bring needle and thread through last purl made.

NOTE: Add quality to a ready-made garment by going over buttonholes with above stitch; this will also add to the life of the buttonholes.

MACHINE-WORKED BUTTONHOLE

Machine-worked buttonholes are made with a buttonhole attachment or on a machine equipped for zigzag stitching. Follow directions in manuals. Use regular thread and needle.

. . . Color of interfacing should come close to color of garment, as it will show at cut edge of buttonhole.

. . . For a stronger, better-looking buttonhole, stitch around a second time, making this second row slightly narrower than the first.

. . . Protect thick, napped or lustrous fabric by covering buttonhole area with cellophane before slipping garment into stitching position under attachment. Then remove cellophane and complete buttonhole. Replace cellophane before sliding out garment.

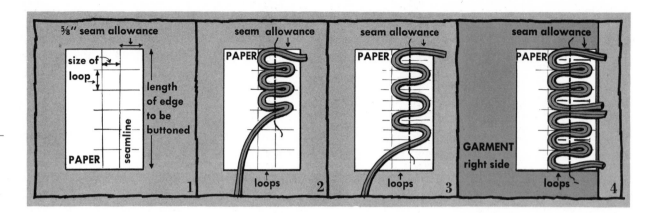

BUTTON LOOPS

Button loops, extending beyond the finished edge of a garment, often take the place of buttonholes.

Any buttons can be used with fabric loops, but the ones most often seen are ball buttons, usually fabric-covered. With braid loops, Chinese ball buttons (p. 44) can, if desired, be made of the same braid. Loops vary greatly in thickness and size, depending on fabric, button, location, etc. They may be part either of decorative or of concealed fastenings.

In decorative fastenings, loops are made of fabric tubing, self-filled or corded, or of round braid. They are used on dressmaker suits, on close-fitting long sleeves or bodices, and on coats and jackets.

In concealed fastenings, a loop, usually single, may be made of thread (as in the neck corner of blouse), or of fabric (for example, in the neck corner of man's sports shirt or underlap of coat).

DECORATIVE FASTENINGS

Row of Loops

Use narrow tubing (⅛″ or narrower), self-filled or corded (see BIAS, p. 30), or round braid.

On an edge to be faced, loops are applied before facing is attached. In this case, the cord should be about three times the length of opening, but it need not be in one piece.

• Cut a piece of sturdy paper about 2″ wide and as long as opening. On one long edge, mark off seam allowance. Determine size of loop needed for size of button. Measure and mark size of loops on paper as shown (1), without or with intervals (2 or 3).

Place one end of paper and one end of cord under presser foot (always keep *seam of cord,* if any, turned *up;* see 2 and 3), and anchor cord with needle on marked seamline. Form first loop; stitch on seamline. Continue, forming loops as you go, until all loops are attached.

• Pin paper to right side of garment, matching edges as shown, loops facing away from edge, as shown (4). Stitch on top of stitching which holds loops. Tear off paper. Apply facing. Trim seam allowances and loop-ends to ¼″. Finish opening (5).

On a finished edge, loops are applied after edge is finished. Cord should be about twice length of opening and must be in one piece.

• Determine size of loop needed for size of button. On garment edge, measure and mark width of loops with pins, as shown (6). On cord, measure and mark size of loops in same manner. Beginning at first mark and matching pins, attach cord to edge with small stitches, sliding needle to next mark through fold of garment. Be careful that seam in cord (if any) is not turned to right side.

Single Loops

Use tubing, either self-filled or corded (see BIAS, p. 30) of a size in keeping with size of button and weight of fabric. Single loops are usually larger than loops in a row. They are always applied to a faced edge, before facing is attached.

With seam of tubing up, pin tubing to right side of garment, forming a loop facing away from edge, large enough to accommodate button (7). Stitch to garment on seamline, as shown. Apply facing and finish.

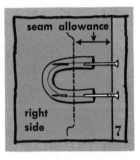

Frogs

Frogs, shown here in two designs, are highly decorative button loops that can be used on any finished front opening. They vary greatly in size, and can be used (I) in pairs (i.e., with the motif repeated on the button side), or singly (II). The button can be a Chinese ball button (p. 44) made with the same cord as the frog, or any shank button.

Use tubing, self-filled or corded (see BIAS, p. 30), or braid. Length needed depends on design. Determine size of loop needed for your button. Draw outline of frog on a piece of sturdy paper (8, 9). Frog will be constructed on this paper right side down, which means that seams on tubing, stitches, and cord-ends will all face up as it is made.

I. Made from one piece of cord. Starting at center, baste cord to paper, following outline (8). Sew cord together at crossings. Secure ends.

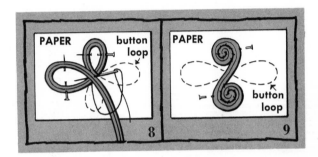

II. Made from two pieces of cord. Begin by stitching together a small, tight spiral, making sure that visible cord-end and stitches all face you. When spiral is the right size, repeat in contrary direction with other end of cord, to fit design (9). Cut off cord-end in center of spiral. Baste to paper. Form loops with a separate piece of cord, basting to outline and joining at center. Sew the two parts together at crossing.

Remove frog from paper; take more stitches if needed. Sew to garment right side up, with garment opening pinned together. Button loop extends beyond edge. If frogs are made in a pair, sew button securely to "button loop" on left-hand side of garment.

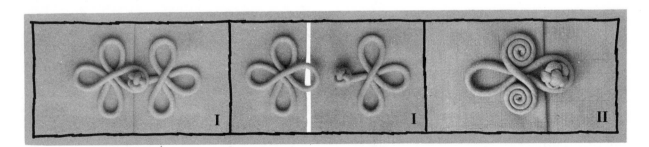

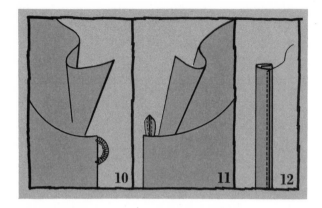

CONCEALED FASTENINGS

Thread Loop—Made after garment is finished (10). See p. 197.

Fabric Loop—Can be bias or straight-grain, and is usually made from garment fabric (11). It is applied before facing is attached—see **Single Loops,** p. 41.
Bias Loop—Made of tubing, either flat or self-filled (p. 30). Size depends on garment.
Straight-grain Loop—Cut a strip on the straight grain, about ½″ x 2¼″. Turn in long edges, fold in half lengthwise, and topstitch (12).

BUTTONS

Buttons, with their companion buttonholes, generally serve as fastenings. They are also, with or without buttonholes, used as decoration—often as counterparts to "working" buttons (as in most double-breasted garments), or for simulating a button closure.

TYPES OF BUTTONS

Buttons may be made of almost any material—wood, metal, plastic, mother-of-pearl, glass, fabric, crochet cotton, etc.—and in many shapes; they may be plain or fancy, worth a fortune (diamond buttons) or sold at a quarter a dozen. From the standpoint of sewing on the button, however, they fall into just two categories:

the **pierced button,** provided with two or four holes through which it is sewed on;

the **shank button,** which has a solid top and a shank or stem underneath for sewing on. The shank may be in one piece with the button or may consist of a wire or fabric loop.

IMPORTANT: Holes or shank must be free of rough edges, which might cut through the thread.

POSITION OF BUTTONS

Position of **buttons in a closure** is marked after garment is completed. Lap opening of garment as it will be worn, with neck, waistline and/or hem evenly lined up. Through buttonhole, place a pin at exact spot where button is to be sewn, picking up a small amount of fabric: near outer edge with a horizontal buttonhole (1); in center of buttonhole with a vertical buttonhole.

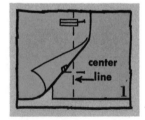

Position of **buttons without buttonholes** (decorative) is marked at the time that all markings are transferred from pattern.

REINFORCING BUTTON POSITION

Buttons need a firm backing. In closures, they usually fall on a faced and interfaced part of garment, but even a decorative button should not be sewn to a single thickness of fabric. When such a button falls in a single-thickness area, or when the existing backing of a "working" button does not seem strong enough for the strain to which it will be subjected, reinforcing is necessary. This is done in one of the three ways below.

For light and medium-weight fabrics—Cut a circle of iron-on fabric a little smaller than button. Before sewing on button, press circle to wrong side of button position (if possible, between garment and facing).

For any fabric—Place a small square of doubled fabric to wrong side of button location and stitch through it as you sew on button.

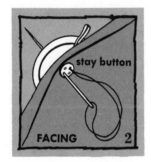

On heavy or tailored garments—Hold a small, flat "stay-button" to wrong (facing) side of garment and stitch through it as you sew on button (2).

CHOICE OF THREAD

Be sure to choose the right thread for the fabric to which button is to be sewn.

For light to medium-weight fabrics—Mercerized regular or "Heavy Duty."

For heavier fabrics—Mercerized Best Cord. This comes in many sizes, of which No. 8 (coarsest) through No. 24 are excellent for buttons. However, it is made in black and white only. Use your judgment in selecting.

For very heavy fabrics—Button & Carpet Thread.

SEWING ON BUTTON

A "working" button always needs a shank, to allow buttonhole to fit smoothly under it. For a pierced button, a shank is made out of thread (see at right).

Length of shank is determined by thickness of fabric: a sheer fabric will need a barely perceptible one, while with a heavy wool it may be necessary to extend even the stem of a shank button.

When attaching a decorative button, which needs no shank, omit bobby pin (or whatever you use) in the instructions below.

Use thread single or doubled, depending on fabric (if thread is doubled, be careful to draw it up evenly with each stitch). Make a small knot at end. On right side of garment (knot will be covered by button), take a small stitch at button position, picking up all thicknesses, but being careful not to let stitch show through facing fabric in a jacket or a coat. Take a second small stitch across the same space.

Pierced Button—Bring thread up through one hole in button. Centering button over stitch, place a bobby pin, matchstick, or toothpick (depending on length of shank desired) between button and fabric (3), and take three or four stitches through each pair of holes. Bring needle and thread out between button and fabric, remove bobby pin or other, and wind thread a number of times around the attaching thread, to form a shank. Take a small stitch in fabric (4). Finish off thread securely. Buttons become detached quite as often through loosening as through breaking of thread. Take several small stitches under button, looping thread over needle to form knots. **Cut,** do not break, thread.

Shank button—If length of shank is sufficient, take 6 to 8 stitches (less if thread is doubled) through shank and finish off as with pierced button. If shank needs lengthening, take a first stitch through shank, then place a bobby pin or other underneath and proceed as with pierced button.

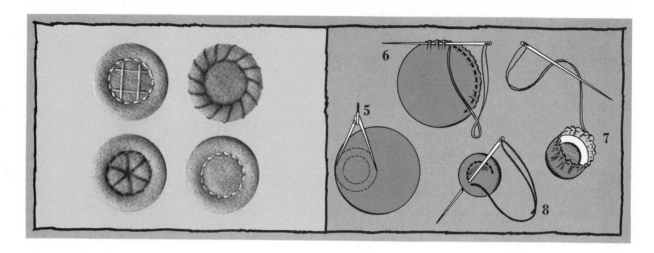

MAKING FABRIC BUTTONS

Whether you have fabric buttons made commercially or make them yourself, have them ready before you make buttonholes. To attach, catch fabric (or cord) underneath and handle like a shank button.

Covered Buttons are made (covered) with your own fabric. You may:

[a] order them from a notions store or counter;

[b] make them yourself, using a kit sold for the purpose (directions with package);

[c] make them yourself, using bone or plastic rings as a base, as follows: Cut fabric circles twice the diameter of rings (5). Gather edge, using doubled thread (6). Draw up over ring (7), and fasten securely. To trim, use matching or contrasting thread and take stitches inside ring, as shown (8). Optional: Cover back with small circle of fine fabric.

Chinese Ball Buttons are made with a length of round cord, which may be either purchased braid or bias tubing, corded or self-filled (see BIAS, p. 30). Here is estimated amount needed for each:

for ⅜″ button:	use ⅛″ cord	6″ length
for ½″ button:	use 3/16″ cord	8″ length
for ⅞″ button:	use ¼″ cord	10″ length
for 1″ button:	use ⅜″ cord	12″ length
for 1⅜″ button:	use ⅜″ cord	36″ length

(fold in half and work double)

Loop cord as shown in diagrams 9 to 11 (shaded sections indicate part looped in previous steps), keeping loops open while working. Then draw them together, easing and shaping into a ball while keeping the two ends firmly together underneath. Trim off ends and sew flat to underside of button.

CASINGS

A casing serves to accommodate an elastic or a drawstring. It may be formed by a **hem,** either turned up or bias-faced (top of apron or skirt, bottom of overblouse, neck and sleeves of night-gown, child's dress, etc.), or by a separate bias strip—an **applied casing**—stitched along both edges to the wrong side of a garment (at the waist of a straight dress with no waist seam, below an edge where a single-thickness heading is desired, etc.). A **heading** is a narrow width of fabric that extends beyond an edge-casing and forms a ruffle when casing is drawn up.

MAKING A CASING

Width of casing: Width of elastic or drawstring plus ⅛″ (more if drawstring or elastic has bulk).

Opening in casing: Read instructions that follow under this heading **before** making casing.

A hem used as a casing is machine-stitched.

Casing in Turned-up Hem—For straight edges only.

• Turn in ¼″ at edge; press. Turn hem to desired depth (width of casing; or casing plus heading). Pin. Machine-stitch as shown (1). On a casing without heading, make a second line of stitching close to fold (optional). On a casing with heading, mark width of casing and make a second line of stitching as shown (2).

Casing in Bias-Faced Hem—For curved edges. Also suitable for straight edges to reduce bulk.

• Follow directions for **Faced Hem** (see p. 104), using bias strip the width of casing alone or casing plus heading (plus seam allowances). After turning facing to wrong side, machine-stitch edge of facing in place. On a casing without heading, make a second line of stitching close to fold (3). On a casing with heading, mark width of casing and make a second line of stitching at that distance from fold (4).

Applied Casing—For any place not an actual edge.

Packaged bias strip of nearest suitable width is generally used. For a casing with a single-thickness heading, actual edge of fabric is finished with a narrow hem.

Mark position of upper edge of casing on inside of garment. Pin strip in place; stitch along both edges (5).

fold	fold	fold	fold	fold
CASING	HEADING	CASING	HEADING	CASING
	CASING		CASING	
wrong side 1	wrong side 2	wrong side 3	wrong side 4	wrong side 5

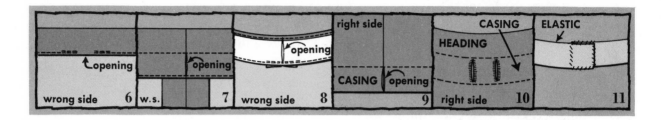

OPENING IN CASING FOR INSERTING ELASTIC OR DRAWSTRING

Elastic—Opening is on wrong side of garment.

In a Turned-up Hem—You may either leave a ½″ opening when stitching down hem, in which case you backstitch at beginning and end for reinforcement (6); or take out stitches in a seam across casing (7).

In a Bias-Faced Hem of an Applied Casing—Fold bias strip under ½″ at beginning and end of application. Make folds meet and overlap stitching at end (5 and 8).

Drawstring—Opening is on right side of garment.

For All Casings—If there is a seam at a suitable location, take out stitches across casing and reinforce end or ends of opening as shown (9). Otherwise, make two worked eyelets or buttonholes in single thickness (outside fabric) of casing, as shown (10).

To insert elastic or drawstring, use a bodkin or a safety pin and push through casing. Be sure not to let elastic twist. To secure elastic, keep the two ends out, overlap and whipstitch together as shown (11), before letting them go into casing.

COLLARS

Collars vary greatly in shape and size. They may have square or pointed corners or a rounded edge; they may be cut in two pieces (upper collar and undercollar or facing), in one piece (folded), or with undercollar in one with garment body and upper collar in one with garment facing (shawl collar). In all the variations of the collar, however, the basic details in the construction are the same. These details are covered in the following pages, the directions being adaptable to any collar, including one cut as part of the garment body.

Interfacing is generally necessary in a collar, and not only for crispness. The interfacing becomes part of the upper collar and the double thickness prevents the seam allowances from showing through on right side of finished collar. If interfacing is not specified in pattern, see INTERFACING for cutting.

MAKING A PERFECT COLLAR

Directions apply to collars made in one section or in two sections.

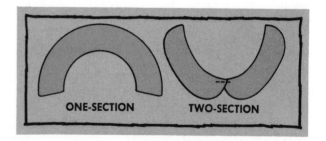

In addition to other markings, make a small clip-mark in seam allowance or cut a notch at center of neck edge on collar (this will ensure accurate placement on garment later).

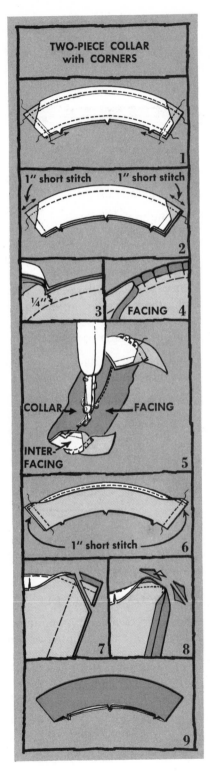

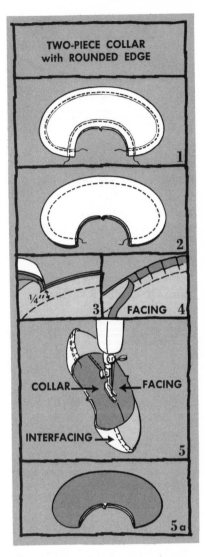

For a perfectly even finished edge, mark seamlines on interfacing. Trim away corners of interfacing, if any.

• Stay-stitch interfacing, marked side up, to wrong side of upper collar (1). This piece will hereafter be handled and referred to as one piece. (To avoid confusion, stay-stitching is not shown in drawings after this step.)

• Stay-stitch undercollar. Pin undercollar to upper collar, right sides together.

• With interfacing side up, stitch outer edge on marked seamline (2). On collar with corners, stitch from edge to edge of fabric, as shown, reinforcing corners by shortening stitch at beginning and end; do not stitch ends of collar.

• Trim seam allowances to ¼", as shown (3).

• Grade seam allowances. Clip at ¼" intervals (4).

• Understitch (5). On rounded-edge collar, understitch entire seam. On collar with corners, start and stop understitching 1" from ends.

• Rounded-edge collar is now finished. Turn to right side and press (5-a).

• On collar with corners, stitch end-seams, shortening stitch at corners as before (6).

• Trim corners (7).

• Press end-seams open with point of iron.

• Trim, grade, and taper end-seam allowances toward corner (8).

• Turn collar to right side, pushing out corners carefully as you do so. Press (9).

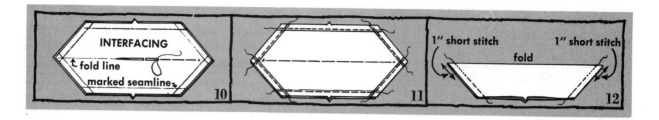

One-Piece Collar

This collar, cut in one piece with its facing and folded on its outer edge, is always entirely straight, with pointed corners. It is best interfaced with very light fabric, cut exactly like outer fabric.

• On interfacing, mark seamlines and fold line.

• Pin interfacing to wrong side of collar, marked side up. Along fold line, catch interfacing to collar with tiny stitches, about ½″ apart and invisible on right side (10). Start and end stitches about 1″ in from outer edges.

• Stay-stitch ½″ from outer edge (11). To avoid confusion, stay-stitching is not shown in drawings after this step.

• Fold collar in half lengthwise, interfaced side out. Stitch ends, reinforcing corners by shortening stitch (12). Trim corners (13). Press end-seams open with point of iron (see **Underpress,** p. 82).

• Trim, grade, and taper seams toward corners (14).

• Turn collar to right side. Press (15).

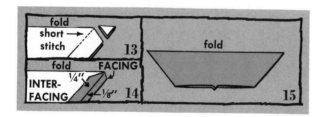

ATTACHING A COLLAR

A collar can be attached to a garment in different ways, depending on the style of the garment. Its neck edge may be caught in a shaped facing all around, or in a shaped facing at front of garment only; or the neck edge may be finished with a bias strip. The pattern primer will tell you what method applies to your garment.

Here, however, are some useful pointers:

IMPORTANT—After a collar is turned, raw edges at neck are no longer even, because upper collar has been brought slightly over outer edge by understitching. Do not try to make these raw edges match—when stitching them to garment, match raw edge of undercollar to neckline. Seam allowance in upper collar will just be a little narrower.

• Always stay-stitch garment neckline, so you can safely clip seam allowance before attaching collar.

• A two-section collar must be anchored together before attaching, to prevent it from spreading. Overlap ends so that edges meet at neck seamline; baste across by hand or machine (16).

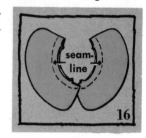

• After collar has been stitched to neck edge of garment, trim, grade, clip, and understitch this seam as you would any facing seam (see FACINGS, p. 82).

MAKING A COLLAR DETACHABLE

Any collar can be made detachable by trimming its unfinished neck edge to ¼″ seam allowance and encasing it in double-fold bias tape. This edge can then be attached inside garment neck edge by means of basting or small snaps. On underside of collar, sew ball part of snaps to bias tape; then—for comfort when garment is worn without collar—sew the socket half of snaps to matching points along the neckline.

CORNERS

Corners, of various kinds and different angles, occur often in clothing, as these illustrations show. The corners must be neatly made, to avoid bulk and to strengthen seams that are weakened by inside trimming and clipping.

Refer to the following chapters for handling the different corners:

Faced Corners (collars, lapels, cuffs, 1 and 4; neckline, 3). See FACINGS, particularly **Processing the Seam,** p. 82.

Patch Pockets (1), lined and unlined. See POCKETS.

Applied Piece (3)—For outside corners, see **Unlined Patch Pocket,** p. 155. At inside corners, stitch through one thickness on seamline and clip into corners before turning seam allowance under.

Bound Corners—See **Corners in Binding,** p. 29 in BIAS.

Corners at Set-in Piece, such as a gusset (1), or at a specially-designed armhole (2). See GUSSETS.

Slashed Opening at neck (5) or in long sleeves. See PLACKETS.

CUFFS

Cuffs on sleeves vary a great deal in design and construction. A cuff cut in one piece with the sleeve is simply a very deep hem which is partly folded up on outside of sleeve. A cuff cut separately may consist of one piece of fabric folded in half, or of two pieces seamed together. It may be folded back over the sleeve (1, 2), or on itself (French cuff, 3), or consist of a plain doubled band into which the sleeve is gathered (4). Cuff-ends may be closed (1), or open (2), or fastened with buttons or cufflinks (3).

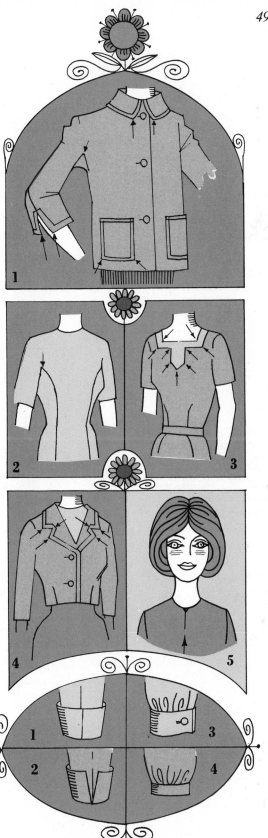

Cuffs should almost always have a certain crispness and body, and interfacing is generally specified in conjunction with a cuff pattern. If it is not, and your fabric seems to require the addition of interfacing, cut interfacing from the cuff pattern.

The pattern primer will tell you how to make and attach your cuffs. However . . .

. . . A cuff with edge-seams is made exactly like a collar. For smooth, sharp edges, follow **Making a Perfect Collar** on pp. 46–47, substituting the word "cuff" for "collar" throughout.

. . . If you are attaching a cuff to a gathered sleeve, be sure, when stitching, to have the gathered side (not the cuff side) up. This allows you to control the gathers more easily.

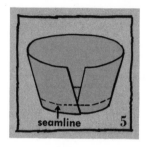

. . . If you are about to attach a cuff with open ends to a closed sleeve, prevent ends from spreading by first overlapping them so that edges meet at seamline; then baste across by hand or by machine (5).

. . . Detachable cuffs are finished like a detachable collar. See COLLARS, last paragraph.

CUTTING

Cutting, with its irrevocable aspect—there's no denying that a mistake in cutting cannot be ripped out like a wrong seam—often makes a person nervous, especially if the fabric is expensive. The thing to do is to proceed without haste, and to follow directions. Study your pattern primer, and take into account all indications on the pattern pieces themselves. What we give you here is the method of procedure.

THE EQUIPMENT

Assemble everything you need:
Cutting surface (large table or cutting board) . . . Shears . . . Tape measure . . . Yardstick and small ruler . . . Pencil . . . Pins and pincushion . . . Fabric (prepared, if necessary—see FABRICS, p. 71) . . . Pattern . . . Iron and ironing board.

PREPARING THE PATTERN

Pick out pattern pieces you will use (depending on what "View" of garment you have selected on envelope). Smooth out pieces with warm, dry iron. Make pattern alterations, if any (see PATTERNS, p. 134).

Small pieces, if printed together, must be cut apart.

Grain line marks, to serve their purpose properly, must extend the entire length of pattern pieces. Using yardstick and pencil, extend grain line arrows on printed patterns (1); on perforated patterns, draw in entire line.

Selecting Your Pattern Layout

On pattern primer, locate and circle your pattern layout: for the selected *view* of your garment, for your *pattern size, fabric width,* and fabric either *"With Nap"* or *"Without Nap"* (2).

. . . See **Buying Fabric** (p. 70) for the fabrics that come under the classification "With Nap," and why (there are many besides actual napped fabrics).

. . . Fabrics that are "Without Nap" have no up or down direction in design, weave, or texture, and may be cut with pattern pieces facing in either direction (3) if they are on grain.

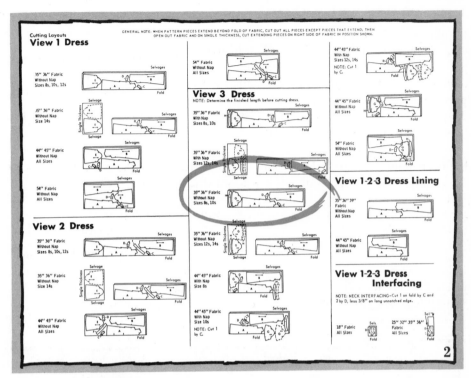

. . . A true napped fabric (wool broadcloth, flannel, camel's hair, etc.) looks best with nap running toward hem of garment (6).

. . . A pile fabric (velvet, corduroy, etc.) has a richer color with the pile running toward top of garment (7). Fake fur varies; hold it up both ways and decide.

. . . Fabrics "With Nap" must be cut with the tops of all the pattern pieces facing the same way (4, 5).

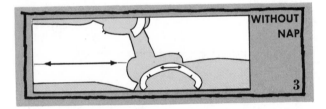

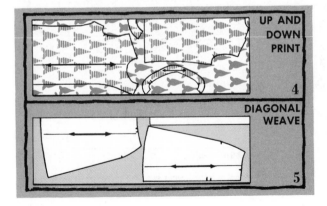

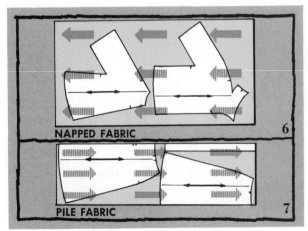

THE FOLD IN THE FABRIC

If your fabric fiber demands it (see FABRICS, p. 71), you will have shrunk the fabric and straightened its cut ends. Press out any wrinkles. Press out center fold to make sure it does not leave a mark. If fold cannot be pressed out, you will have to avoid it as you lay out the pieces. See **A Trial Layout,** p. 54. Carefully refold fabric for cutting, following the grain.

Fabric is almost always folded right sides together for cutting. It is cut right side out if it has a design that must be taken into account and that does not show through to wrong side (printed corduroy, bonded fabrics).

Fold fabric as shown in cutting layout on pattern primer. Never let fabric hang over edge of cutting surface to avoid stretching.

Layout using regular lengthwise fold (A)

Pin matching selvages together in a few places (A-a).

Layout requiring crosswise fold (B)

Regular fold pressed out. Fold fabric across width, as shown; pin matching selvages together (B-a).

Layout requiring new lengthwise fold (C)

Regular fold pressed out. On cutting layout, identify pattern piece which determines width of fold (in layout C, piece 5). Pick out actual pattern piece and measure width. On fabric, spread out singly, measure double this width from selvage and mark with pins (C-a). Fold fabric, bringing selvage to pin-line; smooth out, and pin selvage along line (C-b).

Layout requiring a combination of folds (D)

In such a case, you position only the pattern pieces requiring a certain fold. Cut these out, then make the new fold.

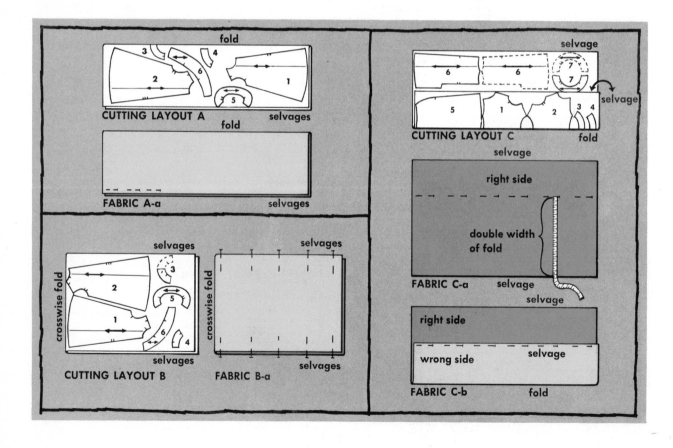

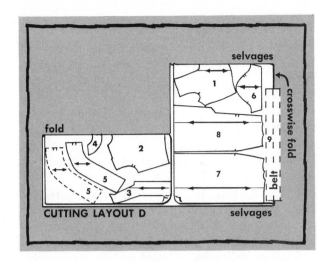

CUTTING LAYOUT D

EXAMPLE: In layout D, two different folds are needed. You would first cut out pieces 2, 3, 4, 5 with regular fold; then press out fold on remaining fabric and fold fabric crosswise. Cut out pieces 1, 6, 7, 8, 9, placed as shown. For piece 9 (belt) open out fold and cut on single thickness.

ARRANGING PATTERN PIECES

If you have bought the correct yardage, as given on pattern envelope, a trial layout will not be necessary (see below for cases requiring a trial layout). Just be guided exactly by the layout you have circled.

. . . When, on a layout, a pattern piece is shown extending beyond a fold line (piece 9 on layout D), cut out the other pieces, then open out remaining fabric to cut this one.

. . . When a pattern piece is drawn with a broken line (second piece 6 on layout C), it means that *after* other pieces are cut you either:

[a] fold remaining fabric (here, crosswise) and cut piece out through both thicknesses, or
[b] cut piece through single thickness, then reverse pattern (printed side down) and cut piece out a second time.

. . . When half of a pattern piece is drawn with a broken line (piece 3 in layout B), it means that the piece is a half-pattern, to be cut on a fold. Cut out all other pieces as laid out, then re-fold fabric to cut each of these pattern pieces.

. . . With a printed pattern, overlap margins to cutting line (8).

. . . With a perforated pattern, place pieces edge to edge (9).

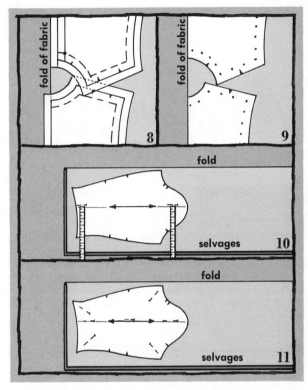

Place first pattern piece (largest piece located at one end of layout) on fabric. To position grain line, measure distance from one end of extended grain line to selvage (10); pin pattern through grain line. Pin through other end of grain line at same distance (10); then through center of line.

Smooth pattern out from grain line and pin at opposite corners, then at opposite sides (11). Keep pins inside cutting line of pattern and don't use too many—they can distort the cutting line.

Repeating the same steps for each, pin in place all the pattern pieces that require the same fold in the fabric.

Plaids and Stripes

Pattern should have few seams, and preferably be designed for plaids or stripes. Because of allowance necessary in matching design, you will need extra yardage.

Plaids and stripes may be even (of symmetrical design) or uneven. The uneven design must be cut "With Nap" so it runs in the same direction on each piece.

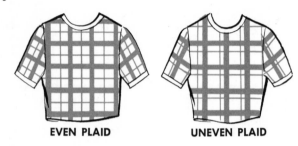

EVEN PLAID   **UNEVEN PLAID**

For cutting, these fabrics must be folded very accurately, with edges pinned together so that corresponding lines are matched.

To match plaids and large stripes, see that notches that correspond on pattern fall on stripes that correspond on fabric (12).

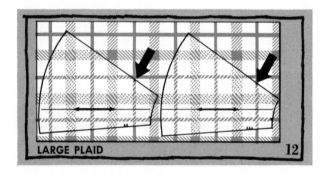

LARGE PLAID   12

Stripes must match at the following places:
. . . sleeve cap notches and armhole notches at front and back,
. . . at shoulder notches on kimono sleeves,
. . . at shoulder seam notches for vertical stripes,
. . . at center seams and, when possible, side seams,
. . . where collars and yokes meet bodice, if they are not on the bias.

Large Printed Designs

Pattern should have few seams. Try to place pieces on fabric so that motifs are arranged for a pleasing effect. Try to match motifs at seams whenever possible.

A Trial Layout

This may be necessary
. . . if your fabric is of a width not indicated on primer,
. . . if your fabric is "With Nap" (see p. 51) and there is no cutting layout "With Nap,"
. . . if you have been unable to press out the fold in your fabric when necessary,
. . . if your fabric has a plaid or other design that must be matched.

To make a trial layout, select cutting layout that seems closest to what you need and place all pattern pieces in proper position, with one or two pins in each. When you have made sure that you have sufficient fabric, *do not cut out* until you have checked each piece for correct grain position, proceeding as directed above and folding fabric as necessary.

CUTTING

Never use pinking shears to cut out pieces—they do not give a reliable cut line.

Cutting lines on patterns are indicated in different ways:
   A printed pattern may have either a single or a double line. Cut exactly outside single line; or between two lines.
   A perforated pattern is cut out exactly along edge.

Keep fabric and pattern flat on table. Never draw fabric toward you to reach a piece.

Cut with long strokes. When cutting into a corner, open shears only wide enough to have points of blades reach end of cut.

Notches are not really notches any longer, although they have kept that name. A notch is now cut, not into seam allowance, but into adjoining fabric, making a **point** on seam allowance. Two or more "notches" are cut in a block, as shown (13), rather than singly.

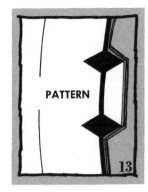

In sections that are at center front or center back of garment, mark center points, top and bottom, with a notch or a small clip in seam allowance.

Do not remove pattern pieces from sections cut. You will need them for the next step, MARKING (see p. 120).

CUTTING THROUGH A SINGLE THICKNESS

Some of the new fabrics require that they be cut through a single thickness at a time.

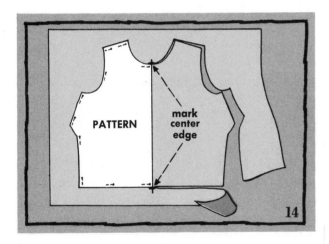

When pattern is to be cut on a fold (usually at center front or center back), trim margin from center ("fold") edge. Pin pattern in place on wrong side of a single thickness of fabric (except for leather, when pattern is placed on right side). With chalk or pins, mark fabric at top and bottom of "fold" edge of pattern piece. Cut around pattern piece except for "fold" edge. Unpin pattern and reverse it, matching "fold" edge to chalk marks. Re-pin and cut out second half (14). When cutting two corresponding sections (sleeves) from a single thickness, reverse pattern for second section.

DARTS

Darts are stitched, pointed tucks that shape the fabric to fit the body. They are clearly indicated on patterns. Since their exact length, depth, and placement have a great bearing on the fit of a garment, they may need some alteration. This, fortunately, is relatively easy (see **Pattern Alterations,** p. 134).

MARKING

Center of dart is usually shown by a solid line. If your pattern does not carry this line, carefully measure and mark center of dart at widest point; then draw a line to point of dart.

Carefully transfer center line and stitching lines to fabric. Make short crosslines (1) to mark point of dart and matching dots (see MARKING, p. 121).

SEWING

Fold dart on center line, then pin or baste.

Start stitching either at point or at wide end. To make sure that point will taper to nothing gradually (as it *must*), take two stitches at point, along fold, as close to fold as possible (2). Tie thread-ends.

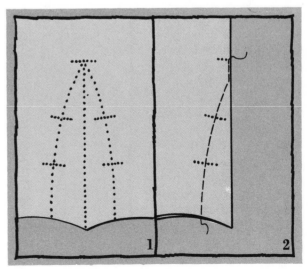

FINISHING

Generally there is no special finish for a dart before pressing; the following cases, however, are the exceptions:

Deep dart—Trim or slash to within ½″ of point (3).

Heavy fabric—Slash to within ½″ to 1″ of point of dart (3).

Lace or sheers, unbacked—Make a second line of stitching ⅛″ from first (4); trim (5).

Double-pointed dart—Clip at widest part; reinforce stitching (6).

Curved dart—Trim to ⅝″; clip at curve; reinforce stitching.

PRESSING

First press line of stitching as is, but be careful not to put a crease into fabric by pressing beyond point. Then open out garment; to maintain shaping, complete pressing over a pressing ham, or end of ironing board, or sleeve board. Trimmed or slashed darts are pressed open like a seam (3). Vertical uncut darts are pressed toward center of garment (6). Horizontal and diagonal darts are pressed downward (7). If fabric marks easily, slip a piece of paper between dart and fabric.

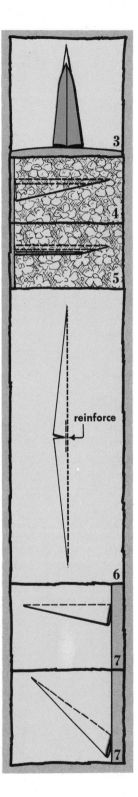

A FEW SPECIAL CASES

Dart in backed garment—In order to keep the two layers of fabric together at fold, machine-baste (on backing side) through center line before folding and stitching dart. Basting must not show beyond point.

Dart in very sheer fabric—"Bobbin-stitching" will avoid a knot at point, where it might show through. Thread machine as usual, and turn wheel to bring needle and take-up lever to highest point. Then:

• Draw out about 20″ of bobbin thread through hole in throat plate.

• Remove thread from machine needle. Thread bobbin thread through needle, in opposite direction.

• Knot bobbin and spool thread together (8). Wind spool, drawing bobbin thread through needle and onto spool (9). Bobbin thread is now continuous from spool to bobbin.

• Stitch dart, starting at point. Rethread machine for each dart.

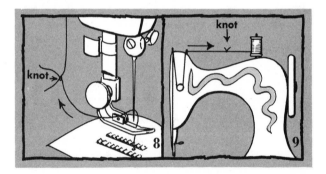

Dart tucks release fullness at one or both ends. Mark and pin or baste as for regular darts. Starting at fold, stitch across to marking; pivot fabric on needle; stitch along marking to edge of garment (10), or pivot again and stitch across to fold (11). Tie the ends. Press toward center of the garment.

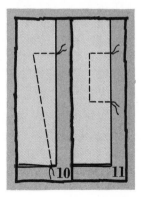

DECORATION

Decoration may be something applied to a garment purely as trimming, or it may be a functional detail, done in a decorative manner. Among the latter are a facing turned to the outside (see FACINGS, p. 85), bias binding and piping (see BIAS, p. 28 and p. 31), and self-fringe. The decorations that follow are of both kinds, selected because they are the ones you are most likely to use. They are in alphabetical order.

APPLIQUÉ

Appliqué (1) is a piece of fabric, almost always small and in a contrasting color, applied as a decoration to a background fabric. Unless the motif is cut out of a print, it is traced on the appliqué fabric with a sharp pencil, on wrong side for hand appliqué, on right side for machine appliqué. It may also consist of bias strips.

For hand appliqué, make a line of machine-stitching, exactly on outline of motif. Cut out ⅛″ outside outline. Pin motif in place. Turning under raw edge along line of machine stitching as you sew, attach edges either with invisible slipstitch (see HEMS, p.101), or with small blanket stitch (see **Embroidery,** p. 58).

NOTE: Appliqués of felt, which does not ravel, are cut out on outline itself and tacked on invisibly (these are often used on sweaters).

For machine appliqué, cut out motif, leaving about 1″ seam allowance all around. Cut an identical piece of a lightweight, heavily sized fabric—the lower the thread count, the better (starched lawn or cheap organdy are very good); place between appliqué and background fabric, and pin. Do not baste, because basting may cause puckering; do not turn edges under. Stitching is done with a close zigzag stitch and with thread matching the appliqué (contrasting thread will show up any imperfection in stitching). Try out stitch length (closeness) and bight (width) on scraps of all layers: background, in-between and appliqué

fabric. The narrower the bight, the easier it is to control the stitching. Stitch at slow speed, even with hand on wheel, if necessary, adjusting and manipulating fabric as you stitch, in order to avoid puckers and distortion. If appliqué consists of several pieces do not stitch any part that will be covered by another piece—machine may jam when going over previous stitching and the stitching would show as a ridge when pressed. At end of each stitching line pull threads to wrong side, tie off and clip before continuing. After appliqué is stitched, trim off excess fabric carefully, cutting each layer separately; don't pick up work but cut flat, pulling loose edge of fabric over scissor blade and cutting close to stitching.

Bias strip appliqué can be anything from satin bias tubing pressed flat (see BIAS, p. 30), to ready-made cotton bias tape. The edges are slipstitched in place—in the case of cotton sometimes machine-topstitched. Large, gay initials can be made of bias tape.

Iron-on appliqué is suitable for cotton playclothes, aprons, and children's clothes. It is sold in packages at notions counters, in a variety of colors. Follow directions in package.

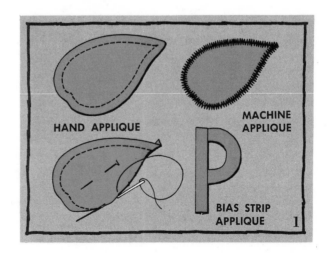

HAND APPLIQUE

MACHINE APPLIQUE

BIAS STRIP APPLIQUE

1

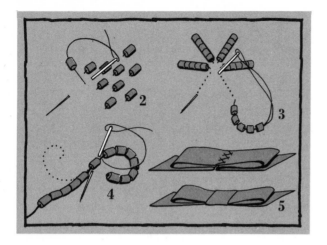

straight lines use thread doubled; take 5 or 6 beads on the needle and sew on as shown (3). A string of beads is attached by taking a stitch over the thread between each bead (4). Always fasten thread-ends securely.

BOW, TAILORED

A tailored bow (5), suitable for a dress or a hat, is made from ribbon or flat tubing (see BIAS, p. 30). Cut a length three times the desired size of bow. Trim ends diagonally—in the case of tubing, turn in end-edges, sew together and press. Fold and tack through center as shown. Fold another piece over center, as shown; sew ends together underneath.

BEADS

Beads are usually attached along an outline lightly marked on outside of fabric. Sometimes they are used to enhance a printed or woven design in the fabric. They can be sewed on singly or in groups, or they can be strung first on a heavy thread for a continuous line. For illustrations 2 and 3 use a very fine needle; wax the thread with beeswax to prevent twisting. Sew on single beads with a backstitch, working from right to left, as shown (2). For short,

EMBROIDERY

Embroidery (6) can be mentioned here only sketchily. **Machine embroidery,** made with zigzag stitch, is described in your sewing machine manual.

Hand embroidery includes smocking, faggoting, openwork, appliqué, and every kind of decorative stitch made on fabric. We give you here the stitches you may find most useful. Six-strand embroidery floss, in which the strands can be divided for finer work, is the thread generally used.

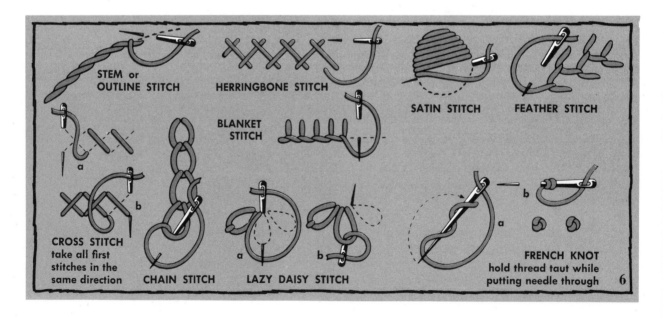

STEM or OUTLINE STITCH

HERRINGBONE STITCH

SATIN STITCH

FEATHER STITCH

BLANKET STITCH

CROSS STITCH
take all first
stitches in the
same direction

CHAIN STITCH

LAZY DAISY STITCH

FRENCH KNOT
hold thread taut while
putting needle through

6

FRINGE

Fringe comes and goes as a fashion finish; the three main types are discussed below.

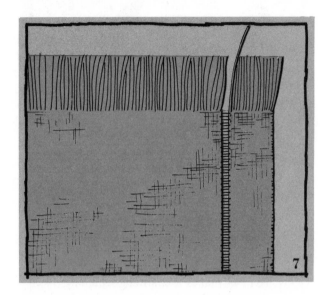

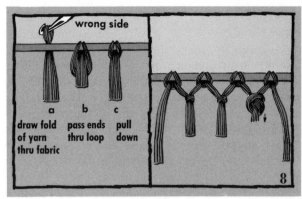

Ready-made fringe, in various widths, is usually made of rayon. Sold by the yard, it is simply stitched on through the heading, which as a rule is decorative and placed on the outside.

Self-fringe (7) can be very chic, especially in woolens. (It is a traditional part of the Scottish kilt, finishing the up-and-down edge at left front). The fabric edge must be absolutely straight-grain. Draw out a thread along edge and trim edge evenly. Using a pin, draw out a thread at desired depth of fringe. Unless fabric is very firmly woven, make a line of machine-stitching, zigzag or straight, along that line. Beginning at stitched line, draw out threads (be sure to trim away first any selvage left at seams).

Knotted fringe (8) is made with a crochet hook, generally using wool yarn. It requires a finished edge. How thick your yarn should be and how many strands you want in each tassel will depend on fabric weight. To determine depth, cut a few strands of yarn, fold and draw through fabric edge with hook, looping as shown. Trim ends. Using this as a guide, cut a piece of cardboard a little deeper than one strand folded in half. Wind yarn around cardboard; cut along one edge. Put the same number of strands in each tassel, place each at the same depth, and space evenly. If you wish, you can make a much deeper fringe and shorten it by knotting together the halves of two adjacent tassels. You can even make several rows of such knots, as is done for Mexican scarves.

LACE

Lace edging or insertion can be applied by hand or by machine. Fabric edge should be finished. If lace is to be gathered to fabric, draw up the heavy thread along straight edge. To sew on by hand, place lace along edge of fabric, right sides together, straight edges matching. Attach with whipstitch, as shown (9). To sew on by machine, lap straight edge of lace very slightly over edge of fabric, right sides up (10). Attach with narrow, not too close zigzag stitch or straight stitch.

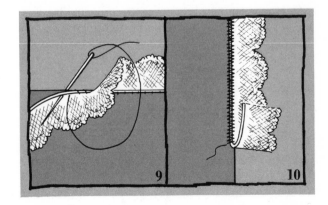

MACHINE-QUILTING

Machine-quilting (11), a very handsome form of decoration, is done before garment sections are assembled if quilting—as is usually the case—is limited to a certain section. Place thin wadding between fabric and lining and baste diagonally all over. A beautiful and very easy design consists of squares on the diagonal. If you get a quilting guide, as shown, you will need to mark only one line in each direction. The others will proceed out from there. Lighten pressure on presser foot. Use Mercerized Sewing Thread or Quilting Thread. Stitch length will depend somewhat on fabric, but you should keep it small.

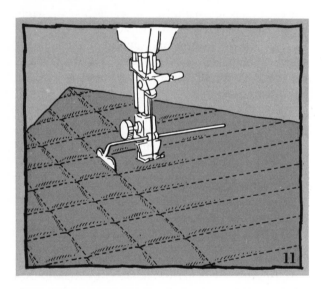

MACHINE-STITCHING

Machine-stitching, i.e., topstitching, can be featured as a decoration by doing it with buttonhole twist instead of ordinary thread. Change to a larger-eye machine-needle and use a long stitch.

POMPONS AND TASSELS

Pompons (12) are made from yarn. Cut a rectangle of cardboard, a little wider than desired diameter of pompon. Along one longer edge, hold a 6″ piece of yarn (doubled, unless yarn is very strong). Then wind a considerable amount of yarn around cardboard, as shown. Tie very tightly with the short

piece; cut through on other edge of cardboard, as shown. Fluff out yarn and trim evenly to form a ball. **Tassels** (13) are started like pompons, but are much less full. After cutting yarn off cardboard, wind another short piece just below fold, as shown, tie and trim. Trim ends evenly.

RICK RACK

Rick rack (14) makes a charming trimming on children's and casual clothes. A single strip of rick rack can be sewn on by hand as shown, or by machine by stitching through center. Two strips of rick rack can be interlocked, as shown, for a special effect. Apply as the single strip.

SADDLE STITCH

Saddle-stitches are even running stitches, ⅛″ to ¼″ long, used to decorate a finished edge, such as on collars, cuffs, lapels etc. Use silk twist or two strands of embroidery floss either in a matching or contrasting color. Take one stitch at a time, making all stitches the same length and distance apart. The thread should be loose enough to lie on top of the fabric.

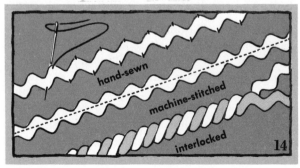

SEQUINS

Sequins (15) are another dressy decoration. They can be bought in ready-assembled strips or "loose."

For a continuous line of sequins, mark design lightly on right side of fabric. To attach a ready-made strip, cut it a little longer than needed. Remove a few sequins at ends and tie thread-ends.

Attach with invisible stitches under sequins. To make a line of single sequins, work from right to left with a backstitch, as shown. Attach single, scattered sequins, with a bead at top, as shown.

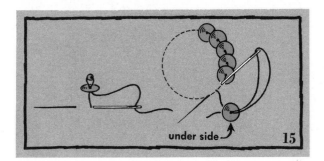

under side

15

SMOCKING

Smocking is most often done on children's clothes. However, where it suits the style, it can add a great deal to an adult garment.

Where a pattern calls for smocking, there will be a transfer sheet with guide-dots, and all necessary instructions. If you wish to add smocking on your own, there are certain things to be remembered:

. . . if possible, keep smocking clear of shaped edges, such as armholes (16). For a beginner, it is easiest to have the smocked section hang from a yoke.

. . . before smocking, fabric must measure three times the finished (smocked) width.

. . . smocking is done before garment is assembled.

There is more than one kind of smocking. What we give you here is English smocking, in which the fabric is first evenly gathered on the wrong side, and gathers (pleats) are held together by embroidery on the right side. Evenness in gathering is essential. Striped (⅛″) or checked (⅛″ or ¼″) fabric provides a built-in guide, and is highly recommended, especially for beginners. With striped fabric, horizontal guidelines must be added on wrong side with pencil and yardstick, placed to correspond more or less with the embroidery pattern.

Gathering—Use a strong thread of contrasting color, with a large knot. On wrong side of fabric, lift each stripe as shown (17). Leave thread hanging at end of each row. When all rows are threaded, pull up threads, forming even pleats (18), to a trifle over desired finished width. Secure threads by knotting two rows together as shown. Holding fabric firmly, pull pleats downward.

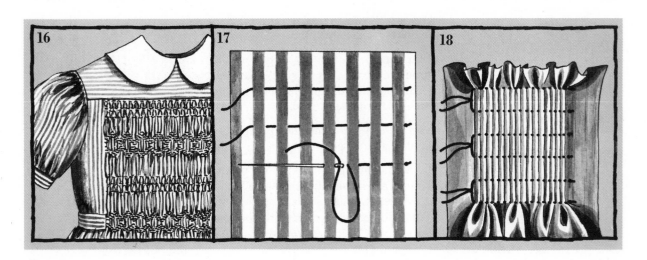

General Rules for Embroidering—Use six-strand embroidery floss. Work on right side of fabric, from left to right. *To start,* bring needle out in first pleat; take two tiny backstitches over fold of pleat to secure thread. *After finishing a row,* bring needle to wrong side through fold of last pleat. Take two small backstitches over pleat; cut thread. *If a new length of floss is needed within row,* finish old length as just described. Make a knot in new length and bring to right side on the same pleat on which old length stopped. *When all embroidery is completed,* snip gathering threads on wrong side and draw out.

Surface Honeycomb Stitch

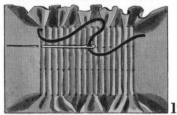
19

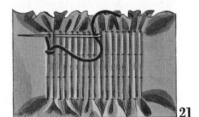
20

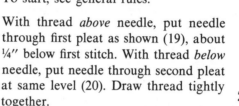
21

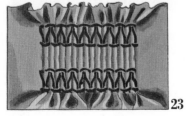
22

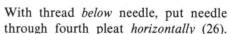
23

Trellis Stitch

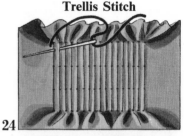
24

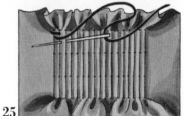
25

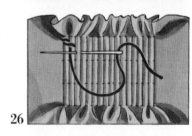
26

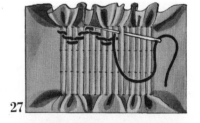
27

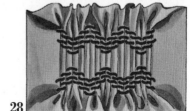
28

A great variety of embroidery stitches are used in smocking, often modified by the pattern they form with the pleats. We give you here the Surface Honeycomb Stitch and the Trellis Stitch.

Surface Honeycomb Stitch

To start, see general rules.

With thread *above* needle, put needle through first pleat as shown (19), about ¼″ below first stitch. With thread *below* needle, put needle through second pleat at same level (20). Draw thread tightly together.

Put needle through same pleat at same level as first stitch (21). With thread *above* needle, put needle through third pleat at same level (22). Draw tightly together. Repeat to end of row. Repeat row as desired (23).

Trellis Stitch

To start, see general rules.

With thread *above* needle, put needle through second pleat (24), slanting, needle slightly downward. Put needle through third pleat in same way (25).

With thread *below* needle, put needle through fourth pleat *horizontally* (26).

Put needle through fifth, the sixth pleats, slanting needle slightly *up.* With thread *above* needle, make seventh stitch horizontal. Repeat this pattern to the end of the row (27). Repeat the row as often as desired (28).

EASING

Easing disposes of small amounts of fullness caused by a fabric edge being longer than the edge to which it is joined (in a seam), or the area to which it is attached (in a hem). For easing a hem edge see HEMS, p. 100.

Easing in seams usually takes place between notches and is indicated on the pattern. A sleeve cap may be eased to the armhole, the back edge of a shoulder seam to the front (1), the back edge of an underarm sleeve seam to the front edge. Ideally, easing should be invisible after pressing. However, fabrics treated for "easy-care" and such can never be pressed entirely smooth, since they resist easing.

THE HOW-TO OF EASING IN A SEAM

Always ease the longer edge to the shorter; *never stretch* the shorter edge.

• The first thing after cutting out (when stay-stitching, if piece is staystitched), make a row of stitching on seamline, using a slightly long stitch (2). A second row (optional) in seam allowance, ⅛″ from the first, will ensure perfect evenness (3).

• When ready to join sections, pin at notches and other marks. Draw up one end of easing thread(s) until edges match. Holding edge as shown (4), work fabric along easing thread with thumb and forefinger until fullness is distributed smoothly and evenly, with no suggestion of pleats. In a sleeve cap, draw up first one half of edge, then the other half.

• Stitch seam with eased edge on top, for better control.

• With edge of iron, press stitched line as is, seam closed, then press seam open.

In *wool*—and wool only—the ease can be shrunk out while pressing the seam open. Work over pressing ham or sleeve board. With a steam iron, hold iron over eased area, and allow steam to penetrate fabric, then lower iron and apply light pressure until ease has disappeared. Use dampened press cloth and touch lightly with hot, dry iron. Other fabrics are handled in the same way, but will not really shrink, although untreated natural fibers may do so to a slight extent. The important thing here is to press seam only, using point of iron, as putting the iron down flat may make creases out of the slight indication of gathers.

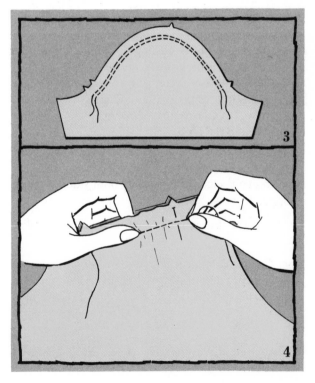

EQUIPMENT

A craftsman is no better than his tools. Try not to stint on the quality of your equipment. Invest in the best and give it your best care. You don't need to buy it all at once. In the listing that follows, we have marked with an asterisk the articles you can't reasonably do without (most are quite inexpensive). You can acquire the rest as you go along.

FOR MEASURING

*Tape Measure (1)—Usually 60″ long, with metal ends. A good tape measure will not stretch, and has measurements clearly marked on both sides, starting at opposite ends.

*6″ Ruler (2)—For marking hem-depth, buttonholes, pockets, etc.

Hem Gauge—Combines a 4″ or 6″ ruler with a movable indicator (3). Another type consists of a thin metal plate with graduated markings (4); the hem is pressed as it is turned over plate to desired depth.

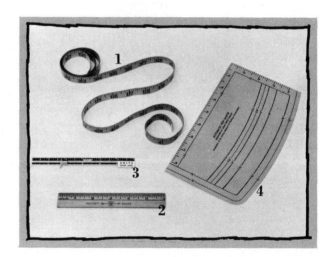

*Yardstick (5)—Indispensable for marking straight long lines; often used for marking hemlines from the floor. Should be firm and straight, with smooth edges and clear markings.

Skirt Marker (6)—Comes in various models. One, worked with a bulb and powdered chalk, allows you to do the job alone. The one using pins is the most exact, but it requires a helper.

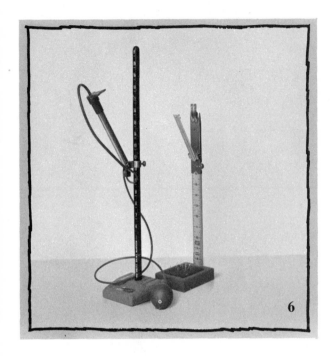

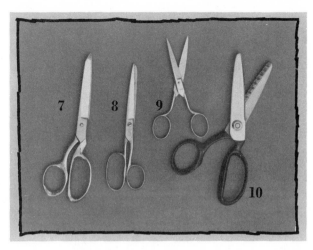

Pinking or Scalloping Shears (10)—For finishing seams (never to be used for cutting out). A 7½″ overall length is good. Left-hand models are available.

*Cutting Surface—Should be at least 30″ wide and 48″ long. Cutting boards are also available.

FOR MARKING

*Dressmaker's Carbon Tracing Paper and Tracing Wheel (11)—For transferring pattern markings to fabric. Paper comes in several colors. Wheels come with or without teeth. See MARKING.

*Tailor's Chalk (12)—Also used for transferring pattern markings to fabric. Clay chalk comes in red, white, and blue, in squares or in pencil form.

FOR CUTTING

Scissors—Good scissors make all the difference, and with care last a lifetime. Buy the best you can afford, and treat them with respect: keep sharp, do not drop or use on heavy paper or cardboard, and use another pair for household chores.

*Bent Trimmers (7)—For cutting out fabric. Bent handles make for accuracy, because they allow fabric to remain flat on table. A 7″ or 8″ overall length is good. Left-hand models are available.

Light Trimmers (8)—For general sewing use, trimming seams, clipping threads, etc. A 6″ or 7″ overall length is recommended.

*Sewing and Embroidery Scissors (9)—Equipped with two sharp points, for cutting buttonholes, clipping, and other fine work. You will find these most useful in a 4″ or 5″ overall length.

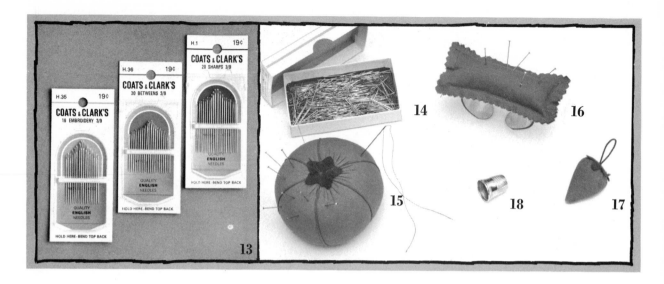

FOR SEWING

Sewing Machine—Your major investment. It may be quite small—good second-hand machines are often available—or quite large. Let your budget—and your sewing ambitions!—be your guide. In addition, you will have to decide whether you want to buy [a] a Cabinet or a Portable model; [b] a Straight Stitch or a Zigzag machine.

[a] . . . A Cabinet or Console model needs room-space of its own. However, it has the advantage not only of being always at hand and ready for work, but also of providing a wide surface, flush with the machine itself, on which to spread your work. Some cabinets also have drawers for keeping gadgets and notions handy.

. . . A Portable model is useful where space is limited. The machine is usually set up on a table. This, however, provides an uneven working surface; fortunately, you can now buy folding tables into which the machine can be set flush with the surrounding surface, allowing fabric to lie flat. When buying a portable, check on its weight, to make sure you can lift it easily.

[b] . . . Whether you buy a Straight Stitch or Zigzag model depends on the kind of sewing you expect to do. The Zigzag model does straight stitch ordinarily, but can swing into zigzag without a separate attachment. If you intend to do decorative stitching (machine embroidery), you will enjoy this feature. Otherwise, zigzag stitch is used mainly for finishing seam allowances and making buttonholes. On a straight stitch machine, a separate attachment makes very good buttonholes.

Whatever type of machine you buy, you will do well to add, right at the outset: 1) a supply of extra bobbins, and 2) a zipper foot.

Needles (13)—For hand- and machine-sewing. Be sure to have a variety of sizes on hand. See THREAD AND NEEDLES.

Straight Pins (14)—Use rustproof brass pins, size 17. They cost more than steel pins, but leave less of a mark on the fabric.

Pincushion (15)—To avoid scattering pins. A wrist pincushion (16) is handiest. You can buy one; or make one by sewing a pincushion to elastic.

Emery Bag (17)—Used to sharpen and remove rust from needles. (Do not leave needles in emery.)

Thimble (18)—For faster, easier hand-sewing, train yourself to use a thimble. Whether it is of metal or of plastic, make sure that it fits the middle finger of your sewing hand.

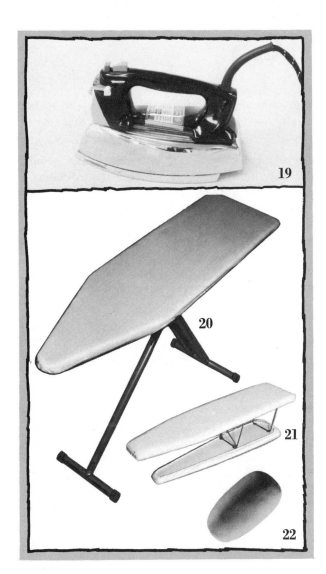

buy a specially-treated cloth; or use a piece of un-bleached muslin, about 14″ x 30″, washed to remove sizing. For dark woolens, use a wool press cloth with a steam iron.

*Ironing Board (20) should be firm and well-padded, its cover clean at all times.

Sleeve-Board (21) is useful for pressing seams in sleeves and other narrow spaces; the ends are good for darts and curved edges. It should be well-padded (add padding as necessary, using old blanket).

*Pressing Ham (22)—A firmly-packed, rounded press-ing cushion, excellent for pressing curved seams, darts, and especially sleeve caps.

MISCELLANEOUS

Dress Form—A form to your specific measurements is helpful, especially if you are hard to fit. A number of kinds are available, varying greatly in price.

The following other sewing aids are particularly help-ful: A **loop-turner** (23), used for turning bias binding and inserting cord into tubing. A **bodkin** (24), for inserting elastic or ribbon into casings. A **needle-threader** (25), if you have trouble threading needles. A **point-presser** (26), for pressing open seams of points in collars and lapels. A **Clapper (Beater** or **Pounding Block)** is very useful for tailoring. Some point pressers have a bottom designed to be used as a clapper (26).

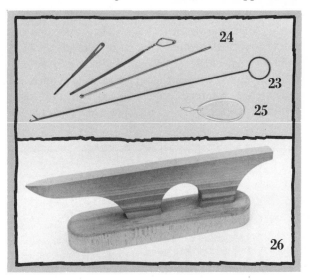

FOR PRESSING

(here you draw on your household equipment)

*A Good Iron (19) must be on hand, set up, and ready for use throughout any dressmaking. A combi-nation steam/dry iron is the most satisfactory.

*Press Cloth—Recommended because most fabrics tend to shine if they come in direct contact with iron, and cloth can be dampened to provide the moisture needed for proper pressing of most fabrics. You can

FABRICS

In the past two decades fabrics have been going through a revolution coupled with an explosion. In the face of all the new man-made fibers, and the new finishes applied to the old ones—a field far too wide to cover here—all we can do is give you such information as will be of use to you in buying and handling fabric.

THE NATURAL FIBERS TODAY

In general, the following improvements may be looked for in the natural fibers:

Woolens, especially the better domestic ones, are now almost always preshrunk, and sometimes washable.

Linens have been made crease-resistant.

Cottons are usually shrink-resistant and, where absorbency (as in terry cloth) is not a factor, have been treated for drip-dry performance—for handling, see **Wash-and-Wear Fabrics,** p. 78.

Silk is much what it used to be, its performance varying with its quality.

THE NEW FABRICS

It would be impossible to enumerate all the new fabrics, let alone describe them. They may consist of 100% synthetics (often a blend of several), or of a blend of man-made and natural fibers. Taken all together, they represent an enormous advance in convenience, wearing properties, variety, and cost-for-performance. They are almost always crease- and shrink-resistant. If they are not always washable, this is due to special texturing rather than to the fiber.

There is, of course, a reverse side to the picture. The new fabrics, and the old ones treated with the new finishes, are not as pliant or absorbent, and are resistant to shaping, often even to pins and needles—see **Buying Fabric,** p. 70, and **Wash-and-Wear Fabrics,** p. 78. Almost all the new fabrics should be handled like **Wash-and-Wear.**

FABRIC CONSTRUCTION

Woven and knitted fabrics—also lace and net—are made from yarn, or thread, spun from one or several of the fibers. Other fabrics, classified as "non-woven," are made from unspun fibers which are felted or bonded together.

Woven Fabrics

Every woven fabric, no matter what its surface is like, consists of lengthwise threads (warp) through which crosswise threads (called woof, weft, or filling) are woven over and under, back and forth. The basic principle is illustrated here (1). Edges (selvages) are reinforced by doubling the number of warp threads at the sides.

Examine the three basic weaves, shown here (2) greatly enlarged. Note how the diagonal effect of twill weave and the smooth surface of satin weave are achieved, with the direction of threads remaining invariably lengthwise-crosswise.

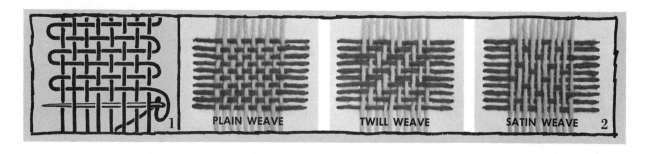

1   PLAIN WEAVE   TWILL WEAVE   SATIN WEAVE   2

The same is true of **nap** and **pile** fabrics. A nap is created by simply brushing up the natural fuzziness of certain fibers. In pile fabrics, the "stand-up" threads are added to the basic weave.

Woven fabric, therefore, always has a lengthwise and a crosswise direction, or "grain." As it comes from the loom, before it is processed with a **finish,** the fabric is "grain-perfect," i.e., the lengthwise and crosswise threads run straight, at true right angles to each other.

Knitted Fabrics

The three basic knits available to the home sewer are shown here enlarged (3).

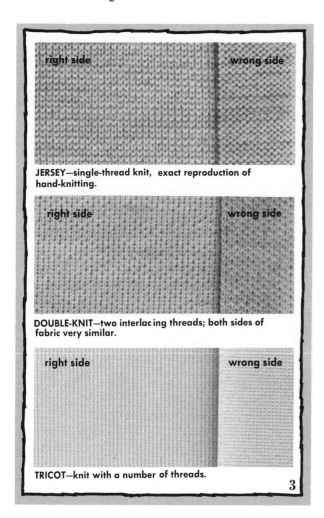

JERSEY—single-thread knit, exact reproduction of hand-knitting.

DOUBLE-KNIT—two interlacing threads; both sides of fabric very similar.

TRICOT—knit with a number of threads.

3

Knitted fabrics are not said to have grain. What they have is a *rib,* visible on the right side or on both sides. It is the rib that gives the true lengthwise direction.

Lace (4) and Net

Lace and net are made on special, very intricate machines, from almost any fiber. Since these fabrics have no grain, you follow the design, if any, for lengthwise or crosswise direction.

Non-Woven Fabrics

The fabrics described as "non-woven" are made of fibers either matted together by steam (felt) or bonded by chemicals (synthetics). Felt, usually wool, lends itself well to steaming and shaping. The synthetics are mainly used for interfacing. Unless these fabrics have a printed design, they can be cut in any direction, and have the advantage of not raveling or curling at the edges.

FABRIC FINISHES

All commercial fabrics (which do not include hand-weaves, imported or other), are processed with a *finish* when they come from the loom. These finishes in the course of application frequently pull the crosswise threads out of line.

Surface finishes such as the application of a print or a glaze, or the raising of a nap, need not concern us here.

Of the other finishes, the only ones of importance to us are the **permanent finishes,** and their presence or absence in a fabric. These are the new finishes that have made such a difference in fabric performance. New ones are being invented every day. They are responsible for wash-and-wear properties, shrink-resistance, stain- and mildew-resistance, "permanent press," etc. With the exception of shrink-resistance, however, these finishes have a drastic effect on the fabric grain, which they lock into position, whether distorted or not.

BUYING FABRIC

Your pattern envelope will tell you what **type of fabric** is suitable and what **amount** you will need.

You will note that yardages indicated are always specified "without nap" or "with nap." "With nap" takes a little more fabric because, nap running in one lengthwise direction, the pattern pieces will all have to be laid out with their top edges facing the same way. "Nap," however, does not cover the situation. Any fabric that looks different when held up or down has the same requirement. This means that the *design* (print, weave, plaid) may go in one direction; or the *weave* (gabardine, twill, whipcord, flannel, satin and sateen) reflects light differently in the two directions; or the *texture* (nap and pile fabrics) looks different.

Still more yardage is needed when a design (plaid or other) is to be matched at the seams—the larger the design the greater the yardage allowance necessary.

See CUTTING for further details.

Irregular designs, such as florals, need not be matched.

The Fabric Properties

Making sure of fabric properties when buying has become a complex problem.

A man-made fiber, simply by the process of becoming cloth, usually imitates one of the natural ones, often so successfully that we cannot tell them apart. Besides, the old fabrics now imitate each other, and all are blended in countless combinations. Fortunately, the law requires that the fiber content of a fabric (in a blend, the percentage of each) be indicated on the label, the hang-tag, or the end of the bolt. As for the finishes that will improve fabric performance—easy-care, crease- and shrink-resistance, stain- and mildew-resistance—if they are present, they will be indicated on the label.

In short, it is the **label** we go by today (5). If it does not carry the information you want, inquire of the salesperson (or you may find it necessary to go as far as the buyer).

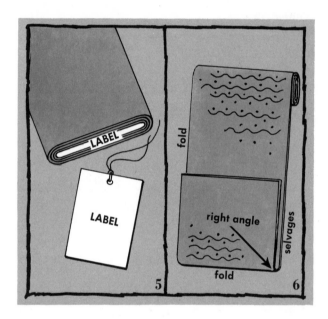

NOTE: In the many small stores where beautiful fabrics are sold, the label may be absent. Here you can only trust your judgment, or go by whatever verbal information you may obtain. Fabric that is 100% synthetic (except rayon) may usually be counted on to have the new permanent finishes. With the other fibers, you should look for specific indication of finish.

Shrink-resistance, indicated by "Sanforized," "Preshrunk," or some other descriptive term, is an unqualified *plus* which does not affect response to shaping, grain correction, etc.

The other permanent finishes—crease-resistance, stain-resistance, "easy-care," "drip-dry," "permanent press," etc., have the effect of locking the grain in position. Where such a finish is present, you are safe with solid colors or overall irregular designs. Where, however, there is a design (plaid, checks, or printed motif) that must be at right angles to selvages (in knits, to lengthwise rib), make sure that the design is not out of line, as it will be impossible to straighten it. Before ordering yardage cut, unroll about a yard from the bolt; fold back half a yard, matching selvages (6). If design is not even with fold the fabric will never give satisfaction (on fabric with a lengthwise center fold, check inside your fold, too).

PREPARING FABRIC FOR USE

A great many fabrics nowadays need no preparation whatsoever (of the fabrics given special notice in the pages that follow, only wool knits, if not pre-shrunk, will need some preparation).

Woven wool, cotton, linen, silk and rayon with no permanent finish (outside of shrink-resistance) indicated on label have a temporary finish only and must be checked for *straightness of grain* and, if necessary, straightened.

Wool, cotton and linen that do not carry one of the non-shrink guarantees (sanforized, etc.), must be *shrunk before using,* whether they are washable or to be dry-cleaned (steam-pressing shrinks fibers).

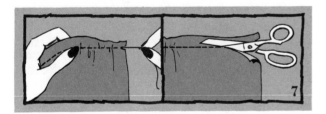

To **straighten fabric,** trim one cut end along a cross-wise thread (if grain is not clearly visible, draw up a thread and cut along pucker, 7). Fold fabric lengthwise, selvages matching. If the two halves of trimmed edge do not match, straighten them by grasping the two selvage edges on the bias (two people are needed for wide fabric) and pulling (8). Repeat at various points until ends are even.

To **shrink fabric,** proceed as follows:
. . . for a washable fabric, leave folded and wet thoroughly (9).
. . . for a dry-cleanable fabric, spread on dampened sheet, fold the two together and leave overnight.

To dry either, hang smoothly over a straight rod; if grain needs straightening, spread fabric flat, smoothing it so selvages and ends are at right angles to one another (check against table-edges).

Another method of shrinking, used particularly with woolens, is steam-pressing. A steam iron, however, produces too little steam for the purpose. Have the job done by a tailor.

HANDLING THE DIFFERENT FABRICS

We don't have to tell you that chiffon requires a more delicate touch than denim. Any fabric, however, even the sturdiest, is better off for being handled as lightly and as little as possible. This is one reason why sewing techniques are always planned for minimum handling.

The directions throughout this book—which, for happy results, you should look up as you go along and faithfully follow—apply to standard fabrics in standard weights. Certain fabrics, however, require special handling. **Bonded Fabrics, Fake Fur, Knits, Lace, Pile Fabrics, Sheers, Stretch Fabrics, Vinyl,** and **Wash-and-Wear** are each given a section, in alphabetical order, in the pages that follow, with instructions as to the points at which they need special handling. Any detail not mentioned should be handled in the standard manner.

Bonded Fabrics

These consist of a face-fabric fused to a backing fabric. This generally makes a backing unnecessary and ensures that a garment will keep its shape through dry-cleaning or washing (the label will tell you which). Bonded fabrics are gaining so rapidly in popularity and scope that the face-fabric may now be woven or knitted out of practically any fiber or blend; the backing fabric is usually nylon tricot, woven cotton or acetate. Lining may be added or not, as desired.

Cutting—Cut with face-fabric up, so you can use its lengthwise grain for "straight of goods," or its pattern for matching.

Pressing—Set iron for the fiber on the side which you are pressing. Test first on a scrap of fabric.

Seams—On unlined coats and jackets, make flat-felled seams as follows: After stitching, separate backing fabric from face-fabric on one seam allowance and trim face-fabric to ⅛″ (10). Trim other seam allowance to ¼″. With full-width seam allowance (backing) on top, fold all seam allowances to one side; fold in raw edge of backing fabric and topstitch or slipstitch fold to garment (11).

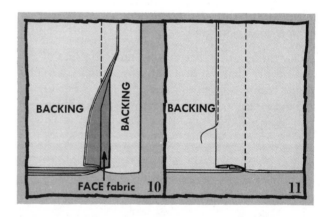

Hem—Sew to backing fabric only.

Buttonholes—Any type buttonhole is suitable.

Fake Fur

Technically described as deep-pile fabric, fake fur has a pile of synthetic yarn, and a back, or foundation, of woven or knitted fabric, synthetic or cotton. Some fake furs are washable, but most require dry-cleaning (label will indicate which).

Pattern—Use simple pattern with few seams, a minimum of detail and darts. Avoid buttonholes—use loops, frogs, or snaps for fastenings.

Backing and Lining—Lining is not strictly necessary except for coats and jackets, but fake fur is more comfortable when lined. If back of fabric is not firmly woven, add backing.

Facings—Facings of self-fabric are recommended only on coats and jackets and when pile is medium-weight. For facing heavy-pile coats and jackets, substitute a suitable lighter-weight fabric (tweed, flannel, etc.).

Preparation of Fabric—Straighten raw edges by cutting along one thread of a woven back; or cut along a line drawn at right angles to rib of a knitted fabric. Be sure to check label for shrinking information.

Pattern Alterations—Trim away pattern margins, if any, to make it easier to cut an even edge on bulky fabric. *Do not cut away seam allowances.* Reduce bulk by eliminating seams wherever possible: When a straight edge is to be faced with self-fabric, cut body section and facing in one piece. When a center seam is on straight grain, cut as if marked to be placed on fold.

Cutting—See **With Nap**, p. 51, and **Cutting Through a Single Thickness**, p. 55. Determine whether you want pile running up or down. Work with fabric spread out wrong side up, and pin pattern to back only.

Marking—Do not cut notches; make marks with chalk on seam allowances, on wrong side. To mark darts, use tailor's tacks, pins, or chalk.

Pressing—Pressing with any iron will mat pile. For seams, see below.

Stitching—Never machine-stitch on right side of fabric. Stitch slowly, going in direction of pile, meanwhile pushing pile out of seamline (toward garment, not toward seam allowance) with blunt end of a long needle. After stitching, use long needle or fine comb to pull out (from right side) any pile caught in seam.

Darts—To eliminate bulk, slash through center fold of dart, stitched as instructed; shear pile from both seam allowances. Slipstitch edges to back of fabric.

Seams—To reinforce shoulder seam, pin preshrunk tape over seamline before stitching and include it in seam. To eliminate bulk, shear pile from all seam allowances. Since seams cannot be pressed, open with thumbnail and catch edges of seam allowances to back of fabric.

Facings—Do not understitch or topstitch a facing seam. To keep facing from rolling, pin facing to garment with a line of pins ½″ from facing seam. Fold facing back on pin-line and slipstitch to garment (12).

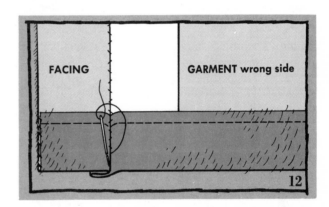

Hems—Catch raw edge of hem to back of fabric.

Zippers—Use a centered application. After closing zipper opening with machine-basting and clipping stitches as instructed, shear pile off seam allowances. Sew zipper in by hand.

Knits

These may be made from any fiber, natural or synthetic; they are appreciated, among other things, for crease-resistance. Their drawback used to be their tendency to stretch and sag, but this has now largely been overcome with "no-sag" treatment (see label on fabric). Wool knits not labeled "preshrunk" will need shrinking before use (see p. 71).

Pattern—Circular skirts and bias cuts should be avoided, since knits do not look right on the bias.

Jersey, which comes in both light and medium weights, has a soft look and is well adapted to dresses with draping or design ease. Select simple designs.

Double-knit fabric comes in medium and heavy weight. It combines flexibility with firmness, and is easy to handle and stitch. It is particularly suitable for tailored styles.

When buying a print with a crosswise design, make sure that the *design* is at right angles to the ribs in fabric—not the *fold.*

Preparation—If fabric comes in tubular form, cut it open at one fold, but follow a *rib,* not the fold. Press out other fold—if it refuses to be pressed out, avoid it when laying out pattern (see CUTTING). Make a line of basting along a rib near center, as a guide for "Straight of Goods," or "Straight Grain."

Seams—To protect unbacked, very lightweight knits (e.g., nylon jersey) against abrasion by feed dog, place 1½″ strips of tissue paper under seams while stitching. Then tear away paper.

. . . Pin-baste or thread-baste seams.

. . . With synthetics use the finest needle the fabric will take.

. . . Zigzag stitch is often found to work well in seams (use smallest bight—see manual).

. . . To stabilize shoulder seams, pin preshrunk tape under seam before stitching; include it in seam.

. . . To prevent seam allowances from rolling, make a line of stitching ¼″ from edge, or finish edges with zigzag stitching.

Bias Binding—The greatest "give" in knit fabrics is crosswise, not on the bias, as in weaves. For bias binding, cut strip across width of fabric.

Buttonholes—Both bound and machine-worked buttonholes are suitable. For either, first stabilize buttonhole area by pressing oval-shaped patch of very lightweight iron-on interfacing to wrong side of outer garment section.

Lace

May be heavy, fine and filmy, or any stage between. Heavy laces usually contain a considerable proportion of cotton; the others are made of all kinds of fibers and blends.

A decorative lace edge to be used as a finish may be present on the fabric when bought, taking the place of selvage on one or both edges. Otherwise, such an edge can be hand-clipped from the lace when there is a regularly-repeated motif along an edge. Working around the motifs, just clip through the short threads that attach the "in-between" lace to the motif (13).

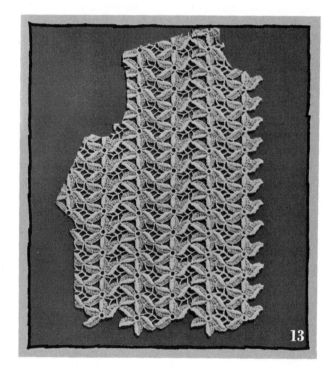

Pattern—Choose a simple design with few seams in order to avoid cutting up lace design. Avoid buttonholes if possible—button loops of lining or backing fabric can be used instead.

Backing and Lining—Any lace garment not worn over a suitable garment or undergarment must be backed—sometimes both backed and lined. Backing may be transparent, sheer, or opaque; lining is usually opaque. Net is a transparent backing. Sheer backing fabrics, most effective in self- or flesh-color, include marquisette, organza, and organdy. Opaque fabrics, suitable for both backing and lining, include taffeta, peau de soie, and polished cotton.

Marking—Where there is an opaque backing, mark backing fabric only. Where there is a net backing or none, mark with tailor's tacks or basting.

Pressing—For heavy lace, cover ironing board with terry cloth; press on wrong side.

Stitching—To prevent very fine lace from catching in feed dog, place 1½″ strips of tissue paper under seams when stitching. After stitching, tear away tissue.

Darts—Make dart as usual. Where fabric, whether it includes backing or not, is transparent, make a second line of stitching ⅛″ from first (14); trim close to second line (15).

Seams—For transparent fabric, finish like darts above.

Edge-Finish—A facing, or a hem, made of a tulle (fine net) strip is practically invisible, and is excellent where there is no backing, or one of net. Cut a tulle strip 2½″ wide on cross grain (tulle has more give on cross grain than on bias). Fold strip in half lengthwise. Stitch raw edges of strip to right side of garment edge, taking a ⅝″ seam allowance. In seam allowance, make second line of stitching ⅛″ from first; trim seam allowance close to second line. Turn tulle strip to wrong side along seamline; slipstitch fold to garment (16).

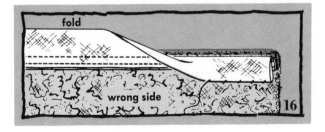

Zipper—Apply zipper as usual, but do last step (outside stitching) by hand.

Buttonholes—Whenever possible, avoid buttonholes. Button loops can be used instead. On backed garments, worked buttonholes are possible. If made by machine, add a hand-finished look by covering with buttonhole stitch done with buttonhole twist or a single strand of embroidery floss.

Pile Fabrics

This usually means cut pile fabrics, such as velvet, velveteen and corduroy (for **Fake Fur,** see that heading). They may be made of any fiber or fibers.

Pattern—Choose a simple design with few seams. For velvet and velveteen do not plan buttonholes unless you have tried one first on a scrap of the fabric.

Cutting—Follow cutting layout "With Nap" (see CUTTING, p. 51). To ascertain the way the pile "runs," brush hand lightly over fabric surface: the smoother feel gives pile "direction," which should go upward in garment for a richer color. When cutting on a fold so that two pieces are cut at one time, only a lengthwise fold can be used. Never follow a diagram with a crosswise fold.

Marking—Corduroy: any method is good. Velvet and velveteen: use tailor's tacks or pins and chalk.

Basting—Hand-basting is necessary throughout, since pile shifts easily.

Pressing—This is a problem with all pile fabrics, velvet being the most difficult, corduroy the least. If fiber content of fabric makes eased seams (such as set-in sleeves) difficult, the fact that there can be no real pressing adds to the difficulty. Here are a few pointers:

. . . Never touch iron to right side of fabric.

. . . Your best help, as good as a "velvet board," is a piece of your pile fabric, placed with pile to pile of garment. When pressing garment on wrong side, place piece on ironing board, pile side up. When pressing right side, place piece over garment, pile side down.

. . . In any case, always use steam, and press lightly, or you will flatten pile.

Zippers—Corduroy and velveteen: Proceed as for any fabric. Velvet: Do first step (anchoring zipper) by machine; finish application by hand.

Buttonholes—Corduroy: any type buttonhole is suitable. For bound buttonholes, cut lips on bias. Velvet and velveteen: avoid machine-worked buttonholes, since attachment marks pile. For bound buttonholes, cut lips on bias.

Sheer Fabrics

No matter what their fiber content, these must be handled carefully. They include dotted Swiss, voile, chiffon, organdy, and batiste, each available in a variety of fibers.

NOTE: A sheer fabric backed with opaque fabric is not handled as a sheer, but as standard fabric. What follows refers to unbacked sheers.

Pattern—Soft, feminine designs with fullness.

Cutting—Where an edge requires a facing, make the entire section double to avoid edges that will show through to right side. A sleeveless bodice, for instance, can be cut double in its entirety. The edges may then be finished with narrow French Binding or a Bias Facing. A shirt-dress type front-facing can be cut in one with the bodice section to eliminate a seam.

Marking—Use Tailor's Tacks. Other marks show through on right side and pins slip out.

Basting—Many sheers, especially silks and synthetics, require hand-basting.

Pressing—Use dry iron on all sheers except cottons.

Stitching—To prevent very fine sheers from catching in feed dog, place 1½″ strips of tissue paper under seams when stitching. After stitching, tear away tissue.

Darts—You can avoid a knot showing at point of dart—see DARTS, p. 56.

Seams and Bindings—Seams are visible from right side, and should be neat and narrow. Make **French Seams** (p. 161) or double-stitched seams (17). If you wish to bind garment edges, do it with a **French Binding** (see p. 28).

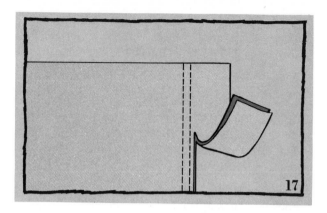

Hems—Anywhere from 3″ to 8″ wide on a full straight skirt; very narrow on a circular skirt. See HEMS.

Zippers—In unbacked sheers, pattern will often suggest snaps instead of a zipper. If a zipper is used, do last step of application (outside stitching) by hand.

Buttonholes—Where buttonholes are made and buttons sewed on, area must be reinforced with lightweight interfacing. Since the patch of a bound buttonhole would show through, worked buttonholes are best—if made by machine, give them a hand-finished look by going over them with hand buttonhole-stitch, done with buttonhole twist or a single strand of embroidery floss.

Stretch Fabrics

The "stretch" property, which allows a garment to "give" while it is being worn and afterwards return to its original shape, is now being added to woven and knitted fabrics of all weights in every kind of fiber—natural, synthetic, or blended. Stretch may be crosswise, lengthwise, or both ways.

Fabrics with *lengthwise stretch,* generally used in slacks and shorts, and *both-ways stretch,* used in swimsuits and foundation garments, are at present found only in ready-to-wear.

Fabrics with *crosswise stretch* are available by the yard. They provide "give," for one thing, across back and hips. Pants, which must have lengthwise stretch, can be cut out of stretch fabric wide enough to allow pattern to be placed on the crosswise grain.

Pattern—Buy same size as for regular fabric.

Backing, Lining, Interfacing—Stretch fabric is never backed, for obvious reasons. For lining, use tricot, or special lining fabric with "stretch," and cut it in the same direction as outer fabric. Use interfacing only where stretch is not needed (waistband, lapels, etc.).

Cutting—Allow fabric to relax for 24 hours before cutting, since it is often stretched from being rolled on the bolt. Cut a waistband in direction opposite to stretch (to avoid its stretching).

Pressing—Set iron according to fiber content of fabric. Press lightly to avoid stretching.

Stitching—See heading **Pressure, Tension, Balance,** p. 115 under MACHINE-STITCHING. When stitching in direction of stretch, feed fabric slowly and evenly through machine.

Basting—Hand-baste slippery fabrics, pin-baste others. When stitching, remove pins as you go along.

Seams—Where no stretch is desired (for example, at shoulder seam), lay preshrunk seam tape over seamline and include it in stitching. To prevent seam allowances from rolling, make a line of machine-stitching ¼″ from edge of each. On ravelly fabric, overcast edges by hand or finish with zigzag stitching.

Hems—Pink or overcast edge and make a Tailor's Hem.

Zippers—Apply zippers in regular manner. When garment has a lengthwise stretch, as in pants, do outside stitching (last step) by hand.

Buttonholes—May be bound or machine-made. Stabilize buttonhole area by applying an oval patch of very lightweight iron-on interfacing to wrong side.

Vinyl

Increasing in popularity for use in garments. There are now:

Opaque vinyl in colors, with either smooth or textured surface (simulating leather). This always has a backing, either woven or knit (with the knit there may be a thin layer of foam between).

Glass-clear vinyl, either unbacked, with surface smooth or embossed, or backed with woven cotton, sometimes a print.

The facts that govern the handling of vinyl are that it has *no grain,* does have a certain *stiffness, cannot be pressed, does not fray* and *marks made on it are permanent.* These characteristics, however, may change at any time. Keep an open mind and don't be afraid to experiment with different techniques.

Pattern—Choose a design with simple lines, a minimum of seams and darts, and raglan, rather than set-in, sleeves.

Pattern Alterations should be made very carefully: Marks from incorrect stitching cannot be removed. To ensure a more even cutting line, trim away pattern margins, if any (*not* seam allowances).

Backing and Lining—Backing is unnecessary. A lining may be added for comfort, unless vinyl-backing is soft. So that garment may be completely washable, use wash-and-wear fabric.

Cutting—Spread fabric wrong side up in a single layer. See **Cutting Through a Single Thickness,** p. 55 under CUTTING. Use pins in seam allowance only.

Marking—Mark on wrong side with dressmaker's carbon, using a tracing wheel without teeth. On clear vinyl, use a tracing wheel with teeth and no carbon paper.

Basting—Thread- or pin-baste through seam allowance *only.*

Pressing—Press seams open with thumbnail.

Stitching—Test very carefully for **Pressure, Tension and Balance** (see MACHINE-STITCHING, p. 115). Machine needle should be of medium size; stitch-length 8 to the inch. When stitching with vinyl face-down, if vinyl tends to stick to feed dog, place 1½″-wide strips of tissue paper under seam. After stitching tear away tissue. Stitch very slowly, turning wheel by hand at difficult spots. For hand-sewing, use a medium-to-fine needle.

Darts—If a dart "pokes out" at the point after it is stitched (which may happen), lengthen it, making a second line of stitching. After stitching a dart, the seam allowances may be topstitched in place.

Seams—To keep seam allowances flat, topstitch along one or both sides of seamline, or make a welt seam.

Facings—Topstitch or understitch edges for a good sharp facing seam. With clear vinyl, facings can be omitted—just turn seam allowance under and double-stitch.

Zipper—Close opening with hand-basting. Using thread doubled or buttonhole twist, do last two steps by hand, taking stitches not smaller than 1/16″ and at least ¼″ apart.

Buttonholes—An area that is to have buttons or buttonholes must be double; opaque vinyl should be interfaced with lightweight non-woven interfacing, clear vinyl with an extra thickness of self-fabric.

The only buttonhole-mark that can be made on right side (use the point of any slightly sharp article for marking) is the position line, unextended. Use masking tape for end-lines (18) and extend position lines over tape, as shown.

A very easy buttonhole—double-stitched and cut out (19)—is possible in vinyl.

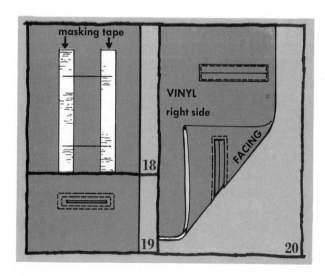

Machine-worked buttonholes can be made on any vinyl; bound buttonholes on opaque vinyl only. See BUTTONHOLES. To finish a bound buttonhole on facing side, stitch around on right side, through facing, as shown (20); then, on facing side, cut out the tiny strip (rectangle) between stitching.

Hem—When turning up hem, secure edge in place with cellophane tape. To finish hem, you have several choices:

. . . topstitch hem near fold, making one or more rows of stitching; then trim away extra fabric,
. . . glue hem in place with waterproof glue,
. . . if vinyl has a knit back, catch hem to backing,
. . . on clear vinyl, double-topstitch as for facings, or trim away entire hem allowance and finish hem edge with binding.

Wash-and-Wear Fabrics

Also described as drip-dry, easy-care, etc., these are woven or knitted fabrics that are washable, quick-drying, and need little or no ironing (the latest addition is one with a "permanent press" finish). Available in a great variety of weights and textures, they may be made of

. . . 100% synthetic yarns
. . . blended-fiber yarns
. . . treated cotton, wool, or rayon.

The "wash-and-wear" finish, valuable in itself, also makes the fabric surface smoother and harder, the fabric less pliable and more resistant to handling. It cannot, for instance, be shrunk or shaped by steaming (as for easing a sleeve cap to an armhole) and it may have a springiness that resists a sharp, clean edge-fold or seam. It also tends to pucker at the seams.

Pattern—Choose an uncomplicated design (you may even wish to avoid set-in sleeves), not broken by too many seams. The tendency to pucker is greater on straight-grain seams than on off-grain or bias seams. Therefore, with hard-finish wash-and-wear such as a "permanent press" fabric, avoid long zippers on straight grain, and cut facings in one piece with body sections to avoid seams on long, straight edges.

Notions, linings, etc.—A wash-and-wear garment must be wash-and-wear throughout: choose any backing or lining accordingly. Use wash-and-wear seam binding or a strip of your selvage for a waist stay, and avoid seam binding on hems. Make shoulder pads, if any, with self-fabric, and stuff them with Dacron* batting; or make them removable.

Cutting—If fabric comes folded through center, try to press out fold before laying out pattern. If it will not come out, arrange pattern to avoid fold (see CUTTING). If the crosswise threads of fabric are off-grain, you can disregard the fact in the case of solid colors, allover prints or irregular designs—just place straight-grain marking on pattern parallel to selvage, as usual. Since the finish holds the shape, the garment will still hang right. If, however, you have made the mistake of acquiring fabric with a design (plaid or other) that should be at right angles to selvage but is not (see **Buying Fabric,** p. 71), *follow the design* in placing pattern. The result will not be really satisfactory, but you have no other choice.

Marking—On a smooth fabric of solid color, the tracing wheel alone (without carbon paper) will often make a sufficiently visible mark (21). If you use

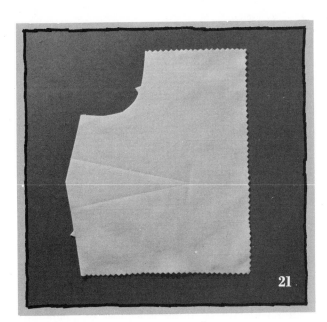

21

*Du Pont T.M.

tailor's chalk, use the clay variety. Otherwise, use markings according to type of fabric—sheers, deep pile, etc.

Stitching—Proper **Pressure, Tension** and **Balance** in your sewing machine are of greater importance with these fabrics than with any others. See that heading on p. 115 under MACHINE-STITCHING.

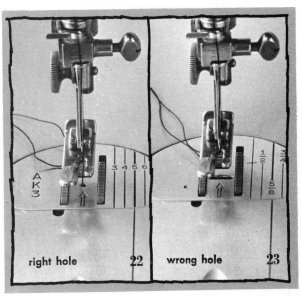

right hole 22 wrong hole 23

Use a throat plate with a round hole (22). The wider oval hole of zigzag machines (23) allows the fabric to be drawn into the hole, and the seam becomes puckered.

Pressing—Three points must be remembered when pressing wash-and-wear:

. . . after setting iron for proper fiber content, *test it* on a scrap of your fabric before using,

. . . creases, once pressed in, stay in. Hence,

. . . be sure of your seamlines (i.e., do your trying on and adjusting) before pressing.

Good sewing techniques are particularly important with wash-and-wear; see chapters on SEAMS, HEMS, FACINGS, etc. If your fabric falls under one of the headings that precede this one, there you will find additional pointers on handling.

FACINGS

A facing is a piece of fabric that doubles and finishes an edge. It is usually a separate piece stitched to the edge (shaped or fitted facing), but may be cut as an extension to the edge (extended facing). A third kind of facing is the bias facing. Complete descriptions follow. A facing is generally on the inside of a garment, but for a decorative purpose may be on the outside (see p. 85). For a lapel, a finished inside facing is partly folded to the outside.

Facings are usually made of the same fabric as the garment. However, a smoother or a lighter-weight fabric may be used to reduce bulk, or for comfort; and a contrasting texture or color may be part of a design.

A **shaped, separate or fitted facing** (1) is a separate piece of fabric cut to match the outer sections, and on the same grain. Shaped facings (usually with interfacing) are used at front and back openings, at neck and sleeveless armhole edges, and at the underside of shaped collars and cuffs.

An **extended facing** (2) is cut in one piece with the outer garment section, from a single pattern piece. Extended facings (generally with interfacing) are used at front and back openings, and as the underside of straight collars and cuffs.

A **bias facing** (3) is made of a bias strip. It is used on gently-curved edges, such as hems, open necklines, and sleeve edges, and is never interfaced.

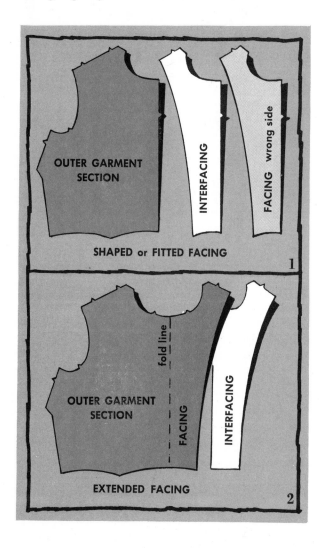

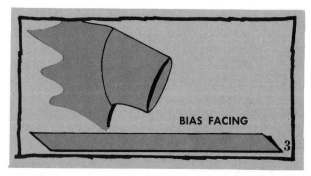

A well-applied facing has sharp, clean edges and smooth, flat-lying surfaces. These are ensured by attention to the small details in the application, particularly in **Processing the Seam**, pp. 82–84.

NOTE: A special application, which eliminates raw edges of facing and interfacing on washable garments with worked buttonholes (blouses, children's dresses, etc.), will be found under INTERFACING, p. 111.

SHAPED FACING
AND EXTENDED FACING

Preparing the Facing

• Stay-stitch curved and bias edges to be seamed: join pieces if there are more than one.

• If free edge (not to be seamed) is not to be covered by a lining, make a line of stitching ¼″ from edge.

Finish according to weight of fabric:

. . . on light or medium-weight fabrics, "clean-finish," i.e., fold raw edge on stitching line and topstitch close to edge (4),

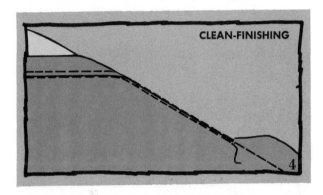

. . . on heavy fabric, pink raw edge outside stitched line (5),

. . . on heavy, ravelly fabrics, overcast raw edge, either by hand (6) or by machine.

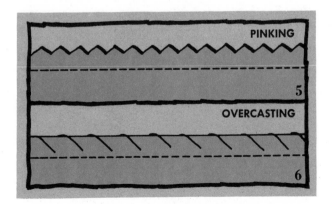

Seaming the Facing

• Pin or baste facing to corresponding outer section, right sides together, edges and construction marks carefully matched.

. . . if facing is smaller than outer section (a neckline facing, for instance), stitch with facing on top for better control (7),

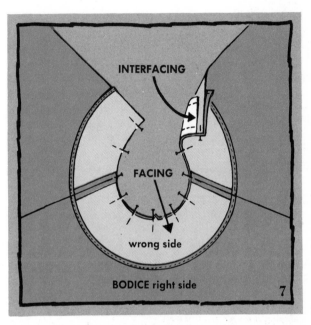

. . . if facing and outer section are the same size, as in a collar, stitch with facing underneath, since the seam allowance has been marked on the interfacing (8).

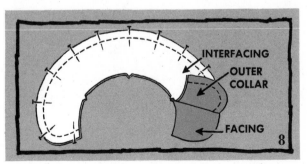

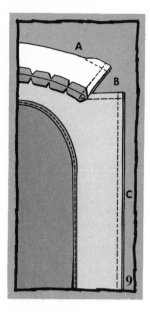

Stitch facing seam as follows:

. . . if seam takes in no outside corners, stitch entire facing to garment in one operation.

. . . if seam takes in outside corners, first stitch the edge between corners and process that seam (i.e., trim, grade, clip, understitch—see p. 83). Then, crossing stitching line at corners as shown, stitch the other edges. In a collar-and-facing assemblage (9), stitch and process the seam in the a-b-c order shown.

When stitching:

• Keep seam even; even a slight irregularity will show on finished edge. Use a seam gauge or mark seamline.

Processing the Seam

Here, in the order in which they are to be dealt with, are the details that make all the difference. Pick out the ones that apply to your seam.

Trim off points close to stitching (12).

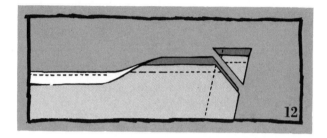

Underpress short seams and lapel seams, neither of which can be understitched (underpressing will flatten seam for a sharp edge in final pressing). Before trimming, open out seam and, working with a point presser (13) or over a pencil wrapped in cloth (14), press seam open with point of iron only.

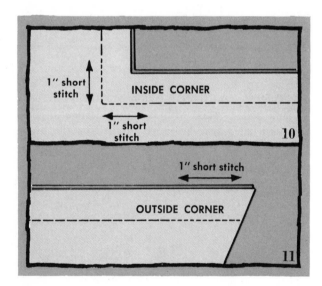

• Reinforce corners by shortening stitch from the regular 12–15 per inch to 20 per inch as shown (10, 11).

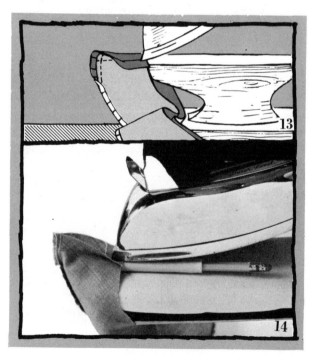

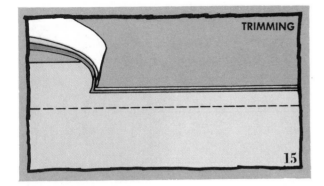

Trim all seam allowances to ¼″ (15).

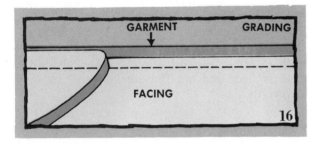

Grade seam allowances, i.e., trim facing seam allowances once more, to ⅛″ (16). If there are more than two thicknesses besides interfacing, trim them to graduated widths between ⅛″ and ¼″.

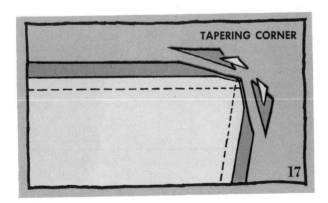

Taper outside corners after grading; i.e., trim toward corner as shown (17).

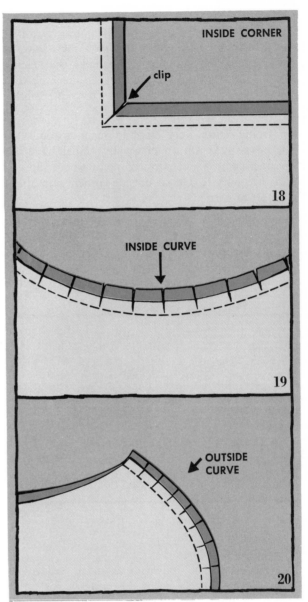

Clip most seam allowances to allow a seam to lie flat after facing is turned. A clip is a straight cut through seam allowance to within a thread of the stitching line. Clip once into a corner (18); clip enough times around a curve to make it lie flat (19, 20). The more pronounced the curve and the firmer the fabric, the more clips are needed. They may be as close as ¼″.

Understitch all facing seams except [a] seams less than 3″ long, such as the ends of a straight collar, and [b] seams where understitching would show, as on a lapel. Understitching guarantees that facing will not roll to outside. Place work on machine with facing opened out, right side up. Turn all seam allowances smoothly under facing.

On facing, stitch very close to seam, through all thicknesses (21). On a facing with a lapel, have understitching stop just short of point where lapel is folded to outside. On an outside corner, stop about 1″ short of corner.

Press all faced edges carefully after folding facing to inside, on seam. To avoid a shine along edges, use a press cloth with a dry iron. On dark fabrics, use a press cloth even with a steam iron.

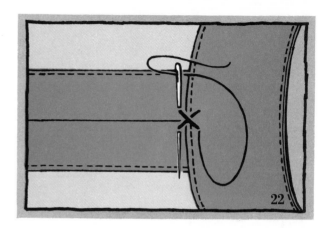

• Anchor facing if fabric is springy or seamed edge will not lie flat. This is done at cross seams (23). Use matching thread. Starting at edge, on outside of garment, machine- or hand-stitch exactly through seam for 1″, or more if desired (24). Pull threads to wrong side and tie. This stitching will not show if correctly done.

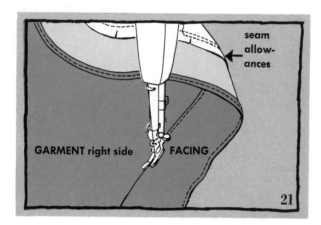

Fastening the Facing

The free edge of a shaped or extended inside facing is never entirely sewn down. However, after garment is otherwise completed, and before lining, if any, is sewn in, the facing and interfacing are fastened in place as follows:

• Catch raw edge of interfacing to finished free edge of facing, taking long stitches on interfacing and short stitches on facing.

• Tack free edge of facing to inside of garment as shown (22) wherever there is more than one thickness of fabric (seams and darts).

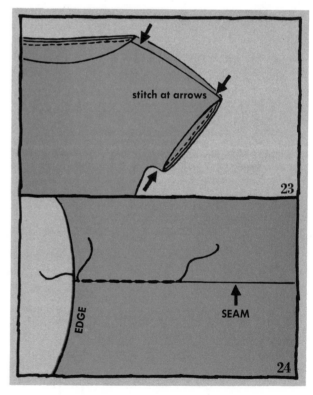

BIAS FACING

A bias facing consists of a bias strip of even width. Join bias strips as necessary (see BIAS, p. 27). If facing is to be applied to a curve, steam-press or "swirl" entire strip into a curve (25).

Make a line of stitching ¼″ from outer edge of strip (edge not taken in seam). Stitch strip to edge of garment, right sides together.

• Process seam as described on p. 82 (i.e., trim, grade, clip, understitch). Fold facing on seamline. Turn raw edge under on stitched line.

Slipstitch to garment as shown (26) or baste and topstitch. Press. If bias facing is to be turned to outside as a decoration, follow instructions which follow for **Facing Turned to Right Side.**

SPECIAL FACING APPLICATIONS

FACING TURNED TO RIGHT SIDE
(decoration)

• Stay-stitch and join pieces as necessary. Along edge not to be caught in seam, make a line of stitching exactly on seamline. Pin or baste right side of facing to wrong side of garment. Stitch. Trim all seam allowances to ¼″; grade by trimming *garment* seam allowance to ⅛″. Clip, if necessary. When understitching, open out facing, turning seam allowances under *garment;* on wrong side of garment stitch very close to seam through all thicknesses (27). Fold facing to outside, on seam. Trim seam allowance on free edge ¼″ outside line of stitching. Turn edge under on stitching line; baste. Slipstitch or topstitch to garment. Press.

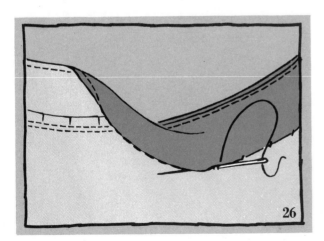

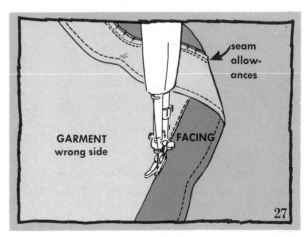

FACING A SCALLOPED EDGE

• When cutting out pattern, do not cut out scallops, either on garment or on facing, but cut edge straight along top of scalloped cutting line (28). Trace stitching line to a strip of tissue paper the same length and width as facing.

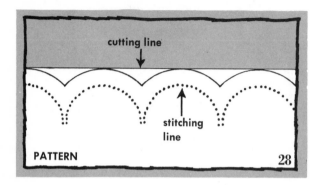

• Pin prepared facing (joined and clean-finished) to garment edge, right sides together. Pin tissue strip over facing, matching edges. Slowly stitch through paper along scallop stitching line, using shortened stitch and taking two very short stitches between scallops (29). Remove tissue paper.

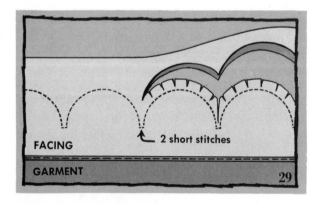

• Cut out scallops, leaving a seam allowance of ¼″ to ⅛″, depending on your fabric. Clip into seam allowance around scallops and into corners between (29). Turn facing to wrong side, carefully bringing seam to edge. Press.

A STEP-BY-STEP DEMONSTRATION

Here, in a shaped neck facing (with or without a collar), is a practical application of some of the procedures described in this chapter.

• Stay-stitch neck edge of facing pieces ½″ from edge. NOTE: To avoid confusion, stay-stitching is not shown in drawings.

• Join back and front facing pieces (30). Press seams open. Trim seam allowances to ¼″.

• Make a line of stitching ¼″ from outer edge and finish edge (31).

• Trim ⅜″ from outer (free) edge of interfacing (32).

• Stay-stitch interfacing pieces to wrong side of garment pieces. Join garment shoulder seams through all thicknesses (33). Trim all interfacing seam allowances to stitching line. Press shoulder seams open.

• Pin prepared facing to garment, right sides together, shoulder seams and notches matched. Stitch around neck edge (34).

• Trim seam allowances to ¼″ (35).

• Grade and clip seam allowances (36).

• Understitch (37).

• Turn facing to inside (38). Catch interfacing to facing. Tack or anchor facing to seams.

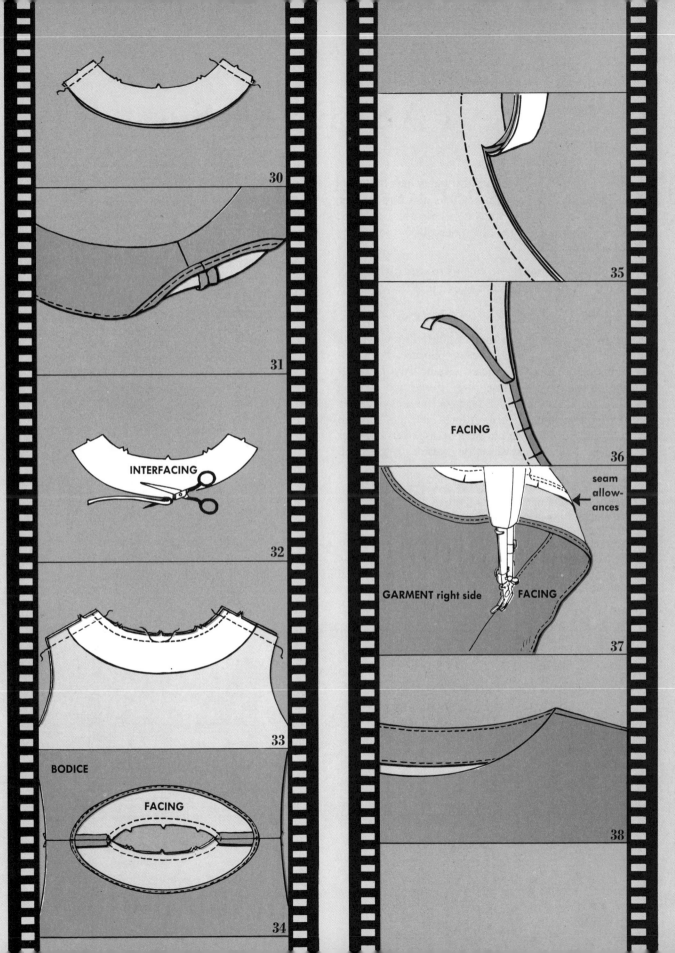

30

31

INTERFACING

32

33

BODICE

FACING

34

35

FACING

36

seam allow-ances

GARMENT right side   FACING

37

38

FASTENERS

With a few exceptions, such as pullovers, slip-on jumpers, tie-on wraparounds, garments have fasteners at openings. Some, such as buttons and buttonholes, are visible, even decorative; others, like zippers, snaps, hooks and eyes, are concealed, and purely utilitarian.

For information on BUTTONS, BUTTONHOLES, BUTTON LOOPS, see pp. 32–44. ZIPPERS, see p. 202.

SNAPS AND HOOKS AND EYES

Snaps are used where there is little strain. Hooks and eyes form a much stronger closure. Both fasteners are attached in much the same way. Depending on weight of fabric, use Mercerized Sewing Thread, "Heavy Duty" thread, or the heavier sizes of Mercerized Best Cord. Attach fasteners through holes provided for the purpose, taking over-and-over stitches that will not show on outside of garment.

Snaps

The two halves of the snap—the ball and the socket—are sewed on separately.

• Place ball half in position on underside of opening overlap. Conceal knot in thread under snap. Take 4 or 5 stitches through each hole (1). Fasten thread securely and cut.

To mark place of socket half, pin opening together. . . . If ball has no hole through center, rub chalk on it and press firmly against underlay. Some fabrics can be marked like this even without chalk. Center socket over mark and sew on.

. . . If there is a hole through ball, push threaded needle (no knot) from right side of garment through hole into underlay. Slip ball-half off needle and thread. Make knot, center socket over it and sew on.

Instructions for covering snaps are on p. 192.

Hooks and Eyes

Place hook in position on underside of overlap about ⅛″ from edge. Conceal knot under hook and take a few stitches to secure bill of hook (2). Pass needle through fabric to eyelets of hook and sew in place (2).

With opening pinned together, mark place for eye with a pin on underlay. Sew eye in place (2). There are three kinds of eyes (3):
Straight eye—Used where there is an overlap (2), as on a skirt waistband.
Round eye—Used where two edges meet (4), as at a waist stay.
Thread eye—The most inconspicuous eye, used in place of the straight eye where there is little strain, as at top of a neck zipper opening. To make, see THREAD LOOPS.

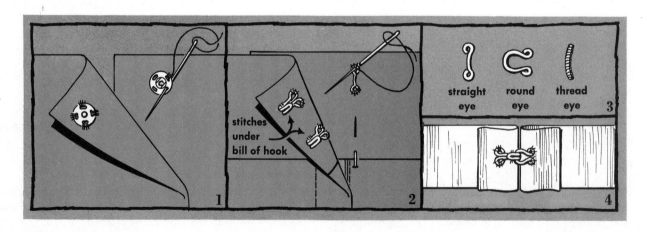

stitches under bill of hook

straight eye   round eye   thread eye

1   2   3   4

FITTING A GARMENT

Fitting a garment while sewing it should be a very small operation, involving small changes, the real alterations (if any) having been made in the pattern (see PATTERNS, p. 134).

If you want to check certain points in your garment (neckline, dart placement), you can try on the section in question as soon as the requisite darts and seams are stitched (in a bodice or a one-piece dress, these would be darts and shoulder seams). Pin-baste side seams.

As a rule, however, fitting is done when all seams are stitched except side seams, waistline, and armhole seams, which should be basted. This will give you the total picture.

FOR PROPER FITTING

. . . Have someone help you. An adjustment is awfully hard to make on yourself. You can't even pin up a back closure by yourself.
. . . Wear the undergarments you will wear with the finished garment—an undergarment can change the shape of your body and consequently, the fit of a garment. And wear heels of the same height as those you will wear with the garment.
. . . Try on garment right side out—fit cannot properly be judged wrong side out. If shoulder pads will go into finished garment, pin them in for fitting.
. . . Pin up opening(s). Put on belt, if any.
. . . The hem, of course, is not yet in, but you can judge fit and hang. Check on the points enumerated as follows, but do not fall into the error so often made by amateur dressmakers: *Do not overfit!* The only place that may be entirely snug is the waistline. At every other point you need ease to look right and move comfortably (just now you're standing still).

CHECKPOINTS

Adjustments are usually made only at basted seams. Remove stitches as necessary and make corrections with pins.

Bustline should be kept easy. A tight or pinched look at this point is particularly sad. Side darts should point to fullest part of bust.

Waistline, while snug, should be so without strain. It may have to be raised or lowered slightly, since all fabrics do not drape in the same manner.

Waist-to-hip area should lie smooth and without strain, with enough ease at hipline so that bending and sitting will not stretch garment. Folds across the back (1) may mean that skirt is too tight, in which case you let out side seams; or that there is too much length between hip and waist, in which case you raise the back at waist (2).

Side Seams, if adjusted (3), should theoretically be altered to the same degree on both sides. In practice, however, the two sides may have to be slightly different for an even hang.

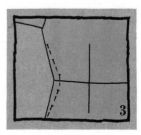

COMPLETING ADJUSTMENTS

• After fitting, remove garment, transfer corrected lines (made on outside) to inside with chalk or pins.

• Re-pin seams on inside and baste new seamlines.

• If you wish, try on again to check alterations; then stitch seams, press, etc.

THE GAPING NECKLINE

This is the case mentioned on p. 144 of PATTERNS. It may be caused by a narrow chest or shoulders, or very square shoulders. The alteration needed is not one of the small ones normally done when fitting, but, since it cannot be determined by measurements, you may not have altered your pattern. A word of caution, however: It is safer not to undertake this alteration if neck finish is anything but a plain facing, because the neck finish will have to be altered to fit.

There are three ways of taking in a neckline:

[a] by taking in shoulder seams (this is done for square shoulders).

• Try on garment before finishing neckline or armholes. Pin up opening. Have someone pin up shoulder seams, taking up an equal amount front and back. This should be not more than ½″ on each side of seam at neck, and should taper to nothing at armhole.

• After taking off garment, mark new seamline on inside. Make same alteration on facing. Stitch new shoulder seams on garment and facing. Remove old stitching; trim seams and press.

[b] by taking tucks around neckline. This may be done on front only, back only, or on both.

• Try on garment before finishing neckline. Pin up opening. Have someone pin small folds at neck to see how much needs to be taken in. Folds might be either:

. . . Two small soft tucks (4), one on either side of center (your taste will have to determine best distance; on a square neck, place them at corners). These tucks, being relatively deep, must be measured and shaped on the body. Stitch in place at edge after removing garment.

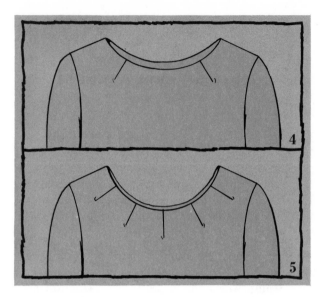

. . . A number of pin tucks (see TUCKS) all around (5). Five on front and two near center back will reduce neckline by ⅞″ (each tuck is 1/16″ deep).

It is best to measure and mark place, direction, and length (1½″ to 2″) of tucks on inside of garment after taking it off. Place equally, one at center and two at each side. Stitch tucks on wrong side.

Whether or not facing will still fit as cut after tucks are added will depend on flexibility of fabric. You may want to cut a new facing, using new neckline as pattern. You can also make adjustments at shoulder seams. In any case, facing must be made to fit smoothly.

[c] by taking in neck at center back (where there is a center back seam or zipper).

• Try on garment before finishing neck. Have someone pin up center back from neck to waist, taking in an equal amount on both sides of center. Neckline should lie smooth, but with ease—do not overfit! Then have pins removed one by one and put back through one thickness only.

• After taking off garment, mark new line of seam or closure, and continue with construction. When applying facing, trim ends to fit.

GATHERS AND SHIRRING

Gathers are formed by drawing up fabric on a line of stitching. They are part of the design of a garment, supplying a soft fullness where needed (1). Shirring, a decorative use of gathers, consists of gathers drawn up on several (three or more) lines of stitching (2).

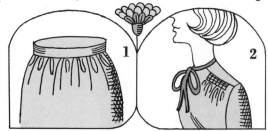

THE GATHERING STITCH

For both gathering and shirring, stitching can be done with hand running stitch (see HAND-SEWING), but is faster and more even when done by machine. To avoid breaking thread when drawing up, use "Heavy Duty" or "Dual Duty" thread. Set machine for longest stitch. Stitch on right side of fabric (bobbin thread is easier to draw up, and gathers look best on side that is not drawn up).

GATHERS

Make a row of machine-stitching on seamline and another ¼" above (3). If edge to be gathered is long (as in a skirt top), divide it into sections and make separate rows of stitching on each (4). Before drawing up gathers, pin edge to be gathered to shorter corresponding edge to which it is to be attached (waistband, for instance), at notches, ends, centers, etc. (5). Grasping both bobbin threads at one end of rows of stitching, draw up one half of gathers to match flat edge, and fasten threads by winding around a pin (6). Repeat procedure from other end of stitched rows. Distribute and straighten gathers evenly. If necessary put in additional pins (no more than 2" apart), crosswise to stitching. Stitch on seamline, gathered side *up*. Make a second row of stitching within seam allowance. When pressing, avoid flattening gathers; work point of iron into them.

SHIRRING

For first two rows of stitching, follow instructions at left. Stitch additional rows carefully as they will remain visible. Make them even and parallel, an equal distance apart. At *one end* of stitching, bring all thread-ends to wrong side and tie ends of each row separately. Cut off thread-ends. At other end of stitching, hold bobbin threads and draw shirring up to desired width (7). Bring all threads to wrong side and tie each row separately. Cut off thread-ends. For a neat, strong finish at each end of shirring, fold fabric on wrong side and stitch a narrow pin tuck as shown (8). When seaming to a flat piece of fabric, have shirred side *up*. Never press shirred area; work point of iron into gathers below it.

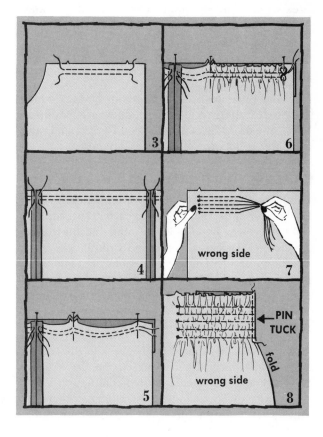

GRAIN IN FABRIC

Grain is the direction of the threads in woven fabric.

THE THREE DIRECTIONS IN FABRIC

Every woven fabric, no matter what it looks like, consists of lengthwise threads (warp) through which crosswise threads (called woof, weft, or filling) are woven over and under, back and forth. In the greatly enlarged detail of twill weave shown here (1), you will see how a diagonal effect is achieved while the threads remain at right angles to each other. The same is true of every other weave, including napped and pile fabrics. The *lengthwise* and the *crosswise* grains, therefore, are the direction in which the threads go (2).

The third direction is the diagonal or *bias* (2), which slants across the threads at the point where they meet. This is the direction of elasticity and "give" and rates a chapter of its own—BIAS.

GRAIN AND THE HUMAN FIGURE

The human figure, like the fabric that clothes it, has two directions at right angles to each other: the perpendicular, or "up-and-down," and the horizontal, or "across" (3). These correspond with the two grain directions in the fabric, a relationship that has a great deal to do with the fit and hang of a garment. Correctness of grain must be maintained, as the fabric is shaped to fit the third dimension, or bulk, of the body by means of seams, darts and gathers.

As a general rule, a garment is cut with the lengthwise grain—which also happens to be the stronger one—on the perpendicular line of the figure. While this is the most logical and satisfactory cut, there are times when a design, for instance, may demand that

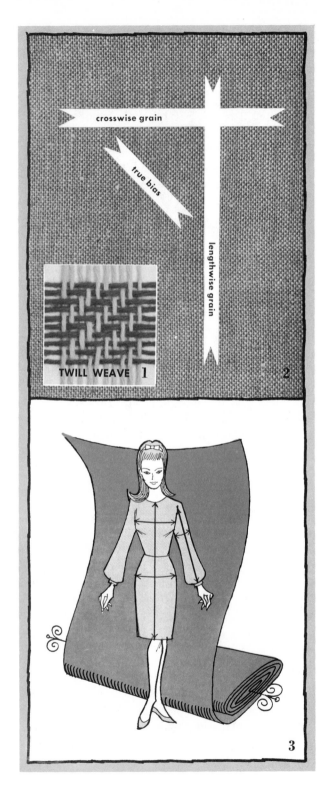

crosswise grain

true bias

lengthwise grain

TWILL WEAVE 1

2

3

the crosswise grain go up-and-down; and in a bias-cut garment the center line will be on the true bias.

In patterns, arrows marked "Straight of goods," or "Straight grain" indicate the lengthwise grain unless there is some special reason for them to mean the crosswise. This is also true of the "Lay on Fold" notation along an edge. Correct placement of arrows means correct direction of grain in your cut sections.

GRAIN AND FABRIC FINISHES

Finishes applied to fabrics after they are woven may be either temporary or permanent. In either case, they often cause the crosswise threads—the weaker grain—to be pulled into a crooked or "off-grain" position.

Permanent finishes (resin treatment, heat setting, and others), except for the shrink-resistance process, lock the grain in position. If the grain is distorted, it will stay that way. These finishes are applied to all synthetics and blends of natural and synthetic fibers; also natural-fiber fabrics labeled "wash-and-wear," "crease-resistant," etc.

Temporary finishes, which consist of sizing, are water- and steam-soluble, and will eventually let the threads return to their natural position. These finishes are present only in the natural fibers and in rayon, and only when these fabrics have not been treated with one of the permanent finishes (see FABRICS, p. 70). In other words, their use is diminishing. If one of the fabrics mentioned is not tagged for a permanent finish its finish will be temporary (we must except shrink-resistance, which is permanent, but does not affect grain).

GRAIN IN MAKING A GARMENT

Permanent-finish fabrics—Make sure, as usual, that the "Straight of Goods" mark on your pattern falls correctly on the lengthwise grain (see CUTTING, p. 53). Beyond that, you may forget about the grain. As we said previously, if it is crooked, it will remain so, and without impairing the hang of the garment.

Temporary-finish fabrics—Any deviation in grain must be corrected before cutting (see **Preparing Fabric for Use,** p. 71) because, the finish being water- and steam-soluble, the threads will eventually return to their natural straight position, and this must not happen *after* garment is finished. When cutting out, pattern indications will place grain correctly. In general, care should be taken not to pull fabric out of shape. See also CUTTING and MACHINE-STITCHING.

GUSSETS

A gusset is a small, three- or four-cornered piece of fabric inserted into a slash to provide ease.

A gusset appears most often at the underarm curve of a kimono sleeve, in a slash cutting across the seam. If such a gusset is four-cornered, it is inserted after seam is stitched. Since it is far easier to insert a gusset *before* seam is stitched, we recommend converting the gusset into two triangles which, added to each sleeve-half, automatically become a four-cornered insert when they are stitched together at the same time as underarm sleeve seam.

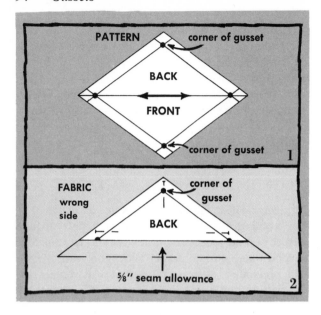

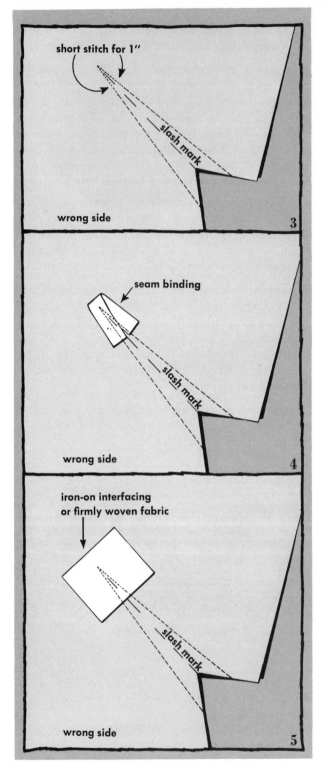

FOUR-CORNERED GUSSET PATTERN INTO TWO TRIANGLES

On pattern pieces for front and back of bodice, compare markings (dots, triangles, etc.) at underarm slash with matching markings on gusset pattern. Mark indicated gusset corners FRONT and BACK, as shown (1). With a ruler, draw a line between the *other* two corners (1). Cut gusset pattern in two on this line.

Pin each triangle to double fabric, allowing for a ⅝" seam allowance to be added at cut pattern edge (this will be underarm seam). Measure and mark this addition (2).

Cut out pieces. Transfer *all* pattern markings, including seamlines, to *all* gusset pieces.

REINFORCING POINT OF SLASH

The point of an underarm slash is subjected to considerable strain, and since there is no seam allowance there, the gusset is liable to pull out. It is extremely important, therefore, to reinforce point of slash before inserting any gusset. This can be done in one of several ways, always *before* cutting the slash:

[a] **Short-stitch machine-stitching** (3) at point may be sufficient with firmly-woven fabrics. Starting at fabric

edge, stitch over marked seamline of slash. At about an inch before reaching point, shorten stitch to 20–25 per inch. Stitch to point; pivot; take one or two stitches across point; pivot again; stitch for an inch, change to regular stitch and continue to edge as shown.

[b] **Seam binding** (4). Fold a 3″ piece of seam binding into a V, and place over point as shown. Mark point with pin. Machine-stitch as described in [a] above.

[c] **Iron-on interfacing** (5). Before using this, test it by ironing a scrap onto a scrap of your fabric, following instructions on package. If results are satisfactory, press a 1½″-square piece of iron-on interfacing over point of slash. Mark point and machine-stitch as described in [a] above.

[d] **Thin firmly-woven fabric.** Place a 1½″-square of fabric over point of slash. Mark point with pin. Machine-stitch as described in [a] above.

INSERTING A TWO-PIECE GUSSET

• Cut slash as far into point as possible without clipping stitching.

• To attach first edge of gusset, pin one edge of slash over one edge of gusset, right sides together, matching point of slash to corner of gusset (2) as marked, and stitched line of slash to marked seamline on gusset (6). With garment side up, stitch over stitched line, going toward point; at about an inch before reaching point, shorten stitches to 20–25 per inch. At point, *leave needle down* in fabric.

• To attach second edge, pivot free edge of slash and free edge of gusset forward and match and pin as before (7). Stitch with shortened stitch, returning to regular stitch after an inch.

• Reinforce seam by topstitching through all thicknesses close to seam (8), again shortening stitch before reaching point. At point, continue for 3 stitches beyond, then backstitch to point. Pivot work, backstitch 3 stitches along direction of next seam, then stitch forward, changing to regular stitch after an inch.

• Repeat with second triangle; stitch underarm seam.

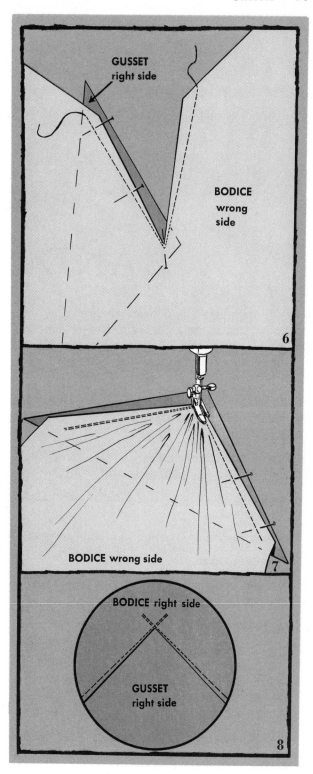

HAND-SEWING

You can be a first-class dressmaker these days, and not know how to "sew a fine seam" (that's what sewing machines are for!). Still, you must know how to handle needle and thread competently. You will need them for:

Basting, where pin-basting is insufficient and machine-basting impractical—see BASTING and PLEATS. Also for MARKING.

Hemming most garments—see HEMS, Blind-stitch, Catch-stitch and Slipstitch on p. 101.

Tacking—see FACINGS, p. 84; for making **Bar Tacks**, see THREAD LOOPS.

Sewing on Fastenings—see BUTTONS, and FASTENERS.

You also need them for:

Overcasting seams in ravelly fabric if your machine is not equipped to do it—see SEAMS AND SEAM FINISHES.

Hand-Worked Buttonholes—see BUTTONHOLES, p. 38.

One further consideration: what with becoming ever less of a necessity, hand-sewing is taking on the elegance of a luxury. Careful hand-finishing (such as doing the outside stitching of a zipper application by hand) will give a garment an expensive look.

You will find on the next page whatever hand stitches are not covered in the chapters named above.

THREAD AND NEEDLE

For any hand-sewing, you generally use the thread you are using in machine-stitching your garment. The needle may be of whatever type you prefer, but pick the size according to your fabric and thread (see THREAD AND NEEDLE CHART, p. 196).

Thread is generally used single. If, for extra strength (sewing on a button, hand-sewing a zipper), you want to use it doubled, make sure that you draw it out smoothly after every stitch, to avoid forming snags and loops.

The working length of any thread, single or doubled, should never be more than 18″ (1).

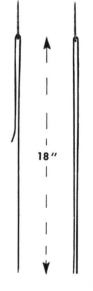

18″

Make a knot at the end of your thread and if you can, tuck knot under a seam allowance, hem, etc. Otherwise, start your sewing with a few tiny backstitches on top of each other. These should be made on the wrong side of your work.

1

To finish, take a few stitches in same way. Do not cut off thread too close. Take a few inconspicuous running stitches (e.g., through seam allowance) before you clip.

THE MOTIONS OF HAND-SEWING

Train yourself to wear a thimble on the middle finger of your sewing hand. You may have been doing without one, but you will find, after an initial feeling of clumsiness, that with this protection you can push the needle forward faster and with much more precision. Except in a very few cases, hold your needle as shown (2).

How you hold your work will depend on what you are doing. In the chapters which are mentioned on p. 96, you will find illustrations for whatever hand-sewing is indicated.

HAND STITCHES

Running Stitch (3) is mostly used for gathering and shirring by hand. With point of needle, take a number of small forward stitches (1/16″ to ⅛″ long, depending on fabric), and slide stitches onto thread as needle fills up. If stitch is used in a seam (this should only be done where there is very little strain—otherwise, it could easily pull out), draw up thread after filling needle, then take a small backstitch before filling needle again. Longer running stitches are used for decoration; they are called **saddle stitches** (see p. 60).

Half backstitch (4)—Good for any seam, and for hand-finishing a zipper application (see ZIPPERS, p. 214). Bring needle and thread out on stitching line. Take a stitch back about 1/16″; bring needle out about ⅛″ from where you first came out. Take another 1/16″-stitch back and continue in the same manner. In a zipper finish, stitches should be tiny and farther apart; it is then called **prick-stitch.**

Backstitch (5) makes strong seams. Bring needle and thread out on stitching line. Take a stitch back about 1/16″, bringing needle out ⅛″ forward (i.e., 1/16″ from where you first came out). To continue, keep putting your needle in at end of last stitch and bringing it out one stitch ahead.

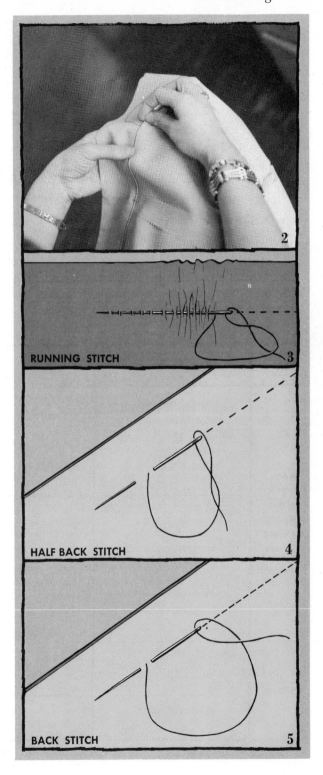

RUNNING STITCH　3

HALF BACK STITCH　4

BACK STITCH　5

HEMS

The hem is the last detail, the step that completes a garment. In something ready-made, or that needs bringing up to date, the hem is often the only place requiring an alteration.

A good hem is one that is inconspicuous and even, and that, while giving body to the bottom edge, interferes in no way with the hang of a garment.

Your first consideration should be the proper choice of hem finish for your fabric and garment cut. For general guidance on the type of hem you should use, follow the chart below.

NOTE: In a case when your fabric is either insufficient or too bulky for a regular hem, make a **Faced Hem** (see p. 104).

Fabric	Cut of Garment		Depth of Hem	Choice of Hem Finish
All types and weights except sheers	**Narrow and Medium Full** Straight Gored Flared		2″–3″	*Suitable for all fabrics:* Hem with Seam Binding Tailor's Hem *Lightweight fabrics:* Turned-and-Stitched Hem
	Full Straight, gathered, pleated		3″	Any of the above; or Machine-Stitched Hem for light- and medium-weight playclothes and children's clothes
		Circular, gored	1″	Hem with Seam Binding Tailor's Hem
Sheers	**Full*** Straight, gathered		3″–8″	Turned-and-Stitched Hem
		Circular, gored	¼″	Hand-Rolled Hem Edge-Stitched Hem

*A narrow skirt in a sheer fabric is usually backed, putting the fabric into the medium-weight category.

MARKING THE HEMLINE

The hemline is the line on which a hem is folded up (i.e., the finished edge of garment). It must be at the *right level,* and it must be *even*—that is, at the same distance from floor all around.

A pattern usually indicates depth of hem. If, through measurement and previous experience, or because you have altered the pattern to fit, you know you can use this hemline, proceed as for the **straight skirt,** below.

As a rule, however, you cannot be sure that the length of a garment is right until you have tried it on. And, the human figure seldom being absolutely symmetrical, a skirt with a curved hemline (gored, flared, or circular), may sag at certain points unless the hemline has been measured up from the floor all around. In other words, for one reason or another, it is usually necessary to put on a garment to mark the hemline. When doing this, wear a proper foundation; put on the belt, if any; wear shoes with heels of the proper height; and stand straight, with arms down and weight on both feet.

A straight skirt, whether full or narrow, is marked at *one point only,* since its hemline is usually on the straight grain.

Mark hemline-level at a seam, on right side. If fabric has a well-defined crosswise pattern, hemline will follow that pattern. Otherwise place garment right side up on ironing board. Set or make a hem gauge for the distance between mark and cut edge. Mark hemline all around with pins or chalk, as shown (1).

A flared, gored, or circular skirt is marked all around, preferably with the help of another person. A circular skirt in a non-treated fabric should be allowed to hang for about 48 hours before hem is marked, to let it stretch. If you use a yardstick, determine hemline-level and mark it on yardstick with a rubber band.

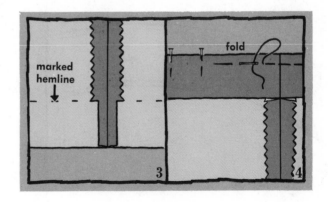

Helper stands yardstick upright on floor against garment, and marks hemline with a horizontal line of pins, about 3″ apart (2). With a skirt marker (see EQUIPMENT) you may or may not need a helper. If you work alone, keep your body straight as you turn, especially when marking the back.

If you wish, pin up hem on a trial basis after marking, and try on garment again, to check length.

For children's clothes of any cut, establish length at one point and proceed as for **straight skirt,** left.

TURNING UP AND MARKING DEPTH OF HEM

NOTE: for **Machine-Finished Hem, Rolled Hem, Edge-Stitched Hem, Faced Hem,** skip what follows and turn to pp. 103–104.

Skirt of any cut—Place garment on ironing board, wrong side out. If fabric is bulky, trim ⅛″ off seam allowances between marked hemline and cut edge, as shown (3). Turn up hem on marked hemline, pinning fold as shown (4) and adjusting fold wherever necessary so line will be even. Then baste close to fold (4), removing pins as you go. Press fold lightly.

For proper depth of hem, consult chart on p. 98, or your pattern. Set or make hem gauge for depth indicated. Measuring from basted fold (5), mark hem all around with sharpened tailor's chalk or with pins *through one thickness of fabric only.* Trim off excess fabric all around on marked line.

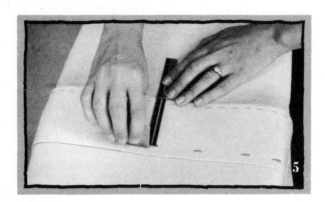

REDUCING FULLNESS IN CURVED HEMS

The excess fullness in curved hems (near seams in gored skirts, all around in circular ones) is eased as follows:

• Make a line of stitching (10 stitches to the inch) ¼″ from cut edge (single thickness), all around. Place garment on ironing board, wrong side out. Wherever there is a ripple, draw up under-thread with a pin (6), forming a group of small gathers, as shown. Place a

piece of heavy paper between hem and garment fabric and press (7), shrinking out gathers in wool and other shrinkable fabrics. On non-shrinkable fabric, press gathers as flat as possible.

METHODS OF SEWING A HEM

To sew a hem, garment is held with hemline up and wrong side of garment facing you.

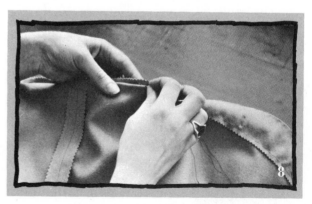

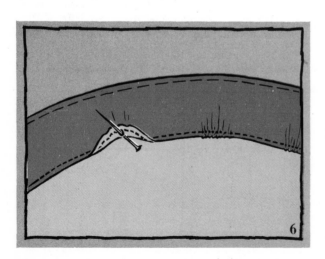

Except for Tailor's Hem (see **Hem Finishes,** p. 102), which is always sewn with inside hemming (8), you have a choice of Inside Hemming or Flat Hemming.

In Inside Hemming, stitches are taken between hem and garment fabric. (Hence, in the finished hem, the thread is protected against friction, the usual cause of a hem's coming undone.) To do this, fold entire hem back against right side of garment, with fold in garment even with machine-stitching in hem edge (9), or ⅛″ below edge of seam binding (11). On garment side, take a small stitch through one thread in fold; on hem-edge, catch machine-stitching (9), or seam binding just below edge (11).

In Flat Hemming, edge of hem is sewn flat to garment, with stitches taken through hem-edge (10, 12, 13), and close to this edge in garment.

STITCHES USED

• For either method, begin hem at a seam, with knot hidden in seam. *Do not pull thread tight,* or outside fabric will show puckers. Take stitches at least ¼″ apart. In garment fabric, pick up just a thread or two, if possible not going through to right side. Finish a thread-length on hem or in a seam (never in garment fabric), taking a few over-and-over stitches. Cut (do not break) thread. When sewing is finished, remove basting and give a light pressing along bottom edge, keeping iron clear of upper edge of hem.

You have a choice of three stitches:

Blind-stitch is used in both Inside Hemming (9) and Flat Hemming (10). Work from right to left. Take a stitch in hem-edge (or line of stitching). Take next stitch in garment, picking up just one thread in fabric and putting needle through hem-edge (or line of stitching) at least ¼″ ahead before drawing up thread. Repeat.

Catch-stitch is used in both Inside Hemming (11) and Flat Hemming (12), and is very good for knit and stretch fabrics because it has "give." Work from left to right, with needle pointing from right to left. Keep thread very loose.

Slipstitch (13) is used only in Flat Hemming where there is a turned edge. It is done like blind-stitching except that the needle is slipped through folded edge of hem instead of being put through edge of hem.

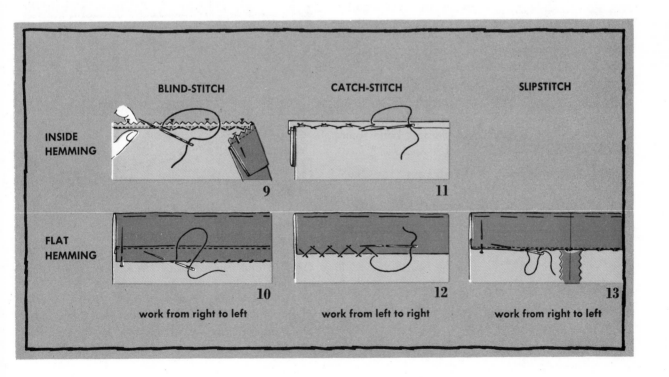

HEM FINISHES

Your garment is ready for one of these three standard hem finishes after hem has been folded up, basted along hemline, and cut to the correct width.

Tailor's Hem (14)—An excellent hem, flat and inconspicuous, particularly suitable for most heavy and medium-weight fabrics. It is always sewn with Inside Hemming.

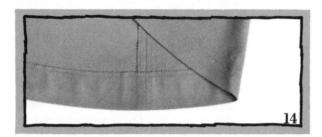

• On a straight skirt, make a line of machine-stitching ¼″ below cut edge through single thickness of hem fabric (on a curved-hem skirt you will already have done it while reducing fullness). On firm fab-

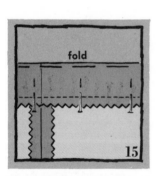

ric, pink edge. If fabric is ravelly, overcast edge by hand or machine. Place work on ironing board, wrong side out. Matching at seams, pin or baste hem in place about ¼″ below stitching line (15). Sew with Inside Hemming, using blind-stitch or catch-stitch.

Hem with Seam Binding or Stretch Lace (16) — Suitable for all fabrics, especially for fabrics that ravel easily.

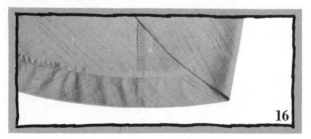

Seam Binding may be either straight or bias.

. . . Rayon seam binding is ½″-wide straight tape with a durable woven edge. Available in regular (see directions below for applying) and iron-on (follow directions on package).

. . . Rayon bias seam binding, particularly good for curved hems, has turned-under edges and is ½″ wide. It can be applied either like straight seam binding (see below), or a ready-made facing (see **Faced Hem,** p. 104).

For use on a **curved hem,** prepare seam binding by steam-pressing it into a slight curve (17).

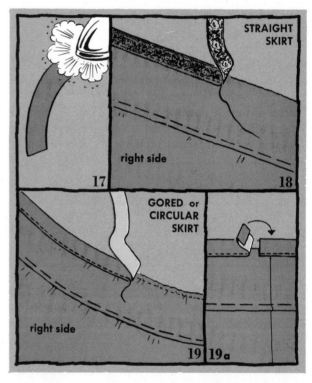

• Topstitch binding to right side of hem about ¼″ from cut edge, as shown, *easing it to fabric* (18, 19). Overlap end, turned under as shown (19-a). Place work on ironing board, wrong side out. Matching at seams, pin or baste hem to garment, just below seam binding. Sew with either Inside Hemming (using blind-stitch or catch-stitch), or Flat Hemming (using blind-stitch).

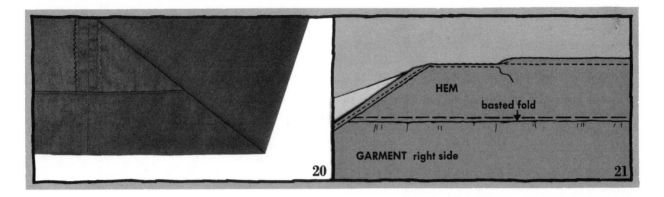

Turned-and-Stitched Hem (20)—Used only on light-weight fabrics in straight or narrow gored garments.

• On a straight skirt, make a line of machine-stitching ¼″ from cut edge, through single thickness of hem fabric (on a curved hem, you will already have done this while reducing fullness). Turn edge to inside on stitching line and topstitch through hem edge only, not garment (21). Place work on ironing board, wrong side out. Matching at seams, pin or baste hem in place about ¼″ below topstitching. Sew with either Inside Hemming (using blind-stitch or catch-stitch), or Flat Hemming (using slipstitch).

Machine-Finished Hem (22)—Quick and easy for hems on straight, full skirts of medium-weight cotton (dirndls, aprons, children's clothes, etc.). Eliminates all hand-sewing while looking like a Turned-and-Stitched Hem. Edge is stitched and hem is caught in place in one operation. Try it first on a fabric sample.

• After **Marking the Hemline** (see p. 99), turn in raw edge of hem ½″ and crease. Fold up hem on marked hemline and press a sharp crease. Pin hem in place as shown (23). Fold entire hem back against right side of garment (24), with hem-edge extending about ⅛″ beyond fold. Stitch on extended edge of hem (10–12 stitches to the inch) and go slowly. Take five stitches, ending with needle **up.** Lifting and lowering presser foot as needed, pivot fabric slightly, let needle down through about a thread of fabric in fold, take one stitch (ending with needle up), and pivot fabric back for another five stitches in hem-edge. Repeat (24).

NOTE: By using a zipper or cording foot in your machine, you can avoid making a crease in the outer fabric as you work.

This hem can also be made with a zigzag machine or a Blind-Stitcher attachment. Follow manufacturer's directions.

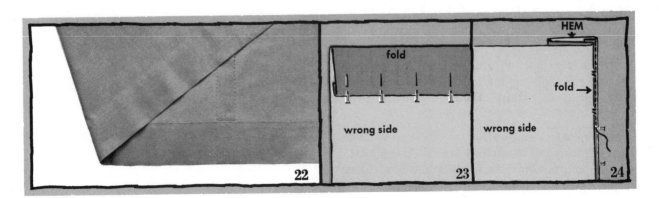

Rolled Hem and Edge-Stitched Hem—These are very narrow hems used on circular skirts of sheer fabric (see chart on p. 98). After **Marking the Hemline** (see p. 99), continue as directed below, following instructions and illustrations exactly.

A Rolled Hem (25)—simplified or other—is an elegant hand-finish for skirts of chiffon, voile, etc.; also for handkerchiefs, scarves, and the like which are made of a sheer fabric.

Simplified Rolled Hem—Trim away excess fabric ¼″ outside marked hemline. Fold in raw edge ⅛″. Slip needle through fold and anchor thread. Take a tiny stitch in garment below raw edge, then slip needle through fold; repeat as shown (26) with stitches about ¼″ apart. After every few stitches, draw up thread, forming a roll.

An Edge-Stitched Hem (27) is done by machine and is quick and easy. Place a strip of tissue paper underneath fabric when stitching. Afterwards, tear away paper.

Make a line of stitching on marked hemline. Trim away excess fabric ¼″ outside stitching. Turn edge to wrong side, folding on stitching line (no pinning or basting necessary) and topstitch on **right side,** a scant ⅛″ from fold. If you want a second line of stitching, make first line a little closer to the edge of fabric.

Faced Hem—A hem is faced with a bias strip (28) if fabric is insufficient; if fabric is too bulky for a regular hem; for decorative contrast; or to stiffen an edge (see Horsehair Braid, next page).

Ready-Made Hem Facing is of taffeta or cotton, 2″ wide, with both edges turned under ¼″ for easy application.

Hand-Cut Facing—Cut strips at least 2½″ wide on the true bias; join until strip is a few inches longer than edge to be faced (see **The Hand-Cut Bias Strip,** p. 26).

Along one edge, make a line of stitching ¼″ from edge. With right side up, turn edge under on stitching line and topstitch. This will be the upper edge of the facing.

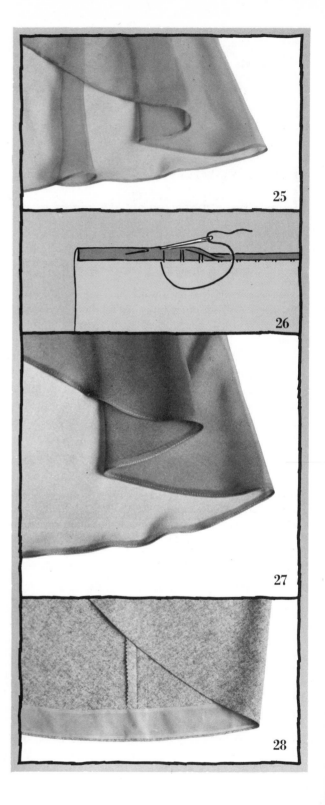

25

26

27

28

Ready-made and hand-cut bias facings are applied in the same manner:

After **Marking the Hemline** (see p. 99), trim away excess fabric ½" outside marked line. Beginning at a seam, place right side of facing to right side of skirt, raw edges even (on ready-made facing, open out edge-fold). For a neat finish later, fold back end as shown (29). Stitch ¼" from edge, or on crease. Overlap ends. Turn facing to inside on marked hemline. Pin fold (30) and baste close to fold, removing pins as you go. Press fold lightly. With work on ironing board, pin free edge of facing in place. Hem to garment with slipstitch. Slipstitch joining together.

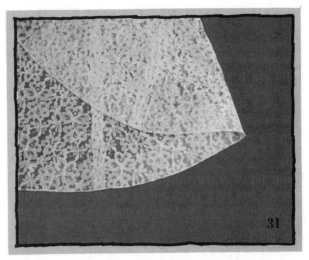

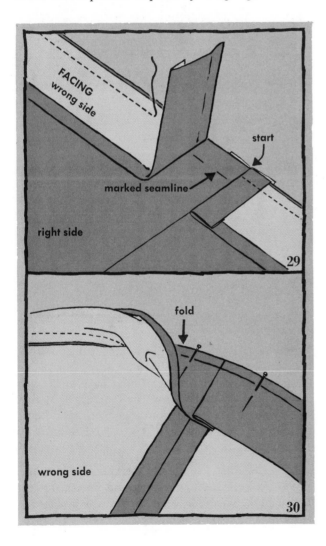

Horsehair Braid is used as a facing to stiffen the hem of a full skirt (31). It comes in several widths.

To apply, trim away excess fabric ¼" outside marked hemline.

Wide Braid—Top edge of braid has a special thread for drawing it up. Topstitch bottom edge of braid to right side of skirt edge with edge of braid at marked hemline, as shown (32). Overlap ends about 2". With work on ironing board, turn braid to inside of garment and pin, then baste close to fold, removing pins as you go. On a circular skirt, draw up free edge of braid on thread mentioned before; pin or baste. Hem to garment.

Narrow Braid—Topstitch one edge of braid to garment. Turn braid to inside of garment and topstitch close to edge through braid and fabric, as shown (33). This stitching, so close to edge, is not noticeable on right side. Catch free edge of braid to seams only.

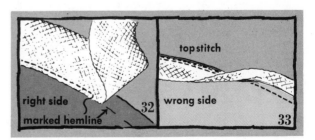

Hem in Pleats—Hem will be a regular hem, as indicated by pattern or by chart on p. 98.

On a skirt pleated all around, complete hem before pressing in pleats.

Pleat with seam in it—Method I (34). Press seam to one side before proceeding with **Marking the Hemline** (see p. 99). Then measure depth of hem on seam above hemline, clip through one seam allowance at that point, and press seam open below it, as shown (35). Within depth of hem, trim seam allowances as shown. Then proceed with turning up and finishing hem.

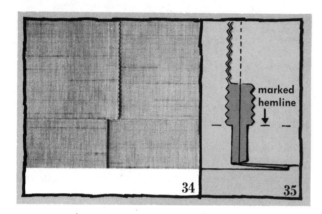

Pleat with seam in it—Method II (36)—Good for hard-to-press fabrics, such as bulky fabrics, wash-and-wear, etc. When stitching seam in pleat, leave seam open for about 8″ from raw bottom edge (37). Complete

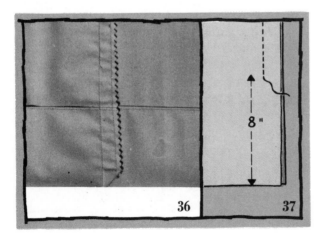

the garment, *including hem.* Be very careful to have both sides even at open hem (38). Stitch open section of seam *through finished hem.* Turn in corner of seam at bottom (39), and whipstitch edges together, as shown. At outside fold of pleat, whipstitch hem edges together for about ⅛″, as shown (39).

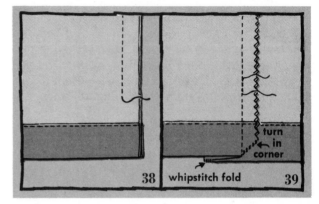

HEM IN A COAT (40)

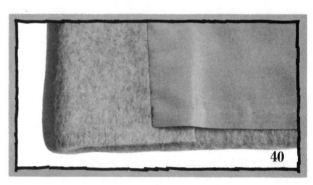

A full-length coat is generally 1″ longer than a dress. On any coat, the hem is 2″ to 3″ deep. It is put in after lining and interlining (if any) have been sewn in to within 8″ to 12″ from bottom edge. At that level, with coat hanging from a hanger, baste lining to coat all around to hold it in place, and let all bottom edges hang free.

• Mark length of coat (see **Marking the Hemline,** p. 99). At both front edges, trim off interfacing just above marked hemline. If an interlining is attached to body of coat, trim it at marked hemline.

• Turn up hem and mark depth as indicated on p. 99, extending hem through open facing (41). If coat has a curved hem, reduce fullness as indicated under **Reducing Fullness** on p. 100.

• Complete hem, making either a **Tailor's Hem** or a **Hem with Seam Binding.** Overcast the two side (facing) edges of hem as shown (42).

• Press facings to inside. Any topstitching should go in or be restored at this point. If front edges of coat are not topstitched, catch facing hem to garment hem ½″ from facing seam (42) to secure facing.

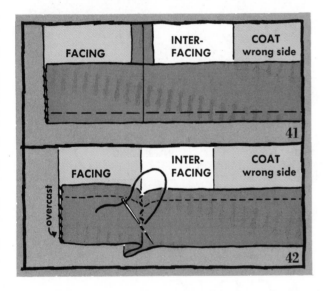

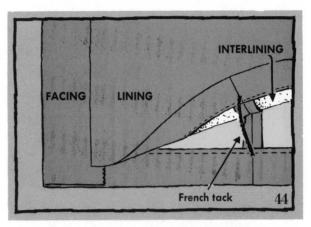

• Finish lining with a 2″ **Turned-and-Stitched Hem,** turning it up over any interlining (44).

• Slipstitch front edges of lining to facings. At each seam, catch lining to coat with a French tack 1″ to 1½″ long (44).

Finishing a Short Coat

• Slipstitch bottom edge of facings to coat (45).

• Check length of lining and interlining, if any. Trim lining even with finished coat edge, interlining to 2″ shorter than lining.

• Turn lining under ½″ and press. Pin fold of lining to just cover hem-edge (upper edge of hem) and slipstitch (46); fold formed by extra length of lining is for ease. Slipstitch front edges of lining to facings, including fold made by extra length.

Finishing a Long Coat (bottom of lining left free)

• Catch facings to body of garment with ½″-long French tack at hem (43).

• Check length of lining and interlining. Trim lining to 1″ below finished coat edge, interlining to 2″ shorter than lining.

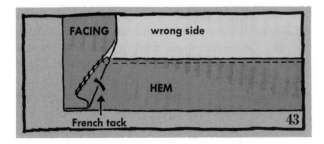

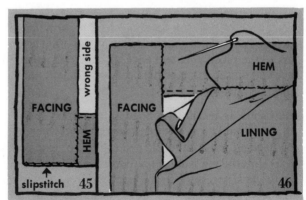

INTERFACING

An interfacing is an extra piece of fabric placed between a facing and the outer fabric of a garment. Its purpose is to reinforce and add body and often crispness to the faced area and edge. It improves appearance and preserves shape. It may be of specially-made fabric or not—see next page.

Interfacing is usually specified in patterns. If it is not, you would do well to consider adding it wherever you have a facing, either shaped (1, 2, 3) or extended (4, 5). Interfacing is essential if your garment fabric is soft; less necessary if you are working with, say, treated cotton, where the finish furnishes a certain

body. Where there are buttons and buttonholes, interfacing is *always* a good idea.

INTERFACING FABRICS

Fabrics used for interfacings may be either specially made for the purpose, or ordinary fabrics with the suitable properties (see chart on p. 109); besides body, these may be firmness, crispness, or real stiffness. Most fabrics used combine certain of these qualities. If different effects are called for in different parts of a garment, you should use more than one kind of interfacing.

All interfacing fabrics are dry-cleanable, some are washable, and some quick-drying—all these are factors to consider when making your choice. If washable interfacing is not preshrunk, it must be shrunk if you are planning to use it in a washable garment.

Woven interfacing fabrics must be cut on the same grain as facing and outer fabric. Most have a certain "give" and can be manipulated. Some, containing wool, can be shaped by shrinking, which makes them ideal in tailored woolen garments. Self-fabric does very nicely with smooth (never nubby or ribbed) wash-and-wear fabrics, smooth cottons, and solid-color organdy. Hair canvas is used only in tailoring (see p. 173).

Non-woven interfacing fabrics, having no grain, can be cut in any direction. They have less "give" than the woven ones, but the so-called "all-bias" varieties can be manipulated to a certain degree.

Iron-on interfacing fabric may be woven (in which case it must be cut on grain), or non-woven. It can be used only where garment fabric is firm enough so outline will not be visible on outside (try it first on a scrap of garment fabric). It is particularly useful for stabilizing ravelly fabric at a buttonhole, or to back a waistband. It is also good for producing a starched effect in a collar. Be sure to obtain directions for use when you buy it, and follow them carefully, especially in regard to amount of heat to apply.

SELECTING AN INTERFACING

It would be impossible to enumerate all the fabrics used for interfacings, and new specially-made ones turn up every day. The chart below will give you the major types, together with what you can expect of them and with what dress fabrics they are suitable. But keep one basic rule in mind: *Interfacing should never be heavier than the garment fabric.*

Interfacing	Properties	Typical Uses
Lawn **Cotton Batiste** **and Muslin**	washable—may need shrinking before use—give body but no crispness	**Lawn** or **Cotton Batiste** with voile, silk, crepe, lightweight linen, broadcloth—**Muslin** with heavier fabrics, generally wool (as in dressmaker suits)
Organdy and Lightweight **Crease-Resistant Cottons**	washable—preshrunk—give crispness to lightweight fabrics	with organdy, silk, shantung, linen, lightweight wool, cottons, jerseys
Woven **Interfacing Fabrics** **(with grain)** **various weights**	may be washable or dry-cleanable, (see labels)—wrinkle-resistant—give body and firmness—shape retaining—some can be steamed to shape	**Lighter Weights** used with wool-type fabrics, shantungs—**Heavier Weights** with heavy fabrics, for tailoring on wool fabrics, for exceptional firmness
Non-Woven **Interfacing Fabrics** **(no grain) various weights**	washable—non-shrinking—depending on weight used, provide gentle firmness or real stiffness	**Lighter Weights** used with linen, heavier cottons and wool-type fabrics—**Other Weights** for exceptional stiffness (bags, belts, etc.)
Iron-on Interfacing **Fabrics** **woven and non-woven** **various weights**	usually washable—depending on weight, provide firmness or real stiffness	used on medium to heavy fabrics

HANDLING INTERFACING

Cutting (if there is no pattern piece for interfacing) . . . For a shaped facing (1, 2, 3), cut interfacing from facing pattern.

. . . For an extended facing (4), pin facing part of pattern to interfacing fabric, with edge of fabric along pattern fold line (6). Cut out. For collars, cuffs, and waistbands, cut lightweight interfacing from the entire pattern piece, as shown (5).

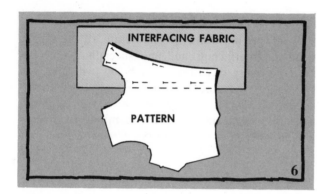

Marking

• Mark center front and back at neck edge on interfacing.

• Mark on interfacing the seamlines that are "critical," i.e., that are curved, or come to points that must match perfectly (collars, cuffs, lapels).

• For marking buttonholes, see BUTTONHOLES, p. 33.

Trimming

• Unless interfacing fabric is very lightweight, outer corners (on collars, cuffs, lapels, etc.) should be trimmed away on interfacing (7) before it is attached to a corresponding piece.

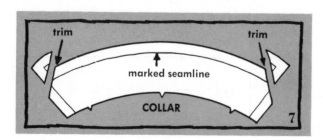

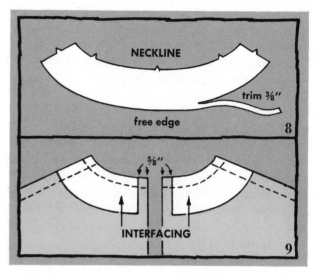

• Trim ⅜″ from free edges (i.e., those that are not to be caught in a seam) of a neck interfacing, front interfacing, etc. (8). If interfacing fabric is ravelly, make a line of stitching ¼″ from trimmed edge.

• On an interfacing that reaches a zipper opening (as at a neck), trim ⅝″ from the two edges that adjoin the opening (9).

APPLYING INTERFACING

Interfacing is applied to a section before section is either stay- or construction-stitched.

. . . For a shaped facing, pin interfacing to wrong side of outer garment section, carefully matching edges. Stitch ½″ from edges (10). When edge is curved or slanted, this serves as stay-stitching.

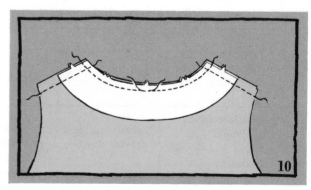

. . . For an extended facing, place interfacing to wrong side of outer garment section, matching straight edge of interfacing to garment fold-line. Catch edge of interfacing to fold-line with loose slipstitch invisible from right side (11). Stay-stitch, taking in interfacing.

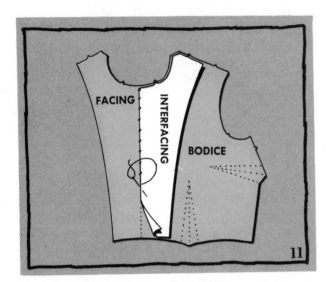

. . . If lightweight interfacing on a collar or cuff has been cut to full outer fabric size, fold interfacing on fold-line, and slipstitch this fold to fold-line of collar with loose slipstitch invisible from right side (12). Open out interfacing and stay-stitch around edges.

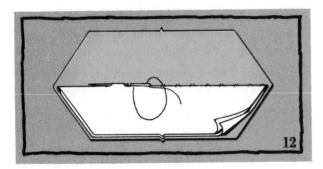

. . . On washable garments with worked buttonholes (blouses, children's dresses, etc.), the following finish for an extended facing is very neat and stands up well under washings:

• Place interfacing to right side of garment facing, edges matching. Stitch ¼″ from outer raw edge; if facing reaches to shoulder seam, stitch shoulder ⅝″ from edge (13). Grade seam allowances, clip if necessary, and trim corners. Turn interfacing to wrong side; press. Stay-stitch, taking in interfacing. Stitch down raw straight edge of interfacing, close to edge (14); on an open neckline, stop stitching before point where it would show on outside (15).

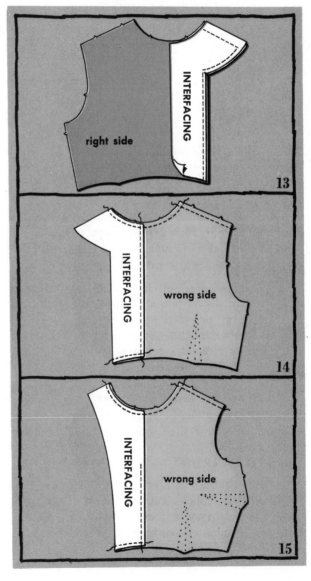

LINING

Lining, like backing, doubles a garment. Unlike backing, its purpose is to provide the inside of garment with a finish. It often helps preserve shape (in pants, straight skirts), but never establishes shape, as backing does. Again unlike backing, which is attached to and stitched with each garment section, a lining is seamed together as though it were a separate garment, and then sewn to garment along the edges.

Since a lining covers all raw seams and edges, it is practically always present in garments that may be worn open, such as coats and jackets—exceptions may be lightweight summer clothes in which seams are carefully finished (see SEAM FINISHES, p. 160), and reversible wraps, which are doubled with a true and equal second garment. In dresses, a lining may be added as a luxury touch, but it serves a definite purpose if garment fabric is irritating to the skin or tends to stretch (like some knits, for instance).

LINING FABRICS

The main requisites of a lining fabric are that it be smooth to the touch, soft and pliable, and light enough in weight not to interfere in any way with the hang of a garment. Silk or imitations thereof in rayon and synthetics—China silk, crepe and taffeta, satin and brocade—are most likely to have these qualities,

while smooth-surface cotton is often suitable as well. In an ensemble, a coat or jacket may be lined with the same fabric of which the dress or blouse is made. In such a case, the sleeves are often lined with another fabric, especially if the coordinated fabric would not allow them to slip easily on and off.

PUTTING IN A LINING

The instructions that follow are for lining a dress, blouse, or skirt where no such instructions are furnished with the pattern (in general, patterns include lining only for coats, jackets, etc.).

• Buy same amount of lining as garment fabric, minus facings, collar, and cuffs.

• Cut lining from garment pattern, omitting the details mentioned, or kick pleat. Transfer all markings.

• Complete outer garment, except for neck edge and hemline. On sleeves, turn up bottom edge and hem. On a sleeveless garment, leave armhole edges unfinished. Leave waistline unfinished on a skirt. Assemble lining in the same way, but leave sleeve bottoms unfinished; leave any zipper opening or location for kick pleat unstitched. Press seams open; to lessen bulk, press lining darts in opposite direction from garment darts.

• Depending on your edge-finishes, attach lining to garment by one of the following two methods:

METHOD I—For use when edges are to be faced, or finished with an edge-finish (braid or bias binding).

• With garment and lining wrong sides out, pin back of lining to back of garment, wrong sides together, seams and waistline matching. With loose basting stitch (1), catch one lining seam allowance to one garment seam allowance *exactly* as shown (study the illustration; if you catch the seam allowance along wrong side of seam it won't work). Join seams loosely in this manner at shoulders, along underarms to within 2″ of sleeve-ends, and down side seams as far as hipline. Leave zipper area free.

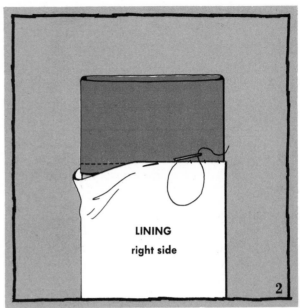

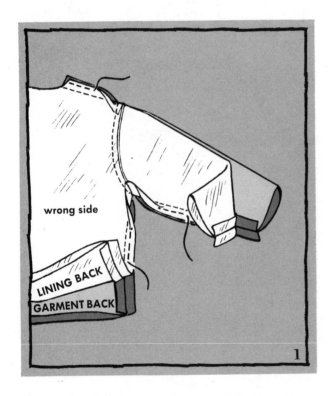

• Baste lining to garment at neckline, at armholes of a sleeveless garment, or at waistline on a skirt. At zipper opening, fold edges of lining under and slip-stitch neatly to zipper tape. At sleeves, trim lining to length of finished edge; turn ½″ under and press. Pin and slipstitch this edge over catch-stitched hem at garment-sleeve (2)—the slight extra length in lining is for ease. At a kick pleat, let lining edge hang free, finished with narrow hems.

• Apply edge-finish—facing, bias binding, etc.—to garment, or waistband to a skirt. On a skirt, dress, or coat, hem hangs free; on a blouse or short coat, lining is attached at hem (see HEMS, **Finishing a Coat,** p. 107, for finishing).

METHOD II—For garments that have a front or back opening (coats, jackets, blouses) and where the lining reaches to and finishes all edges.

• On both garment and lining, mark hemline and cut away hem allowance ⅝″ from marked line (remember that this makes it impossible to lengthen garment later).

• With lining and garment right sides together, baste and stitch around neckline and front (or back) opening; trim and clip seam allowance; understitch.

• Reaching inside lining and through armholes, put your hands through both lining sleeves at the same time and grasp ends of lining and garment sleeves together. Pull sleeves through, turning body of lining over garment. Entire lining will now be right side out, with garment inside.

• Stitch bottom edge, leaving an opening as shown (3) through which to turn garment. Press this seam open; trim corners and grade seam allowance.

• At shoulder- and side-seams, catch one lining seam allowance to one garment seam allowance with loose basting stitch as in Method I. Read accompanying instructions (1).

• Push garment through opening at bottom and bring it right sides out. Reach inside garment sleeves and through lining sleeves; grasp ends and pull lining through.

• Slipstitch opening together. Press garment edge so that lining will not show on right side. To finish sleeves, see Method I (2). On a sleeveless garment, baste lining to armhole and complete with facings of lining fabric.

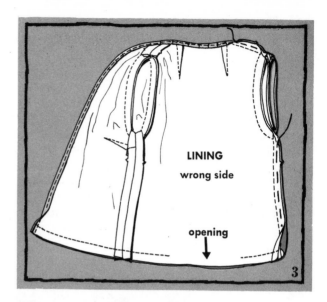

MACHINE-STITCHING

Before going into the various uses—the *why* and *where* —of machine-stitching, let us consider the *how,* which means the handling of your sewing machine.

The key to success in stitching *any* fabric with *any* kind of thread lies in your sewing machine. Take the time to match the pictures in the sewing machine manual with the machine itself, identifying the different parts and familiarizing yourself with their names. Even if you know how to set in the needle, thread it, wind and insert the bobbin, do these things once by following the manual—you may have overlooked some extremely helpful detail. And read up on the care of the machine.

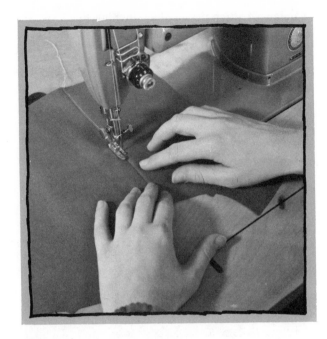

PERFECT STITCHING

Your machine will stitch perfectly if you are particular about certain points in its use (for details see the headings that follow this listing):

. . . a clean sewing machine,
. . . thread and needle chosen to suit the fabric,
. . . pressure on presser foot correct; thread tension correct; stitch balanced,
. . . stitching started and ended correctly,
. . . pace of stitching steady and even.

A Clean Sewing Machine

• Keep your machine covered when not in use.

• Be sure to have a "lint brush" handy; it is inexpensive, and available in most places where sewing machine supplies are sold. Before using machine, whisk brush around each side of feed dog and around bobbin case.

• How often you clean your machine more completely depends on how much you use it. You must do so in any case if you have stitched linty or fuzzy fabrics; also before oiling. Remove throat plate and bobbin case (if removable) and go over machine thoroughly with brush.

• The manual will tell you how, when, and where to oil. One drop in each place is sufficient. Use machine oil, and never over-oil.

• If a scrap of thread is caught in bobbin case, turn balance wheel slightly to release it, then draw thread out (using tweezers if necessary).

Thread and Needle to Suit Fabric

For choice of thread, needle, and stitch length, see THREAD AND NEEDLE CHART, p. 196.

Pressure—Tension—Balance

Pressure on presser foot is regulated by pressure regulator, which may be a thumbscrew on top of machine (1) or a dial inside. Locate it on your machine. Amount of pressure needed varies with weight, finish, fiber, and bulk of fabric. When pressure is correct, the two pieces of fabric—top and bottom—are held firmly but lightly in place and the two travel under needle at the same rate.

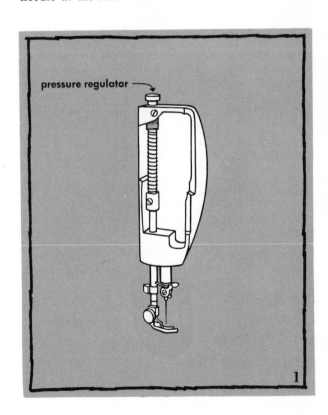

pressure regulator

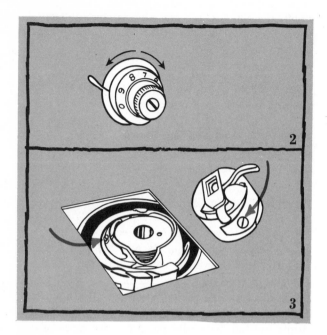

Tension of thread is regulated for needle-thread by tension dial (2), for bobbin-thread by screw on bobbin case (3). Today's fabrics call for rather loose thread tension. Too tight tension causes puckered seams (4).

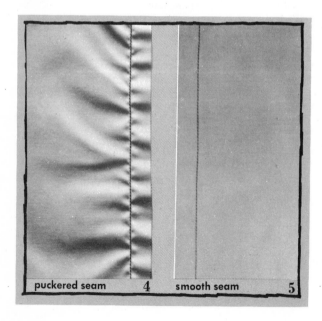

puckered seam 4   smooth seam 5

A balanced stitch means that stitching line looks the same on both sides (needle-thread and bobbin-thread), the two threads having equal tension (6).

Pressure, tension, and balance can be checked and adjusted by means of a single test, which should be made for each new fabric to be stitched.

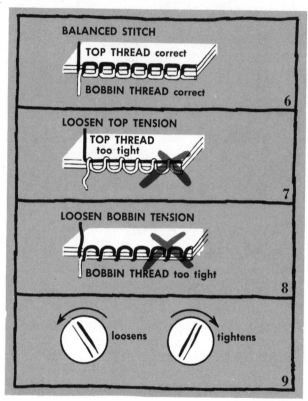

BALANCED STITCH
TOP THREAD correct
BOBBIN THREAD correct   6

LOOSEN TOP TENSION
TOP THREAD too tight   7

LOOSEN BOBBIN TENSION
BOBBIN THREAD too tight   8

loosens   tightens   9

Test-Seam

NOTE: On all screws and dials, a counter-clockwise turn loosens, a clockwise turn tightens (9). To adjust a screw, give it only a *slight fraction* of a turn (equivalent of 5 minutes on clock face).

• Thread machine for what you are about to sew. From scraps of the fabric you are using, cut two strips, about 8″ long, on lengthwise grain (crosswise or on bias for knits, because stitches sink into ribs). Place pieces together, edges even, and pin crosswise at top and bottom. Stitch as shown (10), continuing to bottom pin.

. . . **If a ripple forms** in top layer, as shown (10), pressure is too heavy; loosen pressure regulator. If fabric does not feed through properly, pressure may be too light; tighten pressure regulator.

. . . **If seam is puckered** (4), tension is too tight; loosen top tension and bobbin screw.

. . . **If stitching is tighter on one side** of fabric than on other, stitch is not balanced; loosen tension on that side (either tension dial or bobbin-case screw, 7 and 8).

pressure → regulator

10

If you have made an adjustment, cut off test-seam and repeat test until seam is smooth (5), the same on both sides, and forming no ripples.

Starting and Ending

The following steps, which are essential to good stitching, will become automatic after you have taken them a few times.

Before starting to stitch:

• Be sure that thread-take-up lever is raised to highest point—or thread will come out of needle with first stitch. Turn wheel by hand if necessary.

• Bring needle-thread under presser foot and extend both needle and bobbin thread-ends backward—this prevents thread from snarling in bobbin case or catching in seam.

• Place fabric under presser foot with bulk of fabric to left and seam edge to right. Never let machine run without any fabric under presser foot.

• Before lowering presser foot, lower needle into fabric by turning balance wheel by hand—thus placing needle exactly where you want it.

• Lower presser foot. Stitch.

At end of stitching line:

• Raise take-up lever to highest point, turning wheel by hand—thread cannot be drawn out otherwise, and may break.

• Raise presser foot.

• Remove work by drawing it to the back, then cutting threads—you will find that this prevents strain on needle and leaves thread-ends in the proper place for next stitching.

NOTE: If stitching line needs to be secured at beginning and/or end, take a few stitches in reverse, or leave thread-ends long enough to tie.

• To tie threads, draw needle-thread end through to other side; tie the two ends; clip.

Stitching Pace

• Train yourself to stitch at a steady, even pace, even if you have to go slowly. Stitching done in spurts becomes uneven.

CHECK-LIST FOR TROUBLE SPOTS

Common sewing machine failures usually have a simple explanation. Check the following in the cases indicated:

Thread breakage—Improper threading of either top or bobbin-thread . . . Starting machine with needle in incorrect position . . . Needle improperly set . . . Bent needle . . . Tension too tight . . . Needle too fine for fabric or thread . . . Rough spots on needle eye, throat plate, or bobbin case . . . Lint or thread-ends around bobbin case.

Irregular or skipped stitches—Sewing in spurts . . . Pressure too light . . . Needle wrong size for thread or fabric . . . Pulling fabric.

Machine stuck—Bits of thread caught in bobbin case holder.

Needle breakage—Wrong needle for machine . . . Needle improperly set . . . Presser foot or attachment improperly set . . . Wrong size needle for fabric . . . Stitching over pins . . . Pulling fabric . . . Bobbin inserted incorrectly.

MACHINE-STITCHING APPLIED

There are two kinds of machine-stitching: straight and zigzag (a novelty is chain-stitch). Zigzag, being used mainly for embroidery, seam finishing, and buttonholes, need not concern us here.

Straight stitching, although it has no variations except in stitch-length, is referred to in various ways that describe its application, use, and location. Following are the terms most often used.

Plain stitching, without further definition, is of course the most common. When it is used for joining seams—**construction stitching**—it is good to make it *directional* when possible (see next heading). For selecting correct stitch-length for fabric, see THREAD AND NEEDLE CHART, p. 196.

In general, remember that well-made, expensive clothes have stitches as short as fabric requirements allow, while bargain-basement clothes invariably have long ones.

Topstitching is stitching that is visible on outside of garment. It is done from outside whenever possible, because [a] most machine-stitching looks much better on top than underneath, and [b] stitching-line can be better controlled from visible side. The stitch length is often shortened for the sake of looks.

Edge-stitching is stitching done close to an edge (finished or turned under), and may be either on inside of garment or on outside (in which case it becomes topstitching). For even stitching, guide fabric edge along some point on sewing machine, or along inside edge of presser foot.

Basting Stitch and **Gathering Stitch** simply mean the longest stitch on your machine. See BASTING and GATHERS.

Ease-stitching is the line of stitching that serves for drawing up a piece of fabric to be eased to another. See EASING, p. 63.

Stay-stitching is a line of directional stitching made inside a seam allowance, before construction-stitching, to keep an edge from being pulled out of shape in handling (see **Directional Stitching**, on this and the following page).

DIRECTIONAL STITCHING

Most of the seams you stitch are neither straight-grain nor true-bias. In other words, most seams are "off-grain." In loose-weave fabrics, particularly, such seams are easily pulled out of shape. In order to guard against this, it is good to acquire the habit of stitching *directionally,* i.e., *with* the grain and not against it.

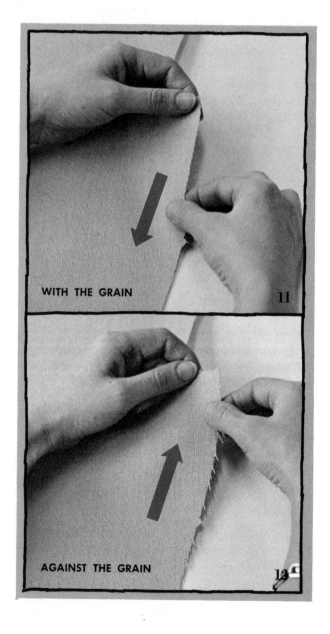

WITH THE GRAIN   11

AGAINST THE GRAIN   12

Some patterns have printed arrows at seamlines to show correct stitching direction. In the absence of these, remember that, where the shape allows, you stitch from *wide to narrow*. For instance,

. . . from *hem to waist* in a skirt,

. . . from *underarm to waist* in a fitted bodice.

At less clearly-defined cut edges, determine direction by sliding your thumb and forefinger along the edge (the "stroke-the-kitty" test):

. . . if edge stays smooth (11), you are going with the grain (smoothing kitty's fur). Stitch in that direction.

. . . if threads at edge get ruffled (12), you are going against the grain (ruffling kitty's fur). Don't stitch in that direction!

In curved seams, the grain naturally changes direction as an edge turns. You cannot, however, change the direction of your construction-stitching. That is one reason why stay-stitching is important with loose-weave fabrics. As you can see by the diagrams at right (13), at evenly-curved edges, stay-stitching is done in two runs, one in each grain direction; at an uneven curve, stay-stitching is done in direction that stays longest with the grain (see armhole curves in diagram).

To sum up, try to make your construction-stitching directional as a matter of habit—loose fabric or firm, edges stay-stitched or not. But forget about it at most curved seams—where fabric is loose-woven, these should be stay-stitched.

Stay-stitching, which is strictly directional, stabilizes the grain at off-grain edges. With loose-grain weaves, it should always be done. On fabrics firmly woven or with a firm finish, it can safely be omitted.

Stay-stitching is done on the separate garment pieces the first thing after cutting and marking. Use matching thread and regular stitch (10–15 per inch). Stitch through a single thickness of fabric, ½″ from cut edge (so it will be outside construction-stitching); at a zipper placket, place stay-stitching ¼″ from cut edge.

Diagrams (13) show where and in what direction to stay-stitch. At any other off-grain edges, straight or curved, "stroke the kitty" to determine direction of stitching.

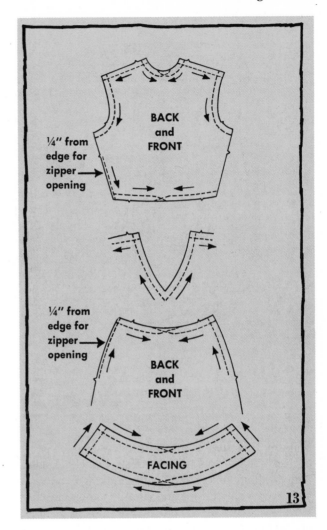

When garment sections are backed, stay-stitching is omitted, because backing is attached with directional stitching (see BACKING), in this case often referred to as stay-stitching.

RIPPING OUT STITCHING

The term seems to imply tearing apart, which is exactly what must *not* be done. With the rather loose stitch used nowadays, controlled stitch-removal is easy. Bottom thread is usually the looser of the two: clip through a stitch about every 2″ and draw out. In bound buttonholes, where very small stitches are used, pick out stitches with a pin or a needle.

MARKING

Marking is a step a professional dressmaker never neglects but a home-sewer resists (which explains many a "home-made look"). It is marking that allows you to sew with precision and safety, without fumbling. Once you have discovered how quickly it is done, and what a help it is in both your work and its results, you will not want to sew without having every pattern-mark on your fabric.

Marking means transferring pattern markings to fabric sections. It is done the first thing after cutting; *do not separate* pattern pieces from sections until you have transferred marks.

Construction details (darts, tucks, reference points for assembling) are marked on wrong side of fabric, or on backing fabric if backing is used.

Position marks for buttonholes, pockets, pleats, and trimming, which must show on right side, are first marked on wrong side. They are then transferred through fabric by means of baste-marking by hand or machine, unless tailor's tacks, which show on both sides, have been used as marks.

WHAT TO MARK

Matching-points—A circle shows where sleeve cap matches shoulder seam, where collar ends at a lapel, where fabric meets in a dart, where outside details are applied.

Center-points—If they are on a fold, mark them in seam allowance (not only on main sections, but on collars, yokes, etc.) if you have not already done so while cutting.

Darts—If you are using tracing paper, make a short crossline (1) at point of dart and at alignment marks (circles). If pattern does not give center line of darts, measure center of dart at widest point and draw line to point. You will fold dart on this line.

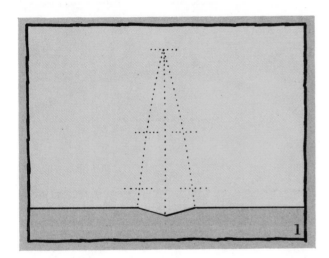

Seamlines on critical outlines, such as curves and points on collars, cuffs, lapels, etc., where two finished edges will face each other and must match perfectly. Also mark inner corners on a square neck so you will know when to pivot. Mark seamline on the section which will be on top when stitching, i.e.,

. . . on facing, when facing is smaller than garment section (e.g., lapel or square neck facings),
. . . on interfacing, when garment section, facing, and interfacing are the same size (e.g., collar or cuffs).

Do not mark arrow showing grain direction. This arrow serves only for placing pattern correctly on fabric.

HOW TO MARK

Printed or perforated patterns allow for any method of marking. Your choice will depend, not only on your personal preference but also to a great extent on the fabric you are using.

Dressmaker's Tracing Paper and Tracing Wheel
Recommended for most fabrics except sheers and lace, where marks would show through; or tweeds and spongy fabrics, on which marks are often unreliable and sometimes don't show.

Dressmaker's tracing or carbon paper, a specially-prepared waxed paper, comes in many colors. Select a color not in too great contrast with fabric, as it will not come out with pressing or washing. Always begin by test-marking a scrap of fabric, doubled as instructed below.

Tracing wheels are available with or without teeth. Wheels with teeth can be used on most fabrics, and will even mark certain plain-weave, solid-color wash-and-wear cottons without tracing paper. The smooth wheel makes a firm, continuous line and is recommended for hard-to-mark fabrics.

Two layers of fabric, with pattern on top, are marked as follows: Fold sheet of tracing paper in half across width, with marking surface inside. Cut off a strip (2) about 2″ wide (each strip can be used many times).

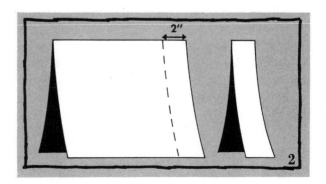

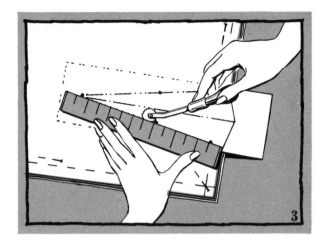

Use a long thread, doubled, without a knot. At point to be marked, take a small stitch through pattern and both layers of fabric. Draw up, leaving a 1″ end. Take another stitch at same point, leaving a loop of 1″ or more (4). Cut thread, leaving a 1″ end (5). When all points are marked, remove pattern. Gently separate the layers of fabric to the extent of the thread loop and cut through threads, as shown (6). Little tufts of thread remain in each fabric layer as marks.

Slip bottom half under fabric and insert upper half between fabric and pattern (remove pins only as needed). In this way, the two marking surfaces will be against the wrong side of both garment sections. Place a piece of cardboard or a magazine under work to protect table surface. Follow lines on pattern with wheel (3), using ruler for straight lines.

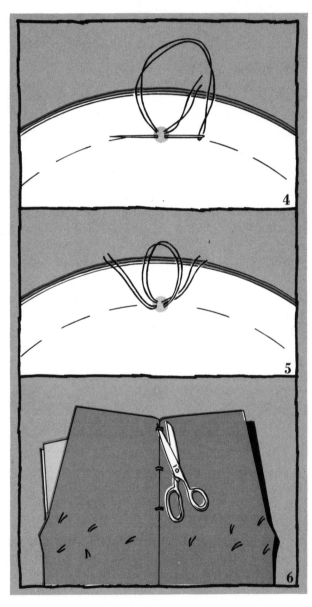

Tailor's Tacks

A slightly slow, but excellent method, suitable for all fabrics, leaving no permanent marks, and visible on both sides of fabric.

Tailor's tacks are made with needle and thread. Darning cotton and embroidery floss are best, because they stay in fabric better than other threads. Mercerized sewing thread is satisfactory, however. Use white or pastel colors.

Pins

Quick, and usable on all fabrics. Be careful, however—pins slip out!

At each point to be marked, put a pin straight through pattern and fabric (7), to stick out on other side. Turn section over and put in another pin, in opposite direction, as close as possible to each pin.

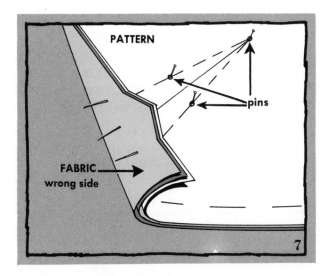

Remove pattern carefully. Separate the two layers of fabric, each one with pins bristling on right side (8).

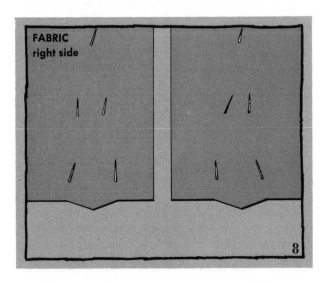

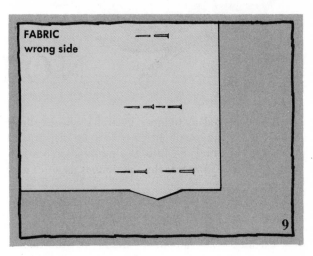

On wrong side, without ever entirely removing a pin from fabric, draw out each pin and pick up a few threads of fabric at the same spot (9). Push pins in far enough so they won't slip out.

Chalk

Chalk-marking is quick and easy, and very useful at times. It does not, however, show on all fabrics, or make reliable marks on nubby weaves. Do not make markings until you are ready to sew.

At each point to be marked, put a pin straight through pattern and fabric, to stick out on other side (7). Remove pattern carefully. On wrong side of both layers of fabric, use sharpened chalk to mark places where pins are. Remove pins. If desired (in darts, for instance), connect marks with chalk lines.

Baste-Marking

Generally used to transfer position marks (for buttonholes, pockets, etc.) to right side. After marking on wrong side, transfer to right side by machine, using longest stitch, or by hand with uneven basting stitch.

NOTIONS

The notions listed as follows, in alphabetical order, consist of all the small articles that, for fit, finish, fastening, etc., may go into the making of one or another kind of garment; thread alone is used for all.

Notions serving as sewing implements are listed under EQUIPMENT. For interfacing, see that chapter.

Belt Buckles are available in metal, plastic, bone, mother-of-pearl, and wood. Fabric-covered buckles can be ordered in notion or sewing stores and departments, or made with the help of a kit (see BELT BUCKLES).

Belting comes in two kinds, each with its own purpose:

Washable Belting is used for backing fabric belts. It is available by the yard in widths from ½″ to 3″, in black and white; also in belt-and-buckle kits (see BELTS).

Grosgrain Belting is used in the waistbands of skirts. It is sold by the yard, in widths from ½″ to 2″, in black, white, and colors (see WAISTBANDS).

Bias Tapes are pre-cut and pre-folded bias strips, packaged in widths most commonly used for binding and facing edges. See chart below.

BIAS FOLD TAPES				
Width	**Name**	**Material and Colors**	**Description**	**Uses**
½″	Single Fold **Bias Tape**	Cotton: black, white and colors, in both fine percale and nainsook; stripes and checks in nainsook	Bias strip, edges folded to wrong side, meeting at center	Binding (¼″), facing, appliqué; can be used with binder attachment on machine. See BIAS.
¼″	Double Fold **Bias Tape**	Cotton: same fabrics and colors as single fold (see above); no stripes or checks	Bias strip, same as single fold plus extra fold just off center	Extra-quick binding (¼″), appliqué. See BIAS.
1″	Quilt Binding **Wide Bias Tape**	Cotton: black, white and colors in fine percale		Facing, appliqué, binding (½″). See BIAS.
2″	Bias Cotton **Hem Facing**	Cotton: black, white and colors in fine percale	Bias strip, edges folded ¼″ to wrong side	Facing, appliqué, binding (1″). See BIAS.
2″	Bias Taffeta **Hem Facing**	Rayon: black, white and colors		
¼″	**Piping** (corded)	Cotton nainsook: black, white and colors	Bias strip (corded), ⅛″ seam allowance	Piping. See BIAS.

Boning and Stays, the modern, lighter substitutes for whalebone, are used where vertical support is needed, as in strapless tops and cummerbunds. Available by the yard or in packages, in black and white. Stays come in 4″, 6″, and 8″ lengths.

Buttons, for fastenings or decoration, come in a great variety of materials, shapes, and sizes. Buttons covered with your own fabric can be ordered in notion or sewing stores and departments, or made yourself with or without the help of a kit (see BUTTONS).

Cable Cord is soft cotton cord used as a filler for corded piping or corded tubing (see BIAS) and for corded buttonholes (see BUTTONHOLES). It comes in many sizes in black and white.

Elastic comes in widths from ¼″ to several inches, in black, white and pink. It is sold by the yard; also in packages.

Hooks and Eyes are the reliable fasteners used at points of strain (see FASTENERS). Regular hooks and eyes are available in sizes from 00 (smallest) to 4 (largest), in black and nickel. Larger hooks come enameled, in colors; or silk-covered.

Horsehair Braid is used to stiffen hems of flared or full skirts (see HEMS). Available by the yard or in packages; in various widths, in black and white.

Lingerie Strapholders are attached on the inside of a garment shoulder seam to hold lingerie straps in place. They are available in black, white and pink, or can be made as shown, using 3″ of narrow tape or ribbon.

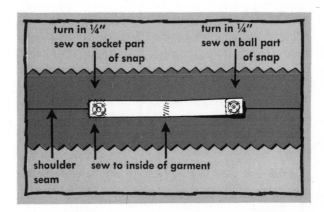

Seam Binding is used nowadays for finishing hems and as a waist stay. See chart below.

Shoulder Pads come and go with fashion, but are always a help to sloping shoulders. They are sold ready-made, covered and uncovered, in many styles and sizes. They can also be made from a pattern. Use washable pads in washable garments.

SEAM BINDING				
Width	Name	Material and Colors	Description	Uses
½″ 1″	Wash-and-Wear Rayon **Seam Binding**	Rayon: black, white and colors	Ribbon-type, straight grain, woven edges, preshrunk	Edge of hem. See HEMS. Waistline stay. See p. 209.
½″ 1″	Iron-on **Seam Binding**	Same as above	Same as above, with heat sensitive adhesive	Edge of hem. See HEMS.
½″	Bias Rayon **Seam Binding**	Rayon: black, white and colors	Bias strip, exactly like single fold bias tape (see p. 124)	Edge of hem on flared skirts, binding, facing. See HEMS, BIAS.
¾″ 1⅜″	Stretch Lace **Seam Binding**	Nylon: black, white and colors	Decorative lace	Edge of hem, sleeves, facings

Snaps, Hammer-on, are used on children's clothes, work clothes, pajamas and sportswear. Sold packaged in various types and colors, with instructions on the package.

Snaps, Sew-on, are good for closings that have a minimum of strain (see FASTENERS). Available in many sizes, from 4/0 (smallest) to 1 (largest); in black and nickel. Also come silk-covered, in two sizes and many colors. Instructions for covering snaps are on p. 192.

Thread—See chapter on THREAD AND NEEDLES.

Twill Tape is strong cotton tape, ¼″ to 1″ wide, used as a **Waistline Stay** (see p. 209), in tailoring (see pp. 174, 179), and for drawstrings. It is sold in packages; comes in black and white only.

Weights are used to give body to the hang or drape of a garment. They may be placed at hems, or, say, in a cowl neckline. They come in various types:

Round lead weights resemble coins, and are of different sizes (weights). Inquire as to reaction to washing or dry-cleaning. They may be sewn permanently within the layers of a garment or, covered with lining fabric, attached in place with a small safety pin.

Lead weight by the yard consists of small flat slugs (in two weights) encased in half-inch tape, or small pellets covered with a knitted sleeve. Attach along top edge of hem before sewing down lining.

Gold chain weight is pretty enough to be tacked along the lining, not covered by it. It comes in various weights, by the yard or packaged.

Zippers are the fasteners most often used. They come with synthetic coils or with metal teeth.

Skirt Zippers (6″ to 9″ in length and also used in pants) and *Neck Zippers* (ranging from 4″ to 30″) open at the edge of a garment. Neck Zippers are so called because they open at the neck, but are used in dresses, usually at center back.

Dress Zippers (12″ and 14″) open within a seam. A bar tack at the top (p. 203) will protect the seam when the zipper is open. If your zipper does not have one, take a few stitches in the tapes above top stop to hold them securely together.

These three zippers—*Skirt, Neck, Dress*—are made in fashion color with synthetic coil or metal teeth.

The newest additions are the *"Hidden"* or *"Invisible"* Zippers (7″-9″, 16″-18″, 20″-22″). They are completely concealed in the seam and therefore come in fewer colors.

Separating Zippers are made in metal only, in two weights: heavy (14″ to 26″ long), in neutral colors for outer wear; and lightweight (10″ to 24″ long) in fashion colors for jackets and dresses.

Zippers for other applications are *Trouser Zippers* which come in two weights, heavier, brass-finished 9″ long for sports and work clothes and lighter-weight enameled 11″ in men's wear colors (they have to be cut to fit the placket); *Blue Jean Zippers,* 6″ long; *Reversible Jacket Zippers,* 16″ to 22″ long; *Slip Cover Zippers,* 24″ to 36″ long. All these come in metal only.

PATTERNS

American dress patterns are probably the most carefully designed, accurately drafted anywhere. To begin with, they are based on data supplied by the U.S. Bureau of Standards, compiled from surveys made of the body measurements of a representative segment of our female population. Basic body measurements, therefore, are standard, and the same in all makes of patterns.

Patterns, however, are not cut to exact body measurements. This would produce skin-tight garments, entirely unwearable. A considerable allowance (ease), especially in the width, must be added for the wearer's comfort and freedom of movement. How much allowance is needed, and how it is distributed, is left to the pattern companies' quite careful discretion, and varies with each; this is why you, individually, may have "better luck" (i.e., a better fit) with one brand than with another.

Patterns are offered in a vast variety of **styles,** in eight different **figure-types,** and in just about as many **sizes** as women and girls come in. Which combination of these is right for you, or how to alter the nearest fit to your figure, is what concerns us here.

THE RIGHT PATTERN FOR YOU

To dispose of the question of pattern-brand: Here you can only proceed by trial. You may prefer the styles of one make to those of another, but no measurements will give you a clue to the subtle differences in line and cut that exist between them. For a first garment, choose a simple style (or a Basic Pattern—fitted bodice, straight skirt, set-in sleeves) in any brand. Unless the fit turns out (miraculously!) to be perfect, try another pattern-name for your next project. In time you will know which make results in the best fit for your figure.

Patterns, incidentally, are never returnable to the store.

Style, figure-type, and **size,** the three other things you must decide upon, are very closely interrelated. To get the complete picture, you should read what follows about all three. Remember that correct choice of figure-type and size not only makes for good fit, but keeps alterations to a minimum.

Style is design, and has nothing to do with fit. Select a style similar to one you have worn before and know is right for you. Here there is no trying on before buying! And, until you are expert in dressmaking, steer clear of complicated designs! Every major pattern company has certain models designated as easy to make.

Figure-Type is what is meant by "Misses," "Half-sizes," "Juniors," and the other categories described, with sizes and measurements, on pp. 130–131. These categories, determined by the variations in our shapes, are very important—even the pattern-books are divided and indexed according to figure-types. They do not *necessarily* represent age-groups. What they are based on is proportion: the proportion to each other

of the different measurements of the body, particularly length in proportion to width. Since it is undeniable, however, that age does have something to do with a person's shape, styles—both in patterns and in ready-to-wear—are usually designed to be suitable for the age-group implied by the figure-type ("Half-sizes," for instance, are designed for more mature women; the whole "Developing Figures" division is for girls in their teens, etc.). This does not make *all* of them unsuitable for other age-groups. This is where your taste and judgment come in.

You have, of course, been buying your ready-made clothes for a certain figure-type. The chances are that your measurements will place you within the same category. If they do not, and you find that your proportions belong to a figure-type well outside your age-group and taste, be extra-careful in choosing your style. If the styles offered in that category are not at all appropriate for you, it is better to look under another figure-type, where the combination of measurements may not come as close to yours, but your taste is satisfied. Of course it may mean an alteration in the pattern.

Size is established by the four measurements—bust, waist, hips, and "back waist length"—which appear as "Standard Body Measurements" on pattern envelopes and are given on our **Chart of Types and Sizes** on pp. 130–131. Correct size ensures a minimum of alterations, if any. In November 1967 pattern sizing was changed by all major Pattern companies to correspond more closely to standard ready-to-wear sizing. New style patterns, issued after November 1, 1967 will have the NEW Sizing. However, it will take some time before all the patterns in the catalogues have this NEW Sizing. Meanwhile you will have to be very careful when choosing a pattern to be sure you buy the right size.

As a general rule, you will be buying one size smaller in the NEW Sizing than you did in the former sizing. However, since the NEW Sizing measurements for bust, waist, hip and back waist length and their proportions to each other have been changed, it is most important that you consult the measurement charts very carefully before deciding on the right size patterns.

The charts in this book represent the NEW Sizing but the method of using them to determine your size is the same for NEW Sizing or former sizing. The former sizing charts will continue to be available in the pattern catalogues until all patterns are made in the NEW Sizing.

On p. 132 you will find instructions for making your **Personal Measurements Chart** in order to check your pattern for fit. Since taking even the first four measurements (the ones just mentioned) requires the help of another person and other preparation, it is a good idea to make this entire chart now, even though you will not need Measurements 5 through 11 until later.

We suggest two ways of determining your pattern size:

. . . If your ready-to-wear clothes fit you well, buy your pattern for the same figure-type and *the same size* for NEW Sizing patterns, but one size larger for former sizing patterns. For example, if you wear a Junior Size 11 in ready-to-wear you may choose a Junior Size 11 in NEW Sizing but Junior Size 13 in former sizing (for safety, compare the first four of your body measurements with the measurements on pattern envelope).

. . . Otherwise, read the description of each figure-type on the **Chart of Types and Sizes** and decide which ones may best be suited to you. On each of these charts, circle the measurements that match yours. If any one of your measurements falls between two on a chart (see example charts for Mary Mythical on p. 131), place the circle between the two; if it is closer to one than the other, circle the closer one.

Now compare the charts marked, and see which one best combines your measurements within one size (again, see Mary Mythical's results on p. 131). The kind of garment you are making, and the comparative ease or difficulty of alterations, make correct measurement more important at certain points than at others. For instance:

. . . In a dress or a blouse, correct **bust** size will ensure against the rather difficult alteration of the armhole-and-neck area. Pattern ease, however, will take care of a bust up to 1″ larger than the pattern.

. . . A straight skirt, shorts, or slacks, should have correct fit at the **hips**—the waist is easy to enlarge or take in.

. . . A full skirt usually goes by **waist** measurement, but, again, an alteration at the waist is easy.

. . . A loose-hanging or semi-fitted garment needs correct **bust** size and nothing else.

You may end up choosing a type and size in which no measurement is exactly yours, but all come reasonably close. In the unlikely event that, after buying a pattern and comparing all its actual measurements with your own (as directed on p. 133) you discover that another figure-type or size would require less alteration, we suggest that you buy this other pattern rather than make elaborate alterations on the first one you bought.

CHARTS OF TYPES AND SIZES
Based on Body Measurements

NEW Sizing

Here are the eight figure-types devised to cover all the variants of the feminine form. All pattern companies make patterns in various types, based on the standard body measurements (proportions) shown in the chart for each, though some companies call the figure-types by slightly different names. We have divided them into two major groups—Developed Figures and Developing Figures—the latter belonging, generally, to young girls. It is between these two groups as a whole that the differences in proportions are the most pronounced. The "Back Waist Length" is the clue to the wearer's height, though this would not hold true for a heavy person, with a rounded back. Styles offered in each are also described.

DEVELOPED FIGURES

Miss and Woman

This is the tallest type, well-proportioned. It is also the most common, offering the largest choice of styles. High-style, special-design patterns are always made in Misses sizes.

Bust	30½	31½	32½	34	36	38	40	Ins.
Waist	22	23	24	25½	27	29	31	Ins.
Hip	32½	33½	34½	36	38	40	42	Ins.
Back Waist Length	15½	15¾	16	16¼	16½	16¾	17	Ins.
Misses Size	**6**	**8**	**10**	**12**	**14**	**16**	**18**	

Bust	42	44	46	48	50	52	54	Ins.
Waist	34	36	38	40½	43	45½	48	Ins.
Hip	44	46	48	50	52	54	56	Ins.
Back Waist Length	17¼	17⅜	17½	17⅝	17¾	17⅞	18	Ins.
Woman's Size	**38**	**40**	**42**	**44**	**46**	**48**	**50**	

Junior

Shorter than the Miss—hence shorter-waisted—but well-proportioned, with a high-placed bust. Junior styles tend to the youthful, without being juvenile, and can usually be worn by all ages.

Bust	30	31	32	33½	35	37	Ins.
Waist	21½	22½	23½	24½	26	28	Ins.
Hip	32	33	34	35½	37	39	Ins.
Back Waist Length	15	15¼	15½	15¾	16	16½	Ins.
Junior Size	**5**	**7**	**9**	**11**	**13**	**15**	

Half-Size

The fraction added to the size indicates narrower shoulders and greater middle-fullness in proportion to height. Styles in the Half-Sizes tend to be on the conservative side.

Bust	33	35	37	39	41	43	45	47	Ins.
Waist	26	28	30	32	34	36½	39	41½	Ins.
Hip	35	37	39	41	43	45½	48	50½	Ins.
Back Waist Length	15	15¼	15½	15¾	15⅞	16	16⅛	16¼	Ins.
Half-Size	**10½**	**12½**	**14½**	**16½**	**18½**	**20½**	**22½**	**24½**	

Junior Petite

Designed for the well-proportioned diminutive figure. Waist is small.

Bust	30½	31	32	33	34	35	Ins.
Waist	22	22½	23½	24½	25½	26½	Ins.
Hip	31½	32	33	34	35	36	Ins.
Back Waist Length	14	14¼	14½	14¾	15	15¼	Ins.
Jr. Petite Size	**3JP**	**5JP**	**7JP**	**9JP**	**11JP**	**13JP**	

DEVELOPING FIGURES

Young Junior/Teen

A size range designed for the shorter pre-teen and teen figure with bust not fully developed.

Bust	28	29	30½	32	33½	35	Ins.
Waist	22	23	24	25	26	27	Ins.
Hip	31	32	33½	35	36½	38	Ins.
Back Waist Length	13½	14	14½	15	15⅜	15¾	Ins.
Young Junior/Teen Size	**5/6**	**7/8**	**9/10**	**11/12**	**13/14**	**15/16**	

Chubby

Designed for a figure not yet developed and with more girth all around than most girls the same age.

Breast	30	31½	33	34½	Ins.
Waist	28	29	30	31	Ins.
Hip	33	34½	36	37½	Ins.
Back Waist Length	12	12¾	13½	14¼	Ins.
Approx. Heights	52	56	58½	61	Ins.
Chubby Size	**8½c**	**10½c**	**12½c**	**14½c**	

Girl

Designed for the flat, immature figure.

Breast	26	27	28½	30	32	Ins.
Waist	23	23½	24½	25½	26½	Ins.
Hip	27	28	30	32	34	Ins.
Back Waist Length	11½	12	12¾	13½	14¼	Ins.
Approx. Heights	50	52	56	58½	61	Ins.
Girl Size	**7**	**8**	**10**	**12**	**14**	

EXAMPLE: Let's see how a "Mary Mythical" goes about finding her figure type and size. Mary has taken her measurements. The first four run:

Bust	33½″
Waist	25″
Hips	37″
Back Waist Length	15⅝″

Next, she turns to the **Charts of Types and Sizes** and reads the introductory paragraph. Whatever Mary's age may be, she happens to know that she does not have a child's figure, and so disregards the whole "Developing" group. Her longer back waist measurement eliminates Junior Petite. As for Half-size, while she is a bit wider in the beam than she likes, and only short-average in height, she does not have the bust-waist-hip fullness and comparatively narrow shoulders that are characteristic of this figure-type. This leaves Miss and Junior, whose styles she likes best anyway. On the two charts she now checks, her measurements fall like this:

Bust	30½	31½	32½	(34)	36	38	40	Ins.
Waist	22	23	24	(25½)	27	29	31	Ins.
Hip	32½	33½	34½	36 ○	38	40	42	Ins.
Back Waist Length	15½ ○	15¾	16	16¼	16½	16¾	17	Ins.
Misses Size	**6**	**8**	**10**	**12**	**14**	**16**	**18**	

Bust	30	31	32	(33½)	35	37	Ins.
Waist	21½	22½	23½	(24½)	26	28	Ins.
Hip	32	33	34	35½	(37)	39	Ins.
Back Waist Length	15	15¼	15½ ○	15¾	16	16¼	Ins.
Junior Size	**5**	**7**	**9**	**11**	**13**	**15**	

On the Misses chart, the Back Waist Length is entirely out of line, which means that the up-and-down points (points of bust, elbow, etc.) will fall in the wrong places. On the Junior chart this measurement is almost perfect, while the important bust measurement is right, too. It is no trick to add a half-inch to the waist and 1½″ to the hips. Mary's pattern will be a Junior 11.

CHECKING YOUR PATTERN FOR FIT

Even if your body measurements and those on the pattern envelope jibe perfectly, this does not, unfortunately, guarantee that the pattern will be a perfect fit otherwise (though there is a good chance of its being so). We are sorry to say that you cannot even depend on a difference in a basic measurement (such as Mary Mythical's 2″ in the hips) being the correct one on which to base an alteration—there is that matter of **ease,** on which pattern companies not only vary with each other, but in which they may make changes without warning.

The only way to be safe with a pattern is to compare *all* its relevant measurements with either:

. . . the same measurements taken from a well-fitting garment of the same design, at exactly the same points, or

. . . your own complete measurements, plus ease wherever called for.

To Make Your Personal Measurements Chart, have someone help you with the measuring. Measure over well-fitting undergarments. Tie a narrow ribbon, tape, or string snugly around your waist to mark exact location of waistline.

Use a full (binder-size) sheet of ruled paper. Mark it off in seven columns (see sample chart on p. 134). In the first column, list the eleven points to measure, as given below. In the second column, enter the measurements, taken as instructed:

1. **Bust**—(measured firmly around fullest part).
2. **Waist**—(at ribbon around waist).
3. **Hips**—(around fullest part, 9″ below waist for Misses, Women and Junior; 7″ below waist for Half-Sizes, Junior Petite and Young Junior/Teen).
4. **Back Waist Length**—(from prominent vertebra at back of neck to waistline ribbon).
5. **Front Waist Length**—(from middle of shoulder over point of bust to waistline ribbon).
6. **Point of Bust**—(from middle of shoulder to point of bust only; note when taking measurement No. 5).
7. **Back Width**—(across back, 4″ down from neck bone, between body folds formed by arms hanging straight).
8. **Sleeve Length**—(from edge of shoulder, where sleeve would be set in, over bended elbow to desired length).
9. **Point of Elbow**—(above measurement to point of elbow only).
10. **Upper Arm**—(around arm, 1″ below armpit; if one arm is larger, use larger measurement).
11. **Skirt Length**—(measure center front of a garment of correct length, from bottom edge of waistband to hem of skirt).

The third and fourth columns are for "Ease" and "Total." Under "Ease," enter the following amounts on the proper line (these are *average* ease allowances, which you can make larger or smaller depending on whether you want your garment loose or snug). The other measurements do not need ease—just make a dash in the column instead.

1. **Bust**—3″ to 4″ for fitted bodice
       5″ to 6″ for loose top or jacket
3. **Hips**—2″ to 2½″ for straight skirt
5. **Front Waist Length**—about ¼″
7. **Back Width**—½″ to 1″
10. **Upper Arm**—1″ to 2″ for fitted sleeve

NOTE: Do not confuse *body ease*, above, with *design ease* (blousy top, full skirt, etc.). The latter is a matter of design, not fit. Fortunately, such loosely-fitted garment-parts practically never need an alteration.

Add up body measurement and ease and enter the total in the "Total" column. Where there is no ease, enter the body measurement.

You now have a basic measurements chart for your figure, which will change only with your weight (or posture). The exception is the skirt length, which is subject only to fashion. Date the chart—you will want to check your measurements against it from time to time.

The Pattern Pieces you will use for your garment must now be selected, with the help of your primer. Smooth out the creases with a warm, dry iron. With pencil and yardstick, extend both ends of grain lines the entire length of pattern.

Measuring Your Pattern must be done with care, of course, but it is not difficult if you go about it right.
. . . Work with pattern piece flat on table.
. . . When bodice front has both waist and side darts, draw a line through center of each dart to just beyond point; where the two lines meet will be point of bust.
. . . When bodice front has only one dart, point of bust will be about ½″ beyond point of dart.
. . . Take all measurements *without* seam allowances.
. . . When only half a pattern is given (main body pieces), be sure to double measurement before writing it down.

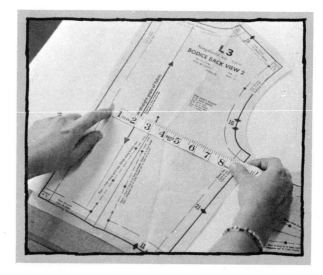

In the fifth column on your chart, enter measurements taken from your pattern as follows:
1. **Bust**—(center front and center back to side seamlines, about 2″ below armhole or at point-of-bust level. Double this measurement.).
2. **Waist**—(copy from pattern envelope—disregard for loose-waisted garment).
3. **Hip**—(center front and center back to side seamlines, at same distance from waist as body measurement was taken. Double this measurement. Disregard for full or flaring skirt.).
4. **Back, Neck to Waist**—(copy from pattern envelope).
5. **Front, Shoulder to Waist**—(middle of shoulder to point of bust and down to waistline).
6. **Point of Bust**—(middle of shoulder to point of bust).
7. **Back Width**—(across back, 3″ below the shoulder edge at armhole seamline).

8. **Sleeve Length**—(center top to wrist edge).
9. **Point of Elbow**—(center top to middle dart or center of ease area in seamline).
10. **Upper Arm**—(across sleeve from seamline to seamline, 1″ below top of underarm seam—disregard for full sleeve).
11. **Skirt Length**—(at front, from waist to hemline—measure off the hem allowance indicated on your pattern, and mark).

Now compare these figures with the ones in column 4 ("Total") and enter the difference, if any, in column 6, as shown in the chart below. For the alteration needed, study the **Pattern Alterations** that follow on the next page.

Below is part of Mary Mythical's chart. It indicates what alterations she will make.

MARY MYTHICAL'S CHART

	Body meas.	Ease	Total	Pattern meas.	Diff.	Alteration
1. Bust	33½″	3″-4″	36½″-37½″	37½″	none	none
2. Waist	25″	—	25″	24½″	½″ needed	Add to seams
3. Hip	37″	2″-2½″	39″-39½″	37½″	2″ needed	Add to side seams
4. Back Waist length	15⅝″	—	15⅝″	15¾″	⅛″ needed	none. diff. negligible

PATTERN ALTERATIONS

The alterations that follow are the ones indicated by the comparison of measurements just made. If you are difficult to fit in ready-made clothes, you may need alterations that we do not have space for here, and it may be very much to your advantage to make a **Muslin Basic,** as described on p. 145, to establish once and for all where—aside from the above measurements—your pattern needs adjustment. Two possible defects that do not show up until the garment, or the Muslin Basic, is tried on, are a neckline or a sleeveless armhole either too wide or too snug. We give the alteration, however, on pp. 144–145, for use on your *next* pattern, or correction of the present one after trying on the Muslin Basic.

All alterations given here are made on a Basic Pattern—i.e., one with fitted bodice, straight skirt, and long, fitted sleeves.

The principle of good pattern alteration is to change the measurements indicated without changing the pattern's essential outline.

Alterations in length and width are made in two locations:
[a] Along cutting lines, when taking off or adding on can be done without disturbing the lines; i.e.,
. . . in **length,** at hem of a plain skirt, a short sleeve, etc. (see skirt alteration on p. 138).
. . . in **width,** when a very small change in each of a number of seams (and darts) will total up to whatever is necessary (see Hip and Waist alterations, p. 140).

[b] Through body of pattern, by folding to reduce size or cutting-and-spreading to increase. This method preserves the shape of the outer pattern, the place of darts, etc., and is described under **Three Basic How-To's,** following.

For Easy and Accurate Altering . . .

. . . make alterations with pattern piece spread flat on table,
. . . for some increases in size, you will need tissue paper,
. . . secure alterations with pins, cellophane tape, or baste-stitching on sewing machine,
. . . try to combine alterations (one operation often takes care of two; see **Shortening and Lengthening of Bodice and Sleeve),**
. . . most patterns have a printed line showing where a skirt, bodice, or sleeve can best be lengthened or shortened (alteration line). If there is no such line, draw one in with pencil and ruler, if needed. Directions for specific alterations on the next pages will show you where to place alteration line.

Remember that after an alteration . . .
. . . pattern must still *lie flat,*
. . . matching seamlines must *still match,*
. . . printed or perforated lines (seam, grain, etc.) broken by alteration must be redrawn as they were before, the straight lines with a ruler, the curved lines by hand (see p. 136).

Three Basic How-To's

How to fold a pattern to reduce size
• Measuring from alteration line, mark amount to be taken out. Draw second line as shown (1), either parallel with first, or on a slant (9, p. 137), as necessary.
• Fold pattern on first line and bring fold to second line. Smooth out pattern carefully (2). Secure fold.
• With ruler, redraw all lines crossing fold to connect smoothly and maintain pattern shape. With a slanted fold (9, p. 137), this means that, beyond fold, lines must be redrawn as a continuation of the original line, and that side edges will be trimmed on one side and added to on the other.

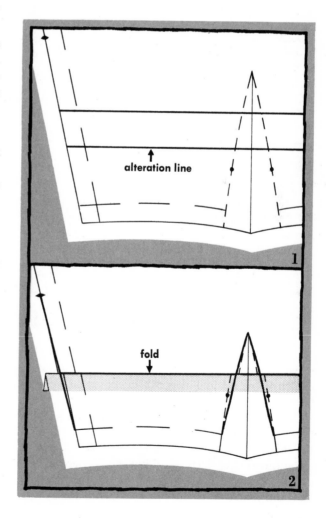

How to spread a pattern to increase size

- Cut pattern piece along alteration line.
- Secure cut edge of main section to a piece of tissue paper (3). With pencil and ruler, extend all straight lines across tissue (grain line, center line, center of dart).
- Measure on tissue amount to be added. To mark amount, draw a line either parallel with cut edge or on a slant (11, next page), as necessary.

How to make a new cutting line after dart alteration

If a dart coming from a seam has been altered in size or direction, cutting line must be redrawn. Pin altered dart together (5) and fold (down at side, toward center at waist). Redraw and cut cutting line across fold (5), with ruler for a straight seam, freehand for a curved seam (waistline). Remove pins (6).

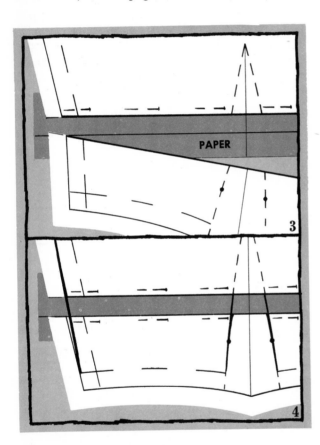

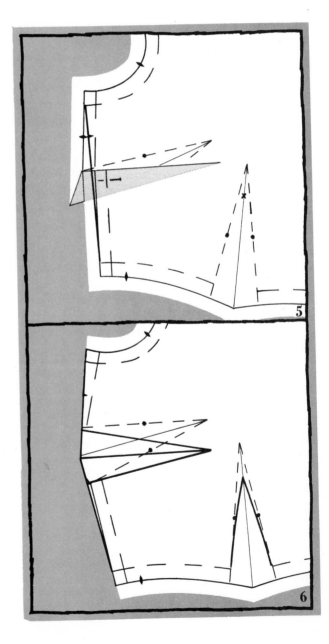

- Secure remaining pattern section to tissue, with cut edge on marked line (4), matching at vertical lines drawn in.
- Redraw all lines to connect smoothly and maintain pattern shape. If inset tapers, this means that, on the smaller pattern section, lines must be redrawn as a continuation of the original line, before section was cut off, and that side edges will be trimmed on one side and added to on the other (11, next page).

SHORTENING AND LENGTHENING

Bodice (Measurements 4 and 5)

If there is no printed alteration line, draw one 2″ to 3″ above waistline, at right angles to center front and/or back (7, 8).

NOTE: When making an alteration in length on bodice front, take into account any alteration needed in Measurement 6.

An alteration line placed *above* the bust dart will take care of at least part of the alteration in length (all of it, if alterations needed for Measurement 5 and Measurement 6 are the same).

See Method II under **Bust Darts,** on p. 139.

Follow **How-To** instructions on pp. 135–136. Matching seamlines will automatically continue to match if alteration is the same for Measurement 4 and Measurement 5 (back and front), and fold or spread will go straight across back and front.

If, however, the alteration is made only on front or only on back, or in both but in different amounts, the fold or the tissue inset, as the case may be, must taper or widen at the seams (9–10, 11–12), depending on which is needed, if you are to keep seam edges matching.

Follow **How-To's** for straightening lines.

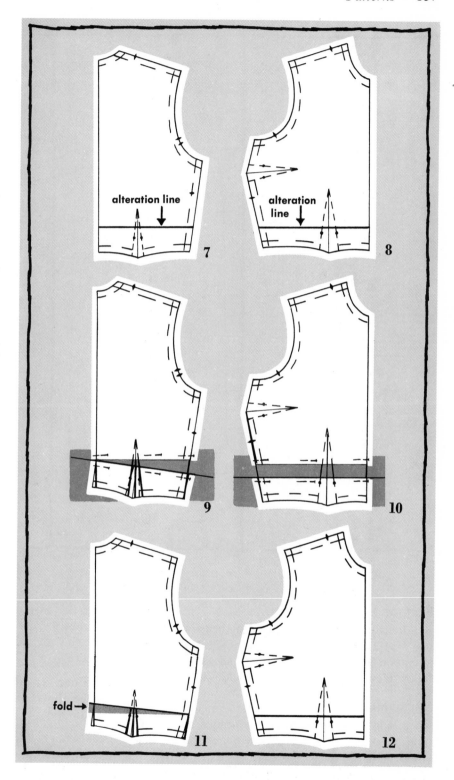

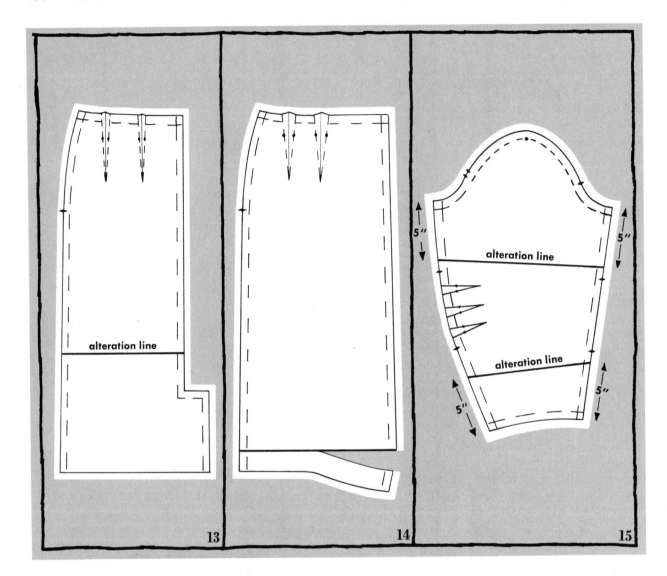

Skirt (Measurement 11)

A skirt is usually shortened or lengthened at hem-line (13). If there is a kick pleat, however, draw an alteration line above kick pleat as shown (14), and follow **How-To** instructions on pp. 135–136.

Sleeve (Measurement 8)

On a long sleeve, if there are no printed alteration lines, draw lines about 5″ below underarm and 5″ above bottom edge, as shown (15).

NOTE: See **Sleeve Darts** on p. 140, and check Measurement 9. Any alteration in placement of sleeve darts may be taken care of while altering length of sleeve.

Using one or both alteration lines, as necessary, follow the **How-To** instructions which you will find on pp. 135–136.

On a straight, short sleeve, make alteration at the bottom edge.

LOWERING AND RAISING DARTS

Darts correctly placed are essential to the fit of a garment.

Bust Darts (Measurement 6)

For a smooth fit, underarm dart should point directly toward point of bust. Moving an underarm dart is a simple alteration which can be done by either of the two methods that follow if bodice length needs no change; or by Method II if it is done in combination with an alteration in bodice length.

METHOD I. If dart is *horizontal* (16), point can be raised as much as 1″, but cannot be lowered; if dart is *slanted upward* (17), it can be lowered 1″ but can't be raised. Mark new point of dart; using ruler, connect point with the two base points at seamline, as shown. Correct cutting line as directed in last **How-To** on p. 136. Raise or lower point of waist dart (if any) the same amount.

17

16

METHOD II. May be used in combination with shortening or lengthening bodice front (see that heading), in which case the lower alteration line would be either omitted or the amount taken out or added would be changed as needed. As described here, the method preserves original bodice length.

• Draw two alteration lines: one 2″ to 3″ above waistline, the other above bust dart—both at right angles to center front. See **How-To** instructions on pp. 135–136.

To lower dart, cut pattern on upper alteration line and spread to amount needed; fold pattern on lower alteration line, taking in the same amount (18).

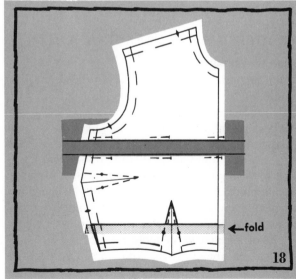

←fold

18

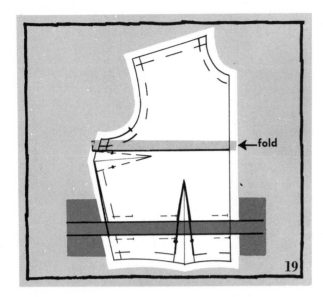

To raise dart, fold pattern on upper alteration line, taking in amount needed; cut on lower alteration line and spread to the same amount (19).

• On waist dart, if any, draw new lines from point to two base points.

Sleeve Darts (Measurement 9)

See **Shortening and Lengthening Sleeve** (Measurement 8). Middle dart, or mid-point between notches, should be directly at bend of elbow (Measurement 9).

REDUCING and INCREASING WIDTH

Hip (Measurement 3)

A hip alteration must be carried all the way to the hem.
. . . For an alteration of 2″ or less:
Add or take off at side seams. *One-fourth* the amount of alteration (½″ for 2″) added to or taken off each edge will add up to total. Measure down from waistline to point of hip measurement. Mark alteration at that point; then, using yardstick, redraw line down to hem, parallel to old line. Above altered point, draw a line tapering to waistline, as shown (20).
. . . For an increase of more than 2″:
Add 2″ as above. Then, with yardstick, draw an alteration line through dart to hem, on back and

front sections (if there are two darts, go through dart nearest side seam). Spread each piece one-fourth the total amount needed. Adjust waistline by taking deeper darts.

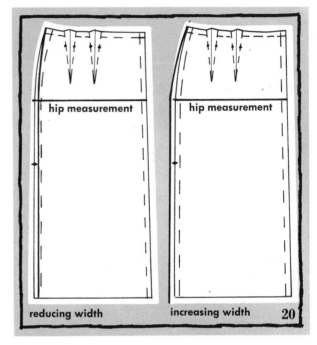

Waist (Measurement 2)

A waist alteration must be made on both bodice and skirt.
. . . For an alteration of 2″ or less:
Add or take off at side seams. *One-fourth* the amount (½″ for 2″) added to or taken off each edge will add up to total. Then draw new cutting lines: on skirt, taper to join existing cutting line at hip; on bodice, pin up bust darts, if any, and use ruler to draw new cutting line from underarm to waist.
. . . For an alteration of more than 2″:
Alter side seams as above to take out or add 2″. Divide *remaining* amount by number of waist darts. Then draw new stitching lines for darts: *inside* existing dart for an increase in size (21), *outside* existing dart (22) for a decrease (a change of ⅛″ at each stitching line—i.e., ¼″ added to each dart—will make a change of 1″ on a garment with 4 darts).

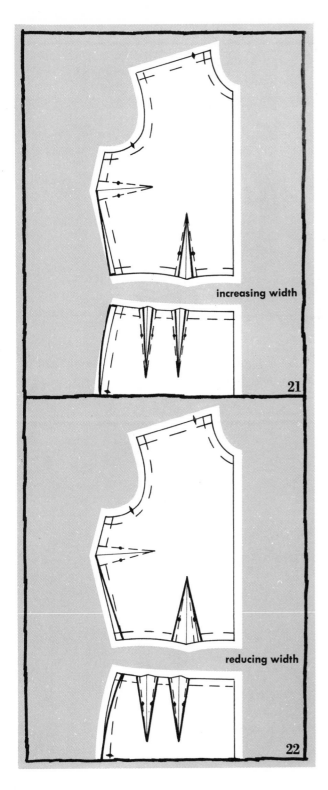

increasing width

21

reducing width

22

Bust (Measurements 1 and 7)

A bust alteration is generally divided equally between front and back of bodice. If you are either full-busted or flat-chested, alteration may need to be made entirely on the front. If your back is very broad or very narrow (Measurement 7), it may need to be made entirely on the back. Or it may be divided unequally between front and back.

NOTE for both **Front** and **Back:** After completing alteration below . . .
• Restore original waist measurement by measuring the amount that pattern has been overlapped or spread at waistline level; then add or trim away an equal amount at side seam and draw new cutting line with ruler.

• Redraw waistline to conform with original line, shortening pattern when there was a decrease in width, lengthening for an increase.

Front—Using ruler, draw lines as shown (23) . . .
. . . from point of waistline dart [a], to ⅛″ from point of underarm dart [b], then to armhole seamline near notch [c],
. . . through center of underarm dart, if not printed on pattern [d-e].

Cut up along outer line of waistline dart (nearer side seam) and along drawn line to points a-b-c. Do not cut beyond armhole seamline.

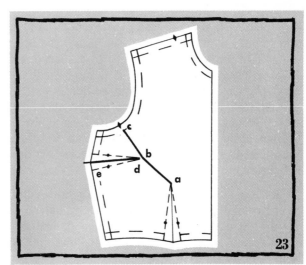

23

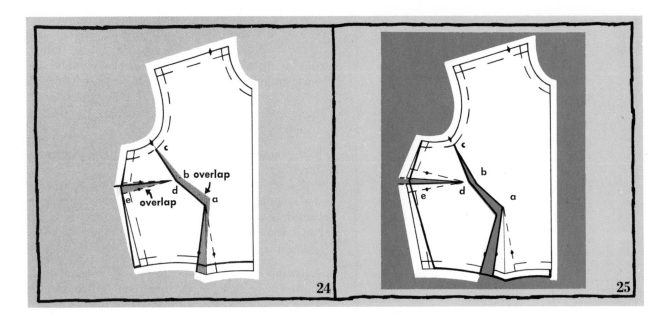

... *To reduce size,* measure one half of total front alteration out from cut, just above point b; lap edge with waistline dart on it over as far as mark, smooth out pattern carefully, and secure overlap at this point. Cut through center of underarm dart (d-e). Shift bottom section of pattern so that bust dart and waist are altered about the same amount. Secure overlaps (24). Restore original waist measurement and waistline. Waistline dart remains original size while bust dart is decreased.

... *To increase size,* slip tissue paper under pattern. Spread out cut, measuring on tissue, just above point b, one half the total alteration for front. Secure cut edges to tissue at this point. Cut through center of underarm dart (d-e). Shift bottom section of pattern so that bust dart and waist are altered about the same amount (25). Secure all cut edges to tissue. Restore original waist measurement and waistline. Waistline dart remains original size while bust dart is increased.

Back—Using ruler, draw a line from point of dart to center of shoulder (26). Cut up along outer line of waistline dart (nearer side seam) and along drawn line to shoulder seamline. Make sure that you do not cut beyond seamline.

Amount of alteration is measured at a level 1″ below top of underarm seam.

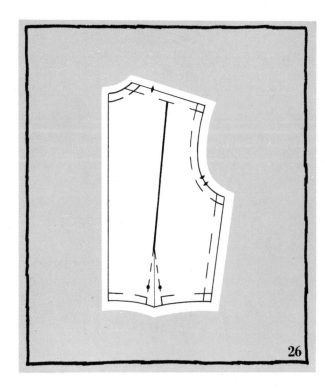

Sleeve (Measurement 10)

A sleeve sometimes needs widening, practically never narrowing. Tightening the lower part can be done by taking in seam after trying on garment. A short sleeve can usually be widened or narrowed at the underarm seam, as shown (29).

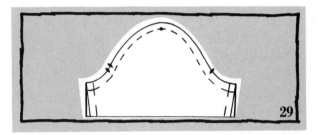

Upper part of a long or three-quarter sleeve can be widened as follows. Since it leaves armhole untouched, not more than 1″ should be added by this method.

• Using yardstick, draw a line parallel with grain line from center of sleeve cap to center of wrist; and a line across as shown, 1″ below top of underarm seam (30). Cut along both lines, stopping and starting *inside* seamlines (do not cut into seam allowance).

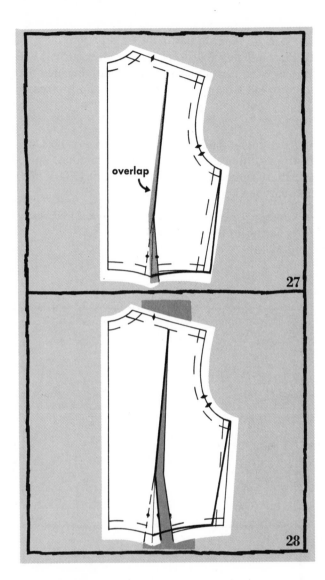

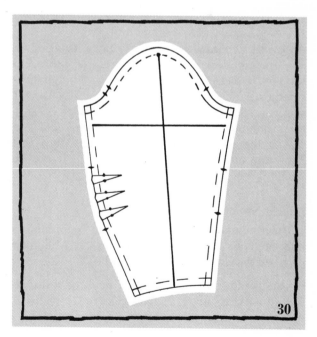

. . . *To reduce size,* measure one half of total back alteration out from cut; mark. Lap dart edge over as far as mark; smooth out pattern carefully and secure overlap (27). Restore original waist measurement and waistline. Waistline dart remains original size.

. . . *To increase size,* slip tissue paper under pattern. Spread pattern to one half of total back alteration and secure cut edges to tissue (28). Restore original waist measurement and waistline. Waistline dart remains original size.

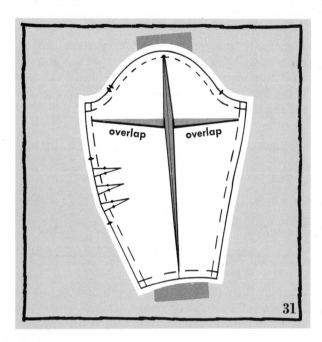

• Cut along outer line (nearer side seam) of waistline dart, to point of dart *only*. Fold pattern on pencil line, bringing fold to alteration mark at neckline and tapering to nothing at point of dart. Secure fold. Pattern will have spread on cut line; slip a piece of tissue paper under gap in pattern; secure cut edges to tissue.

• To restore original waist measurement, measure in from cutting line at side seam an amount equal to pattern spread. Draw new cutting line (33). Waistline dart remains original size.

• Reshape neckline curve, adding tissue if necessary. Alter facing to fit new neckline.

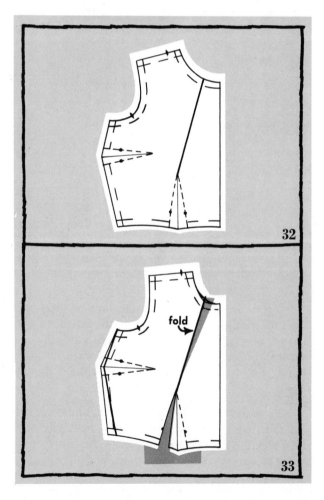

• Slip tissue paper under pattern. Spread the lengthwise cut the necessary amount, meanwhile letting crosswise edges overlap to keep pattern flat. Secure all cut edges. Draw new grain line through center of tissue insert. Redraw cutting line at wrist (31).

MISCELLANEOUS

As mentioned earlier, the fact that a neckline or an armhole in a sleeveless garment is either too wide or too snug cannot be established through measurements. You may know from your ready-to-wear that your clothes tend to have these defects. In anything home-sewn, they will not show up until you try on the garment (or Muslin Basic). Once you know the alteration is needed, however, it can be made in the pattern.

Gaping Neckline

• Determine amount to be taken out by pinning a tuck at center front and/or center back. Alteration on pattern will be half this amount.

• Using ruler, draw a line from point of waistline dart to neckline, about 2″ from center (32). At neckline, measure and mark amount to be taken out.

**High Neckline or Sleeveless Armhole
Too Snug or Too Wide**

A neckline close to the neck or an armhole in a sleeveless garment may not fit properly because they are either too snug or too loose. In such a case the pattern is altered by re-drawing the cutting line, placing it higher (34) or lower (35) as the case may be.

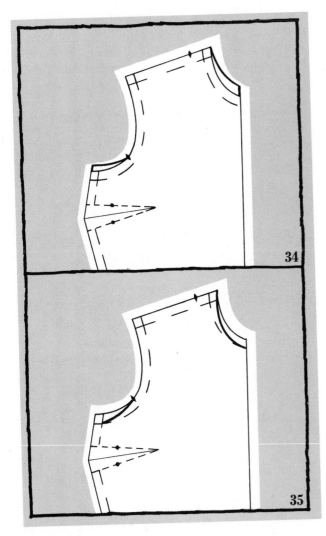

Any alterations made on the bodice must naturally be repeated on the facings and on the collar, if there is one.

MAKING A MUSLIN BASIC

A Muslin Basic is a partly-finished trial garment, made out of preshrunk, firmly-woven cotton (unbleached muslin or an old sheet), for the purpose of taking any uncertainty out of size and fit. To be really "basic," it should be made from the Basic Pattern (from which actual garments can be made in several variations) to establish all your measurements, the alterations you may need and so on, for future reference. You may, however, wish to make "a muslin" before cutting out any dress, especially if the cut is tricky and/or the fabric expensive.

• Do not, just because this is a muslin, omit any of the preparations—this, in fact, is where you will try them out. Select your pattern as directed in the preceding pages, check it for fit, and carefully make the alterations indicated.

• See CUTTING, pp. 52–53. After cutting out muslin, transfer markings from pattern to muslin as directed in MARKING, p. 121. In addition, mark all seamlines, so that any alterations made on muslin will be easier to transfer to pattern.

• No edges (neck, hem) will be finished. To check fit of neckline or a sleeveless armhole later, make a line of stitching directly on seamline, and clip around through seam allowance to stitching.

• For construction, use long stitch to facilitate opening seams (it may be necessary), and follow pattern primer. Leave edges, zipper opening, etc., unfinished (when trying on, pin up opening).

• Try on muslin (have someone help you). See if pattern alterations have come out right. *Do not overfit!* But if additional alterations are needed, do not hesitate to mark and slash into the muslin to remove or add fullness where needed, as indicated in the foregoing **Pattern Alterations.**

• When you are satisfied with the fit of the muslin, transfer any alterations you have made on it to the paper pattern, and make a note of them on your personal measurement chart. Unless your figure changes, you will now know exactly what alterations to make on your patterns.

PLACKETS

- For lap, cut a strip of fabric, either on straight grain or on bias, 1⅞″ wide and twice as long as opening.

- Spreading out opening as shown (2) and matching edges evenly, pin wrong side of opening edges in a straight line over right side of strip. Stitch, with regular seam allowance. Where seam allowance is clipped, reinforce by doubling stitching for about 2″, as shown. Trim seam allowance to ¼″.

- Press strip and seam away from garment. Turn in free edge of strip ¼″; press. Folding strip in half lengthwise, topstitch free edge over first stitching (3).

A placket is a partial opening (i.e., closed at one or both ends) that allows a garment to be put on and taken off. It is most often in a seam, but may be cut as a slash in the fabric. For zipper plackets, see ZIPPERS. Other plackets may be finished with a strip of fabric or a facing. See the following.

PLACKET WITH CONTINUOUS LAP

This may be in a seam, as when it forms the lower part (skirt portion) of a child's dress placket; or in a slash, as in long shirtsleeves.

Placket in a Seam

- At bottom of opening (end of stitched seam), clip through seam allowance to seamline (1).

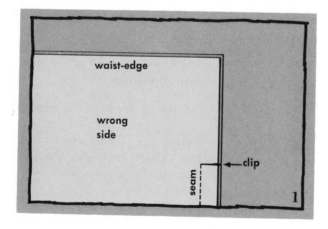

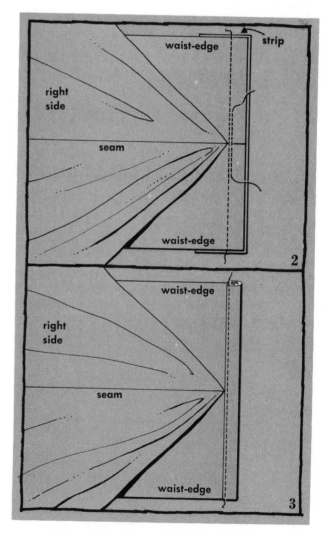

• From inside, fold lap (4); stitch diagonally across fold as shown.

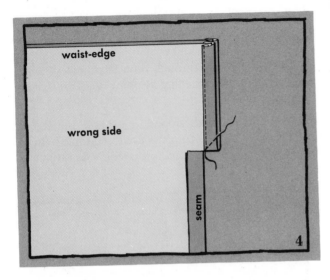

• Fold one side of lap (left edge on a center back opening) along seamline and press (5).

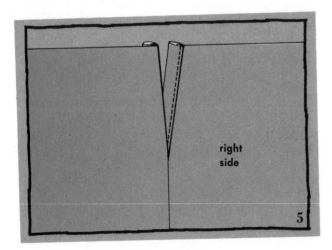

Placket in a Slash—NOTE: *Do not* slash until you have reinforced point with stitching.

• If stitching line is not indicated on pattern, use ruler to draw lines as shown (6), from end of slash line to ¼″ on either side of line at fabric edge.

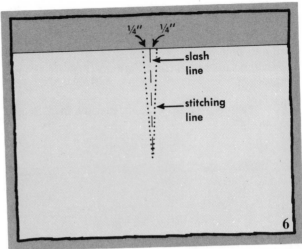

• Using small machine stitch (20 to the inch) for reinforcement, stitch on marked line, taking two stitches across point. Cut on slash line, being careful not to clip stitching at point.

• For lap, cut a strip of fabric, either on straight grain or on bias, 1½″ wide and twice as long as slash line.

• Pin wrong side of one edge of slash over right side of strip, keeping stitched line on slash ¼″ from edge of strip (7).

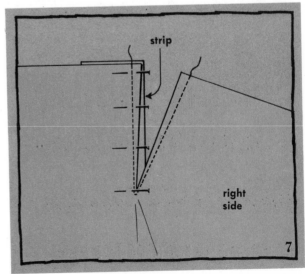

• Still using small stitch, stitch just outside existing stitched line, going toward point. At point, *leave needle down* in fabric. Bring other edge of slash forward and match end to end of strip, so that stitched line is lined up as before. Continue stitching to end of slash (8).

• For finishing, see 3, 4, 5, in **Placket in a Seam,** pp. 146–147.

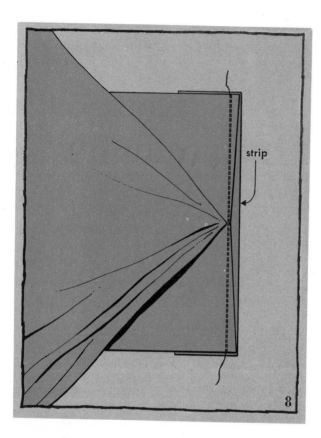

FACED PLACKET IN A SLASH

Used at necklines that may be intended for zipper closure, or for a button or hook at top. Also on long shirtsleeves.

NOTE: *Do not* slash until after facing is applied.

• If stitching line is not indicated on facing pattern, use a ruler to draw lines as shown (6): from end of slash line to ¼″ on either side of line at fabric edge.

• Pin facing (free edges finished, as shown) to garment, right side to right side. Using a small stitch (20 to the inch), stitch on marked line, going toward point. At point, leave needle down in fabric, pivot, take two stitches across, pivot again, and stitch down other edge (9).

• Cut on slash line through both thicknesses, being careful not to clip stitching at point (9). Turn facing to inside; press.

• Finish placket with zipper, or a hook, button, or snap at top. Unless a zipper is used, reinforce bottom of opening with a bar tack on wrong side (10).

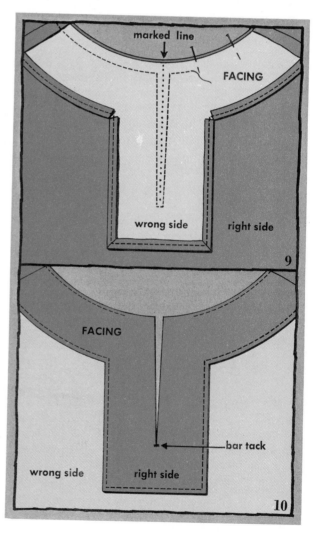

PLEATS

Pleats are folds in fabric providing controlled fullness. They may be placed in a garment singly or in a series.

For a single pleat in a dress or skirt, you need only follow the directions of your pattern primer. What we give you here is general information on pleats, and the principles of all-around pleating in skirts; all are meant to supplement, not replace, the directions in your primer. We also give you directions for a Simulated Kick Pleat, which has several advantages over a regular one. For useful pointers on finishing a regular kick pleat, see HEMS, p. 106.

KINDS OF PLEATS

NOTE: The first three pleats (Knife, Box, Inverted) described at right can be either pressed all the way down, stitched down part of the way, or left unpressed; they may also be edge-stitched along one or both folds. Pressed pleats can be done commercially.

Knife or Side Pleats (1) have folds all turned in one direction. Folds start across back from left to right, automatically becoming right to left across front, with last pleat covering placket.

Box Pleats (2) consist of two equal folds turned away from each other, with under-folds meeting in center underneath.

Inverted Pleats (3) consist of two equal folds turned toward each other and meeting.

As you can see, Box and Inverted Pleats are two sides of the same pleat; hence, they look alike on both sides when made in a series (4).

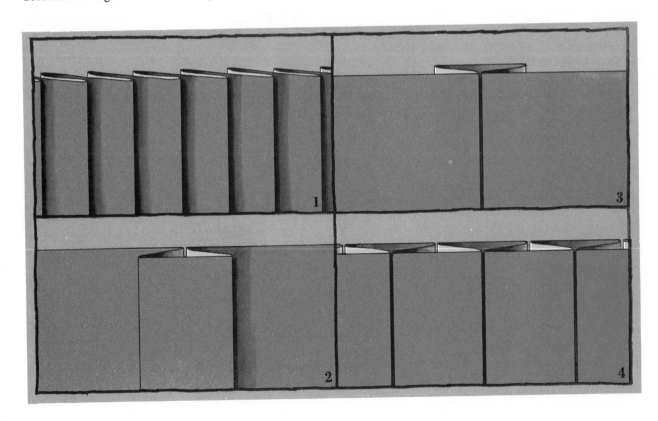

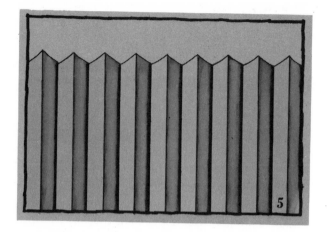

Accordion Pleats (5) are narrow pleats opening out to resemble the folds in an accordion. They can only be made commercially, are always pressed all the way down, and are never stitched.

FABRIC IN RELATION TO PLEATS

Synthetic fabrics (except rayon) and blends usually hold a well-pressed-in crease perfectly, even through washing. Wools and heavy silks hold a crease well. Cotton, lightweight silk, and rayon do not as a rule hold a crease too well; but they do so better if they are treated for wash-and-wear. Pleats in such fabrics can be edge-stitched for sharpness.

SKIRT WITH PLEATS (PRESSED, UNPRESSED OR STITCHED) MADE FROM PATTERN

Pattern for a straight pleated skirt is bought by hip measurement, since pleats should hang straight from hips. Waistline may be adjusted if necessary.

Alteration in width, if any, will be made while forming pleats. See p. 151.

Cutting is done on single thickness of fabric, with pattern placed right side up on right side of fabric.

Marking is done on right side of fabric, since pleats are formed on right side. Pattern gives two lines for each pleat: one on which fold is made, another to which fold is brought. One of these lines may be solid and the other broken, or they may be

otherwise differentiated—pattern or primer will indicate which is which. Before unpinning pattern to cut next section(s), mark position of all pleats with a type of broken basting called **Simplified Tailor's Tacks,** as follows:

Indicate the two different fold-marks just described by using two colors of thread, one for each. Use thread longer than the skirt (forget the 18″ rule for once). Take a small stitch through pattern and fabric at beginning of fold-line, leaving a 1″ thread-end. Take a small stitch about every 3″ all the way down line. When all lines are basted, snip thread between stitches (6), and carefully remove pattern. Repeat on next skirt section(s).

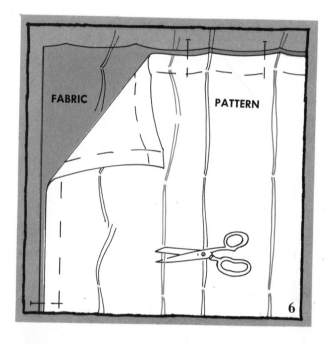

Follow your primer for seaming, etc. If your pleats are to be pressed, you will note that the skirt is hemmed before pleats are put in. For a smooth hem where there is a seam at the underfold of a pleat, see **Hem in Pleats,** p. 106. Determine length carefully, but play safe on the long side, because skirt can be shortened a little at waist later, but not lengthened. With unpressed pleats, hemming is the last step, as usual, and presents no special problem.

Forming Pleats is done on ironing board, with skirt right side out. Start at placket opening and work around. If an alteration in width is necessary, distribute it through all pleats so their width will remain uniform. A very small adjustment in each pleat will take care of the 2″ (difference between pattern sizes) which would be the maximum alteration. For broader hips or waist, bring fold not quite up to mark; for narrower hips or waist, bring it slightly past mark.

To secure pleats for pressing, use diagonal basting across center of pleat (7), through all thicknesses. *Do not remove this basting* until skirt is finished.

Pressing Pleats is done with steam on both sides, using a press cloth on right side (see PRESSING).

Stitching Pleats, if desired, is done before applying waistband and after placket is finished.

. . . *Stitched-Down Pleats* are stitched between waist and hipline (8). To ensure proper hang, start at hip and stitch toward waist: slide skirt under presser foot with hem away from you; topstitch through all thicknesses, along edge of each pleat. At bottom end of stitching, pull thread-ends through to wrong side of garment and tie.

. . . *Edge-Stitched Pleats* are stitched on one fold or both to keep creases sharp. Such stitching is done mostly on children's and sports clothes. If done on underfold only, it is invisible and can be used on any clothes. To edge-stitch, place edge of fold alone under presser foot and stitch, going from waist through hem (9).

It is possible to edge-stitch the lower part of a stitched-down pleat. First edge-stitch upper fold of pleat from hipline through hem, then turn skirt around and topstitch through all thicknesses from hipline to waist as described above.

Follow your pattern primer to apply waistband and finish skirt.

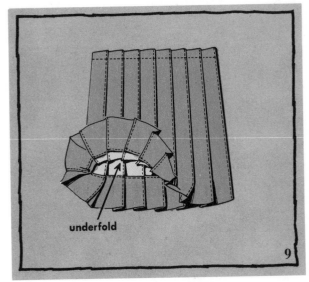

underfold

SKIRT WITH COMMERCIAL PLEATING

To find a firm doing commercial pleating, look in the Yellow Pages and in fashion magazines, or inquire from your notion store or department. Check as to which types of pleats they can make. Some pleating concerns do "pattern pleating," which means that they will taper the waistline to your measurements. Find out how wide a piece of fabric is needed and how it should be prepared.

Since pleating must be done flat, the usual procedure is to stitch all skirt seams except the one that is to contain placket, and to put in the hem.

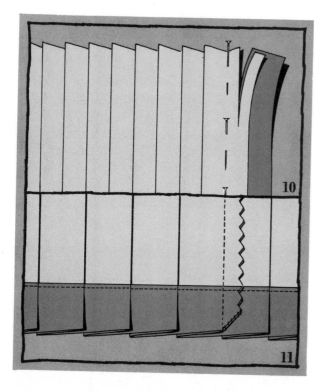

To finish skirt when it returns from pleating—Baste pleats in place across hipline and see if measurement conforms with yours. Make sure that remaining seam forms the underfold of a pleat; if necessary, trim fabric to make it so (10). Carefully matching at hem edge, stitch seam *through hem.* Turn in corners of seam at bottom (11), and whipstitch edges together, as shown. Finish placket.

• Measure pleated waistline on skirt; taper pleats to fit your waist measurement. When doing this, keep top fold on straight grain, making adjustments underneath. Stay-stitch around waistline. Press.

• If desired (except in the case of Accordion Pleats), stitch pleats as described in **Stitching Pleats,** p. 151.

• Apply waistband.

SIMULATED KICK PLEAT

We are all familiar with the spectacle of a kick pleat that has "tucked out." Or with a kick pleat that is bulky to sew or wear. These troubles can be avoided by making a pretend pleat—a slit with an underlay, the underlay being attached to the partial lining you will in any case put in the back of your skirt to prevent its "sitting out."

To convert a kick pleat into a simulated pleat, construct skirt back as follows:

Altering Skirt Back Pattern—At center back, trim away pleat allowance, keeping a ⅝″ seam allowance as shown (12).

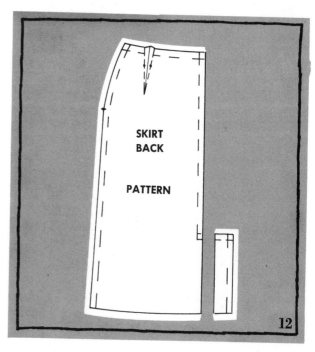

SKIRT
BACK

PATTERN

Cutting—*Outer Fabric:* Cut the two back sections from altered pattern. For underlay, cut a rectangle 18″ in width and 13″ in height.

Lining Fabric: Cut back sections from same pattern, 12½″ shorter than outer sections.

Sewing—*Outer Fabric:* Stitch darts. Stitch center back seam, starting 10″ from bottom (to reinforce this end, first stitch in reverse for about ½″). Join edges of slit by hand- or machine-basting on seamline. Press seam open from top to bottom. Press darts. At basted slit, topstitch an 11″ length of seam tape to edge of each seam allowance. Blind-stitch free edge of tape loosely to garment.

• On rectangle for underlay, make a 1″ hem along each 13″ edge. Press.

Lining: Stitch darts and center back seam; press. Pin underlay to lining as shown (13): wrong side of underlay to right side of lining, centers and raw edges matched. Stitch ½″ seam, extending stitching across lining edge as shown. Fold seam up on stitched line and topstitch (14).

Joining Outer Fabric and Lining: Match lining and outer sections, wrong sides together; pin. Stay-stitch waist and side edges. From here on, handle this lined section as a single piece.

Complete skirt except for hem. Remove basting at slit. Hem, making underlay ½″ shorter than skirt (15).

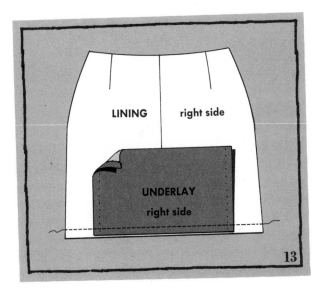

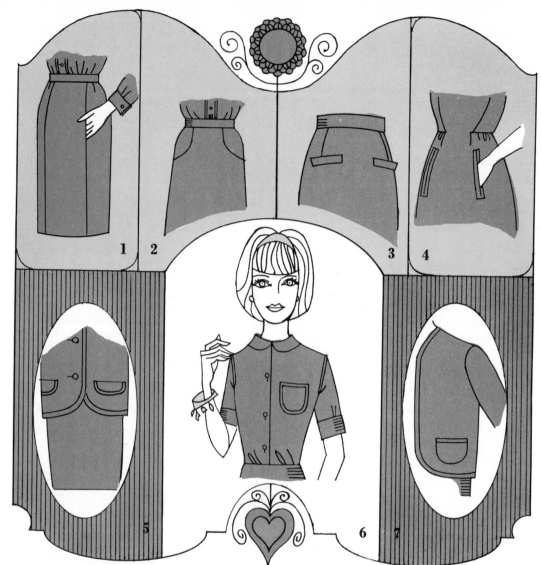

POCKETS

Pockets are part of the design of a garment and may be functional, decorative, or both.

Sometimes the presence of pockets is betrayed only by an edge-seam, as in Pockets in a Seam (1) and Hip Pockets (2). However, Welt Pockets (3), Bound Pockets (4), and Flap Pockets (5) have an outside finish that is a point of interest in the general design.

Patch pockets, placed on the outside and either unlined (6) or lined (7), are made of garment fabric. Inside pockets are made of lining fabric, usually with strips of garment fabric at the opening.

Pockets must be made with precision if they are to enhance, and not spoil, the looks of a garment. The extra time this takes is well spent.

A FEW POINTERS

The pattern primer will tell you how to make your pockets. A few additional pointers, however, may help you to achieve the precision you want.

. . . Position markings for all pockets except 1 and 2 must be transferred to right side of garment with a line of hand- or machine-basting.

. . . Interfacing the opening edges of pockets is generally a good idea; whether or not it is a necessity will depend on the texture and body of your fabric.

Pocket in a Seam and Hip Pocket (1, 2)—For sharp edge-seams, follow **Processing the Seam**, p. 82 under FACINGS. Interface, trim, grade, clip, and understitch as directed (8). NOTE: If you have a pocket in a side seam with a zipper, make your life easier by moving zipper to center back, if possible.

Welt Pocket, Bound Pocket, Flap Pocket (3, 4, 5)—The openings of these pockets are constructed on the same principle as a patch buttonhole. It will help you to refer to the BUTTONHOLES chapter.

Patch Pockets (6, 7)—The procedures that follow ensure neat curves and corners—painlessly.

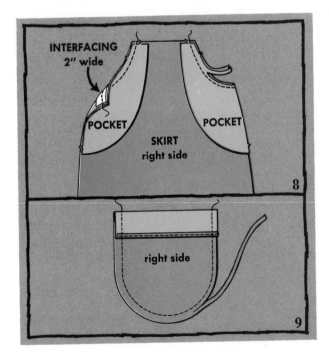

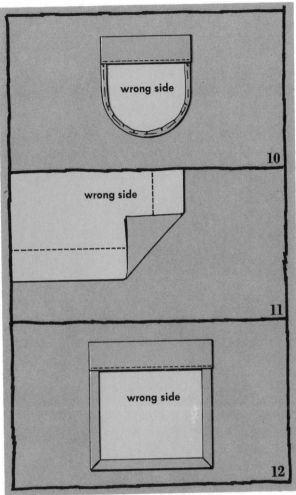

Unlined patch pocket

Turn raw top edge of pocket section ¼" to wrong side and stitch. Fold hem to *right* side, on fold line indicated on pattern. Stitch along seamline around remaining edges, as shown. Trim seam to ⅜", and trim corners at top fold (9). Turn hem to wrong side.

. . . On a rounded pocket, clip through seam allowance at curves. Turn to wrong side on stitched line, baste and press (10).

. . . On square pocket, fold corners to wrong side (11); press. Turn seam allowance on stitched line; miter corners by folding as shown (12); baste and press the pocket.

Baste pocket to garment; topstitch. To reinforce top corners, you can either . . .

. . . Stitch a triangle (13).

. . . Make close zigzag stitch, about ⅛″ wide, for ½″ (14).

. . . Backstitch for about ½″ (15).

Fold top edge of pocket over lining on fold line indicated on pattern; pin. Stitch on seamline around raw edges, as shown. Trim and grade seams; trim corners at top (17). If pocket is rounded, clip through seam allowance at curves; on square pocket, trim corners.

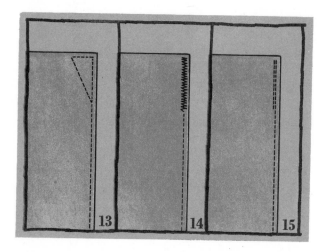

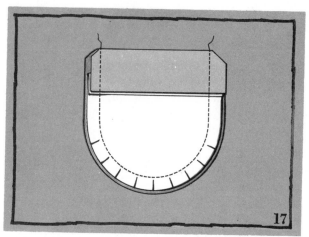

Lined patch pocket (if you desire a lining not indicated in pattern).

Cut lining from pocket pattern with top edge of pattern folded on fold line. Press top edge of lining ¾″ to wrong side. Pin to pocket, right sides together, side and bottom edges even (16).

Turn pocket right side out, carefully pushing out corners and seams. Press carefully.

Slipstitch lining to hem (18).

Baste pocket to garment. Either slipstitch in place, or topstitch, following directions for unlined pocket.

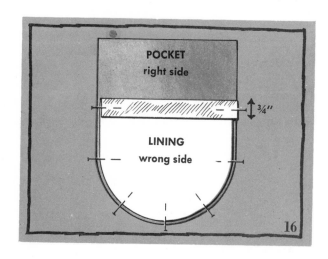

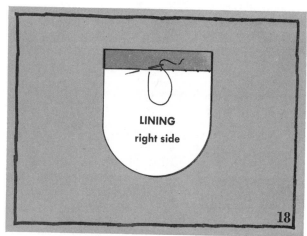

PRESSING

Stitch-and-Press—the practice of pressing a stitched seam before it is crossed by another, and all details as they are finished—is perhaps *the* Golden Rule of Good Dressmaking, the process you cannot afford to neglect if you want professional-looking work. Besides, the fine aspect of the work as you go along gives you continual satisfaction, and the final pressing—otherwise a very complicated procedure—is reduced to almost nothing.

See EQUIPMENT for what you need.

PRESSING PRINCIPLES

Pressing is part of sewing—hence directions for pressing specific sewing details will be found in their covering chapters (SEAMS, EASING, BUTTONHOLES, etc.). Following are the general rules.

• Have iron and ironing board set up and ready before you start on any sewing project. You will need them to smooth out your pattern, and perhaps press out creases in fabric before cutting (see PATTERNS, CUTTING, etc.), and continually thereafter.

• Do not confuse pressing with ironing, the hearty, bearing-down and stroking operation that follows laundering. In pressing, you lower the iron, in most cases lightly, lift and lower it again a little farther on; or you use a light, sliding motion without ever letting the full weight of the iron rest on fabric (this might leave an impression, or, if done on right side, cause a shine). In seams, you work only with tip of iron (1). On most fabrics, pressing action comes from a combination of steam and partial weight of iron.

• All construction pressing (pressing of construction stitching) is done on wrong side. Pressing done on right side, or final pressing, is kept at a minimum.

• Stitch-and-press does not mean that you have to press each seam, dart, etc., immediately after it is stitched. Just make sure it is pressed before either end is caught in another seam. You can usually press several seams at one time.

• Never press over pins—they will scratch your iron and may make an indelible impression on your fabric.

• Remove basting whenever possible before pressing. Always remove it before final pressing, because even the thread may leave a mark.

• Most irons show clearly what heat setting to use with what fabric (fiber content)—linen taking the highest, synthetics the lowest. What with all the new blends and finishes, however, play safe by trying the iron on a scrap of fabric before touching it to the garment itself. Whether or not to use steam will depend on fiber and weave (see following).

• If fabric is of a type that will mark through to outside, place a strip of brown paper between an edge (seam allowance or other) and garment fabric before you press (2).

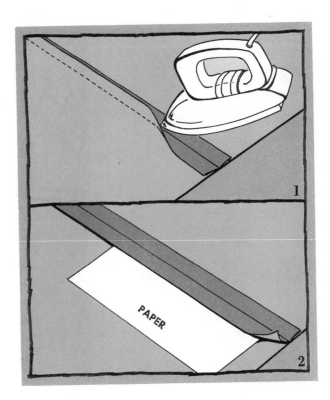

• In any pressing done on outside, a shine is likely to occur on *any* fabric at details with bulkier parts, such as zipper placket, facing, pocket, etc. To avoid this, use a dry press cloth with a steam iron. With a dry iron, use a press cloth dampened like this: wet half of it, wring out, fold damp half over dry, and place on garment with dry side down.

• If you have faithfully pressed as you went along, final pressing should be just a matter of touching up here and there.

PRESSING THE STANDARD FABRICS

For special-handling fabrics (Wash-and-Wear, Knits, Bonded and Stretch Fabrics, Pile Fabrics, Fake Fur, Sheers, Lace, Vinyl), see pp. 72–79 in FABRICS.

Cotton presents no problem. Except when it is of dark color (when it may tend to shine), it can be pressed on either side, either with a steam iron, or with a dry iron after being directly dampened with a sponge.

Linen is as easy to press as cotton, but is more apt to shine if pressed on right side. With dark colors, use a press cloth.

Wool requires considerable steam in pressing. It responds excellently to the steam iron, or to a dry iron with a press cloth, used half-damp, half-dry as described at left. It lends itself to shrinking and shaping by means of steam (see EASING). If used on right side, press cloth should preferably be of wool, especially with dark fabric. NOTE: With wool crepe, use very little steam, or it will shrink, even if preshrunk. Never let iron rest on crepe, as it will leave an imprint.

Silk is handled according to its weight. Heavy and medium-weight silk is handled like wool. Sheer silk, such as chiffon, is pressed entirely dry. The note for wool crepe also applies to silk crepe.

Rayon requires a moderately warm iron. Press on wrong side. Do not apply direct steam.

SEAMS AND SEAM FINISHES

A seam is the line of stitching, usually done by machine, that holds two pieces of a garment together. It may be decorative as well as functional, and outlined by added topstitching, or by cording or piping inserted between the two pieces of fabric (see BIAS, p. 31). The great majority of seams, however, are plain.

Seams can be made in different ways and with different finishes, depending on fabric, design, and purpose of garment. On wash-and-wear fabric, be careful about using seams with outside stitching, as they may pucker.

The seam allowance is the fabric between seamline and raw edge; after a seam is made, seam allowances are on wrong side of garment. Standard seam allowance in commercial patterns is ⅝″, sometimes trimmed afterwards, for one reason or another, to a narrower width.

To maintain the size and lines of a garment, it is very important to keep seam allowances even and at given width. Some machines have guidelines etched on the throat plate, along which you guide the raw edge of the fabric as you stitch. Seam guide attachments are also available. Otherwise, you can make

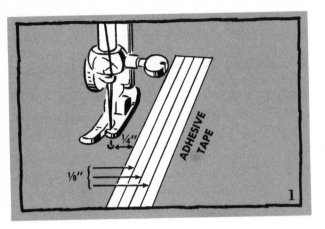

your own guide, or gauge, with a strip of adhesive tape. Tape ½″ wide will give you graded guidelines for seam widths from ¼″ to ¾″. Cut a piece 3″ long. Place on machine exactly ¼″ from needle, parallel with presser foot. Measure and draw lines on it ⅛″ apart, as shown (1).

Stitch length in seams will depend on fabric, type of garment, etc. (see chart on p. 166 in THREAD AND NEEDLES). For general use, 12 to the inch is a good stitch length. A seam on the true bias, however, needs to be reinforced by a shorter stitch.

PLAIN SEAM

This is the simplest and most commonly-used seam. All other seams begin with a plain seam.

• Place the two pieces of fabric together, wrong sides out, edges even (2).

• Stitch on seamline.

• First press line of stitching without opening seam (3), then press seam open with point of iron only, applying slight pressure (4). Then lightly press open seam. Even if a seam is to be pressed to one side, press it open first—the seamline will be much smoother.

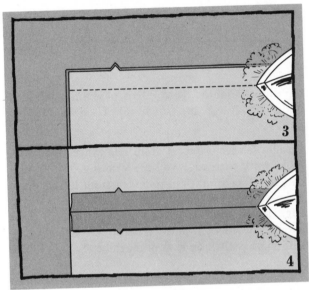

SEAM FINISHES

For neatness, and to prevent ravelling, a plain seam is finished unless garment is lined. Use the finish suited to your fabric. With firmly woven fabric, the seam allowance can be left as is.

Most fabrics: Trim seam allowances with pinking shears, or stitch-and-pink (5).

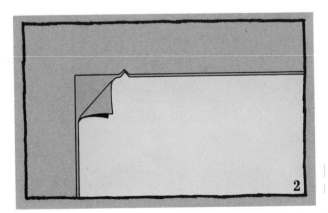

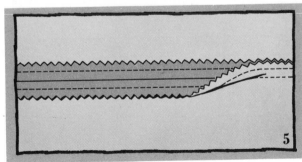

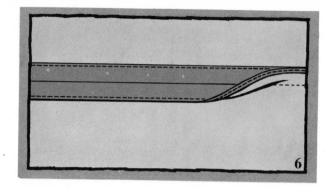

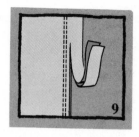

Sheer fabric or lace: Do not press seam open. With seam allowances together, make a second line of stitching in seam allowance ⅛″ from stitched seamline. Trim close to second line (9). Press to one side.

Lightweight fabric: Turn edges of seam allowance under about ⅛″ and stitch (6). Used in unlined jackets.

Ravelly fabric: Overcast seam allowances by hand. Hold work with edge you are working on up. You can go either from right to left or from left to right. Take stitches (⅛″ to ¼″ deep and ¼″ apart) over edge as shown (7), putting needle through from wrong side to right side of fabric. Or finish edges with zigzag stitch on sewing machine (8).

Heavier fabrics in unlined jacket or coat: Enclose edge of each seam allowance in Double-Fold Bias Tape. Insert edge between edges of tape with narrower tape-fold on top. Edge-stitch (10).

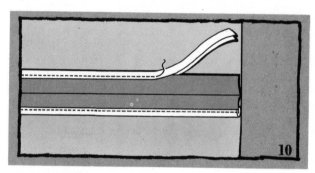

TOPSTITCHED SEAM

A decorative seam, used mostly on sports clothes.
• After pressing a plain seam open, turn work to right side and topstitch on either side of seamline, being very careful to have both sides equal (11). Width of stitching varies according to thickness of fabric and preference.

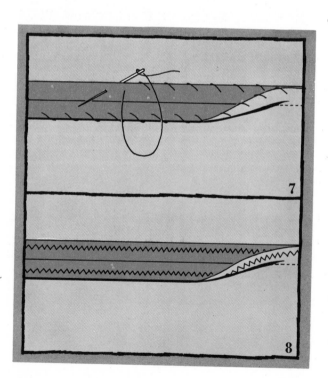

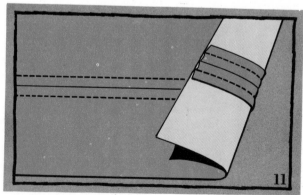

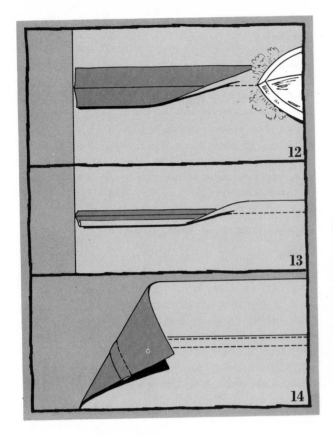

WELTED SEAM

A variation of the Felled Seam, used on heavier fabrics, for strength and for the decorative addition of the line of stitching. It is topstitched from outside, after seam is made on inside.

• Make a plain seam. After pressing seam open, press it again with both seam allowances turned in one direction.

• Trim away under seam allowance to about ¼". On outside, topstitch along side of seam with allowances underneath (15).

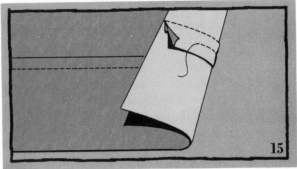

FLAT FELLED SEAM
(also called Felled Seam or Fell Seam)

A strong, neat seam, good on garments that are laundered often. It can be made on inside or on outside of garment. The fell (stitched-down overlap) appearing on the outside is a feature of sports clothes, pajamas, etc. You can fell an armhole seam only if top of sleeve is almost straight, as in a shirtsleeve, with a very shallow cap and no ease.

• Make a plain seam, as on p. 159 (right sides out, if you want an outside fell).

• After pressing seam open, press it again with both seam allowances turned in one direction (12).

• Trim away under seam allowance to about ⅛" (13). Fold in top seam allowance to half its width (with some fabrics, you may wish to hand-baste or press this before stitching). Edge-stitch fold (fell) to garment (14).

FRENCH SEAM

Another very neat seam, used on sheer fabrics, where a raw edge would show through. The first line of stitching is done with right sides out.

To make a very narrow French seam:
• With fabric right sides out, stitch a plain seam a *scant* ½" from raw edges. Trim seam allowances to ⅛" (16).

• Press seam allowances to one side. Fold work on stitched line, wrong sides out. Stitch again (17), ⅛" from fold (this will be on regular seamline allowed).

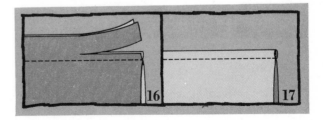

SLEEVES

Sleeves and the way they are set in—high or low on the shoulder, widening or narrowing the shoulder-line, emphasizing or playing down parts of the silhouette—are one of the focal points in the changes of fashion (sometimes even by their absence). While they may be of every length and width, and vary greatly as to shape, sleeves fall into just three basic categories:

The set-in sleeve, cut separately from garment body and seamed into an armhole. This sleeve may have a smooth cap, a darted cap, or a full, gathered cap.

The raglan sleeve, cut separately from garment body, but continuing to neckline over shoulder and seamed to a modified armhole extending from underarm to neck.

The kimono sleeve, cut in one with garment body; it sometimes has an underarm gusset.

The lower edge of any sleeve is finished by a cuff, a hem, a facing, etc., as indicated in pattern. For additional help see those chapter headings.

THE SET-IN SLEEVE

A perfectly set in sleeve—so important in the looks of a garment—depends on three relatively simple pre-conditions:

[a] exact line-up of matching points (underarm seams, notches, shoulder seam to mark on sleeve cap),

[b] evenly-distributed ease in sleeve cap—*see directions below,*

[c] stitching around armhole kept even and with correct seam allowance.

Setting in a Smooth-Cap Sleeve

• Before seaming sleeve, make a row of ease-stitching (10 stitches to the inch) on seamline of sleeve cap, between notches. To help control fullness, stitch a second line within seam allowance, ⅛″ from first one (1).

• Stitch underarm seam; press open. Finish bottom of sleeve (cuff, hem, or whatever).

• With garment wrong side out, place sleeve in armhole, right sides together. Pin together at underarm seams, notches, dots, shoulder seam; then place a pin ½″ to either side of shoulder seam (2), as shown (this inch in top of sleeve cap is straight-grain and has no ease). Gently draw up threads between notches and these two pins until cap loosely fits armhole (do not pull too tight). Distribute ease evenly. Pull all thread-ends through to wrong side and *tie securely.* Remove pins and take out sleeve.

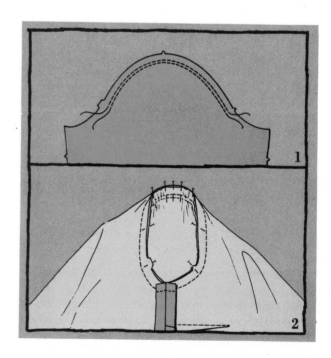

• Handling sleeve carefully, place sleeve cap, right side out, over end of sleeve board or pressing ham. With point of steam iron, press sleeve cap (3), shrinking or smoothing out fullness (depending on fabric).

• Pin sleeve into armhole as before, adding pins all around at intervals of not more than 1½″—unless you prefer to baste sleeve in. Starting at underarm seam, with sleeve side up, stitch around carefully, removing pins as you come to them. Make a second row of stitching within seam allowance ¼″ from first (4).

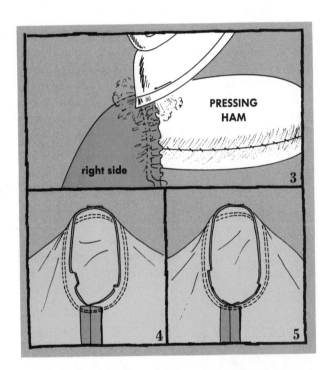

• Between notches at underarm, trim away seam allowance close to stitching (5). Trim remainder of seam to ½″. Press stitching line without opening seam. Then turn seam into sleeve, without pressing.

THE RAGLAN SLEEVE

Raglan sleeves are cut in two sections shaped by a shoulder seam, or in one section shaped by a large curved dart tapering from neck over top of arm. Mark and stitch this dart carefully (see DARTS). When seaming sleeve to garment body, be careful not to stretch seam.

THE KIMONO SLEEVE

Kimono sleeves are usually shaped by a shoulder seam, and may or may not have a gusset at underarm (for handling gusset, see GUSSETS). When pattern calls for no gusset, reinforce underarm seam by one of the following two methods:

METHOD I—Shorten stitch at curve of underarm. Then clip seam allowance and press seam open. Baste a piece of seam tape 3″ to 4″ long over opened seam (or pin, putting pins through *from right side)*; stitch on right side of garment ⅛″ from each side of seam (6, 7).

METHOD II—Before stitching underarm seam, pin a piece of seam tape 3″ to 4″ long over seamline (8); if there is a sharp curve, fold tape as shown (9). Stitch seam with shortened stitch. Clip seam allowance *without clipping tape.* Press seam open.

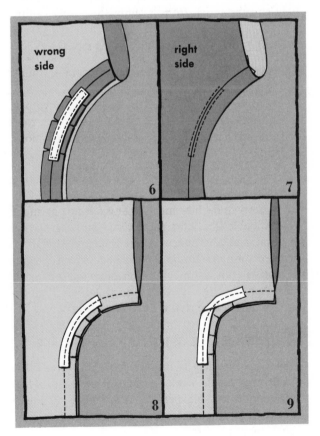

STITCH IN TIME
MENDING

The prudent stitch, taken in time to prevent damage or to repair it, is not as out-of-date a notion as many believe. Small repair work is unavoidable if we would be neat and well-groomed. More extensive work on a garment or other article **that is worth it** will pay for itself many times over. A few general points may be made about mending:

. . . Most of it is done by hand.

. . . It often calls for self-fabric. Naturally, you save the pieces left over after making a garment. Save, also, whatever scraps may come off ready-to-wear (when shortening, for instance).

. . . There are various kinds of mending, ranging from light to substantial, from inventive to purely skillful.

TO MEND OR NOT TO MEND

The small mending jobs essential to neatness should be done without question. They consist of repairing what has **come undone,** and include loose or ripped-off buttons, snaps, hooks and eyes; thread loops, worn or torn out; hems or lining loose or hanging undone; open seams.

Whether or not to undertake more extensive mending depends on a number of factors: How successful the job is likely to be; how much wear is left in a garment; how valuable it is; how much time you have at your disposal; and your budget. There is no point in laboriously repairing an article that can be replaced cheaply, or that will not last much longer in any case. On the other hand, if you can save a good garment you are fond of it, it will be well worth a few hours' work.

PREVENTIVE MENDING

Preventive mending is the true "stitch in time", but is not real repair work, because it is done *before* damage occurs. Inexpensive ready-made garments should be gone over for this kind of mending even before they are worn.

Dangling Threads—Thread the ends into a needle, bring to inside of garment and tie.

Hem—If stitches are loose or if fabric is pulled off grain, remove stitches and resew (for hemming stitches, see p. 101 in HEMS). Resew any section that may be loose.

Buttons, Snaps, Hooks, Eyes that are not properly attached should be resewn. If the existing thread has not begun to come loose, it need not be removed —just sew over it. In the case of **buttons with a shank** however, it is better to remove buttons and scraps of thread entirely and start afresh as described on p. 43 of BUTTONS.

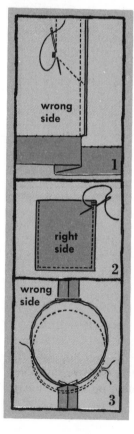

Buttonholes—You can double the life and improve the looks of machine-made buttonholes by going over them with a hand-buttonhole stitch, or a zigzag-machine stitch (see pp. 38, 39 in BUTTONHOLES).

Zippers — Overcast any loose or fraying fabric edges that might catch in zipper.

Kick-pleat and Pockets — Strengthen with a few firm overhand stitches at top of pleat (1) or pocket (2), as shown.

Seams — Sleeve and crotch seams can be strengthened with a second line of machine-stitching on top of the existing stitching (3). Do the same with narrow or crooked seams, or any overly-large stitching.

Underarm seams of raglan and kimono sleeves, which are put to extra strain, should be reinforced with seam tape: place tape over seamline and stitch through it (4); if there is a sharp curve, fold tape as shown (5).

Areas of Hard Wear can be reinforced either when garment is new or when areas are beginning to show signs of wear.

Knees, elbows, seats of pants, especially in children's clothes—Place iron-on patches on inside.

Thinning elbows on wool sweaters—Run matching yarn invisibly through back of knitting for reinforcement, as shown (6).

IMAGINATIVE MENDING

This may mean using contrasting rather than matching fabric for patches, and repeating the patch on an undamaged elbow, knee, or other corresponding area in order to make it plausible. It may mean placing a decoration over the damage, adding a strategic pocket where none was intended, ironing or sewing on a flower (7), adding a braid or frill to frayed sleeve edges (and repeat it on the neck edge!). Needless to say, whether or not such mending is suitable will depend, not only on the garment, but on the location and nature of the damage.

Iron-on Patches can be wonderful cover-ups for spots and tears on play-clothes and children's clothes. Cut them out in gay colors and attractive shapes (coloring books may provide you with outlines). **Appliqués** in contrasting fabrics can be quite sophisticated. **Embroidery** should be done boldly, in a simple design, and should extend beyond the damaged area. **Braid, lace, ribbon** and other trimmings can be used to camouflage mishaps (see DECORATIONS).

IRON-ON MENDING

This is quick and easy. Iron-on fabrics come in plain weave and jersey and in many colors, which are particularly useful in imaginative mending (see the foregoing heading). There are ready-cut patches in denim, twill and corduroy; also strips that can be used for pressing on the wrong side of a tear. The large white pieces are excellent for mending sheets.

In every case, round off corners of patches or designs (sharp corners have a tendency to lift off), and follow package instructions exactly. Be sure to apply enough pressure and heat.

FASTENINGS

Resewing fastenings is the first *must* mending.

Buttons, Snaps, Hooks and Eyes, Thread Loops, must be removed entirely before resewing, including **all** scraps of thread. For resewing, see chapters on BUTTONS, FASTENERS, THREAD LOOPS.

If fabric under a **button** is torn or worn, mend or reinforce it with iron-on fabric in matching color. Remove button. Snip frayed threads around torn spot. Cut two identical circles of iron-on fabric, slightly larger than hole. Spread facing open, wrong side up, and attach circles over button locations on both outer fabric and facing (8). Follow package instructions. Close facing and sew on button. (See other ways of reinforcing button position on p. 43.)

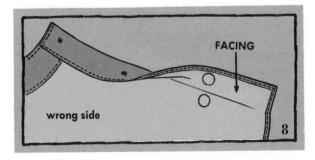

Worked Buttonholes that show signs of wear should immediately be gone over with hand-buttonhole stitch or by machine (p. 39).

Badly-ravelled buttonholes can be renewed from scratch, if the garment is worth it, as follows:

• Carefully remove all stitches with sharp, pointed scissors. Steam-press buttonhole.

• *If you finish buttonholes by machine*
. . . baste buttonhole edges together with diagonal basting (9), *or*
. . . back buttonhole slit on both outer fabric and facing with a lightweight iron-on patch.

• *If you finish buttonholes by hand*
. . . make a line of very small machine stitching on each side of slit, as close to edge as possible.

• Refinish buttonhole edges (see pp. 38, 39).

Zipper—If zipper stitching is ripped, baste zipper back in place and machine-stitch with matching thread. For how to replace a zipper, see p. 216 in ZIPPERS.

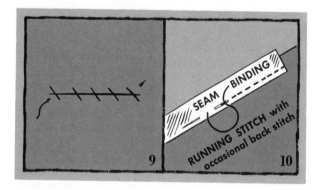

HEMS AND SEAMS

This is another series of small *musts*.

Ripped Hem—When this is simply a matter of loosened thread, remove loose thread and sew hem-edge back (for hemming stitches, see p. 101). If, however, the seam binding is worn through, the worn length must be replaced. Remove it neatly, then edge-stitch the new binding over the raw hem edge, either by machine, or by hand with a running stitch and an occasional backstitch (10). Turn ends under. Attach top edge with one of the hemming stitches.

Ripped Lining—This usually occurs at the hem. Fold lining under and hem invisibly in place. If lining seams have come undone, join as explained below.

Open Seams should be sewed up at once, preferably by machine stitching, which is stronger. Otherwise, do it with a hand-backstitch (11). In either case, you work, of course, on inside of garment and you begin and end about ½" beyond split.

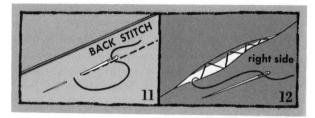

If *garment is lined* or the split has occurred at a facing, it can be sewed up from right side with invisible hand sewing. Use a single thread with a knot at end (knot to be trimmed off when mend is completed). Work needle back and forth between the two edges of split, catching two or three threads in fabric at a time (12). Draw up thread, take a backstitch through edge, and repeat. To finish off, run thread along seam well beyond end of split; clip.

For *split underarm seams* in raglan and kimono sleeves, sew up and reinforce with tape on wrong side, as shown in PREVENTIVE MENDING.

In **Gloves,** open seams should be mended in the manner of the original stitching—whipstitch (13) or running stitch (14). Even if you cannot duplicate this exactly, a mended seam is not one tenth as conspicuous as an open one. Use needle and thread of a fineness or coarseness suitable for the glove material. Start without a knot; secure stitching carefully, and conceal thread-ends inside glove.

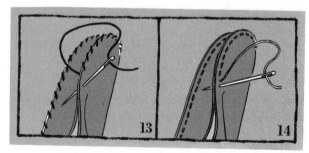

POCKETS

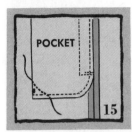

A Hole in a Pocket must be repaired for obvious reasons. A small iron-on patch will do the job. However, if the hole is in the corner, round off corner with hand- or machine-stitching (15). Pockets damaged beyond this easy repair can be replaced with the handy pocket-replacement kits sold at most notions counters.

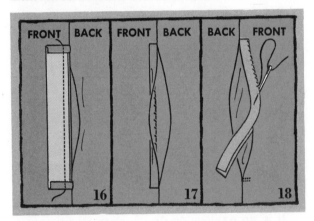

Pocket Edges on Pants can be renewed as follows:

• From a seam allowance or inside of cuff, cut a strip ¾″ to 1″ wide and the exact length of pocket openings plus ½″.

• Press ends under ¼″. Pin strip to edge, right sides together, and stitch about ¼″ from edge (16).

• Turn strip to inside, turn raw edge under and sew down (17).

Pocket Edges on Sports Slacks can be covered with a narrow strip of suede or leather.

• Cut strip about 1″ wide, fold over edge and hem down (18) on outside and inside.

DARNING

Darning is most often done to strengthen weak spots or repair tears. It is also used to fill small holes in an imitation of reweaving or knitting.

Machine-darning is faster and stronger than hand darning, but can only be done where appearance does not matter, as in sheets, work clothes, etc. As machines differ, see your sewing machine manual.

Hand-darning is done with color-matched thread or darning cotton. The best is thread drawn out of the fabric, either from left-overs, or from a straight-cut seam allowance. In woolens, single human hairs make a strong, inconspicuous darn in the tears shown below. For jersey, knits, and stretch fabrics, use Dual Duty® thread, which has "give". Use a needle as fine as possible; use thread short and single (drawing out a long thread pulls fabric out of shape). Make no knot on thread, but let end extend on wrong side. Work on **right side**. Never pull thread up tight.

Tears—Draw fabric together with fishbone stitch (19) before darning. Bring needle to right side ¼″ from tear. Make rows of tiny running stitches, back and forth, as shown (20) keeping in line with weave of fabric and making the outside edges of darn irregular. In L-shaped tears, reinforce corner by darning in both directions, as shown (21). Do the same on diagonal tears (22).

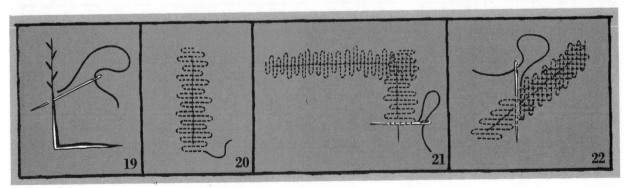

Snags and Small Holes—Trim away ragged edges only, without changing shape of hole. Fill in lengthwise threads as close together as the original weave or knit (in socks) as possible; then weave over and under threads crosswise (23). Be sure to run stitches far enough beyond hole to include all weakened spots.

A darn can be reinforced with a piece of thin fabric placed on underside and caught in the stitches. This, however, should only be done where the extra thickness and slight stiffening will not matter. When pinning on the piece, make sure that the grain runs in the same direction as garment grain. When darn is completed, trim away excess fabric (24).

Chain-Stitch Darning is used for sweaters and other knitted garments, as it reproduces the knitted stitch (stockinette). Lightly steam-press the damaged area. Clear away (pick out) worn stitches around holes, so you have straight edges. Use matching yarn and darning needle. Work from right side. Run yarn invisibly through surrounding area, then work it crosswise across hole, one line to a row, as shown (25).

Starting at top, chain-stitch down across threads, as shown (26). Run thread back invisibly, over and under, to top, and start second row. Repeat until hole is filled. Steam-press.

PATCHES

A patch is used for mending a large hole or tear, or with washable fabrics where darning would not be strong enough. Fabric must match. If garment has faded, the patch may be faded by washing in soap suds and baking soda and drying in the sun. Bear the following in mind for *any* patching:

1. It is **always** done on straight grain, the damaged area being trimmed all around to make a square or rectangular hole, strictly following lines of weave or design.

2. Patch must be cut on exactly the same grain and placed so that lengthwise and crosswise threads match the surrounding area. With a design, match it before cutting out patch.

3. Use matching thread.

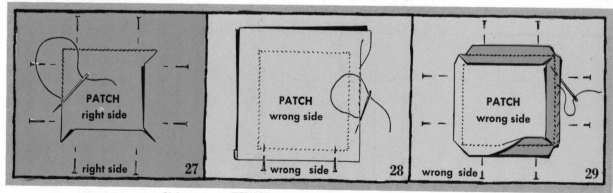

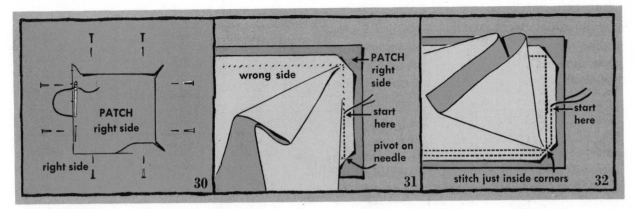

Hemmed Patch—Cut patch 1″ larger than hole on all sides. Pin it under hole with right side showing through. Make a ¼″ diagonal clip into each corner of hole. Turn under raw edges of hole around sides and press carefully.

• Hand-hem edges to patch with fine, invisible stitches (27), taking several stitches at corners.

• On washable articles, trim patch edges to ½″, turn under and hem down (28). On others, trim to ¼″ and hem raw edge lightly in place.

• For a flat, almost invisible patch, trim away patch seam allowances to about ¼″; trim off corners; then press seams open. Overcast raw edges (29).

Set-In Patch (hand or machine)—Install in place exactly like the hemmed patch above.

Instead of hemming the edges down, slip-baste in place, as shown (30): take ¼″ stitches alternately in edge-fold and in patch, always putting needle in at point exactly opposite the one where it came out.

• Fold garment fabric back as shown (31) and stitch on wrong side along line of basting, pivoting at corners (this can also be done by hand).

• For additional strength, make a second line of stitching ⅛″ from first, through the two seam allowances, stitching across corners as shown (32). Trim away fabric to about ¼″ around patch.

• This patch can also be top-stitched in place (33).

• If you want the patch to be inconspicuous, stop after making the first line of stitching (31), trim away patch seam allowances to ¼″, trim off corners, and press seams open as shown in ill. 29. Overcast raw edges.

Darned-In Patch—This is a flat, inconspicuous and fairly sturdy patch, good in wool and similar fabrics. Cut patch to fit hole exactly and baste patch to a piece of net extending 1″ on all sides. Place patch in hole from wrong side, face down, and pin net to surrounding fabric (34). Darn the raw edges together all around (35) following instructions given under DARNING.

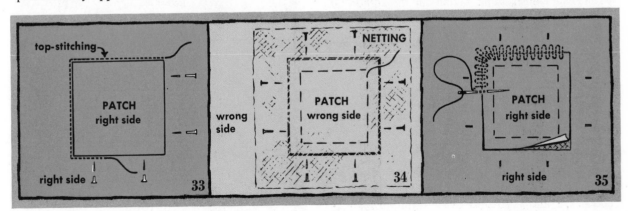

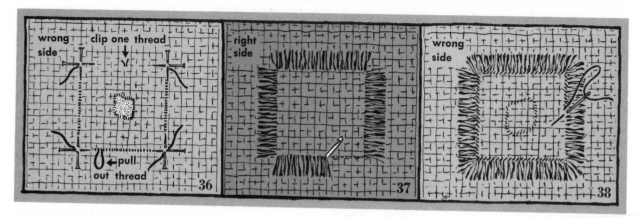

Woven-In Patch (for loosely-woven wool)

Woven-In Patch (for loosely-woven wool)—This is not fitted into an opening, but placed on top of the damaged area. It is neat and quick, and is particularly good for small holes, such as moth holes or cigarette burns.

• Work on wrong side. Around hole, mark out a straight-grain square with pins at each corner. This will be the size of the patch. With pointed scissors clip through **one** thread at center of each side of square, as shown. Draw out these threads as far as the corner pins (36). This is the outline for the patch.

• Out of matching fabric, cut a square 1″ larger on all sides than marked-out square. Draw threads out on all four edges until you have center exactly matching outline (be accurate!), surrounded by an inch of fringe.

• Pin patch to right side of garment, matching outline. Using a fine metal crochet hook, draw a raveled thread-end to wrong side through each corner of outline. Then draw the rest of the ravelings through to wrong side along outline, taking one thread at a time and advancing one thread at a time (37).

• Fasten fringe in place on wrong side with fine hemming stitches along outline (38). Steam-press.

TURNING COLLAR AND CUFFS

Turning a collar and French cuffs, which fray long before the rest of the shirt or blouse shows wear, is as good as getting a new shirt or blouse.

• Fold collar (or cuff) carefully in half and place pins as shown (39, 40), in collar and neckband, and in cuff and sleeve, all placed close to the seamline. On neck-band, mark positions of front collar edges with pins.

• Carefully take out stitching attaching collar to neckband or cuff to sleeve. Remove all thread scraps.

• Reverse collar and reinsert into neckband, matching center pins. Baste through all thicknesses along original seamline, matching ends to front pins (39). Machine-stitch on inside of band over old stitching line.

• Reverse cuff and insert sleeve-edge into it as before, matching pins (40). Baste and stitch as for collar, on outside of sleeve.

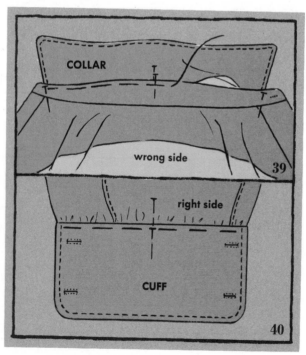

TAILORING

The word tailoring defines itself: it means sewing, not like a dressmaker but like a tailor—a term that immediately brings to mind garments, mainly suits and coats, of firm shape, excellent fit, precise outline, and perfect detailing; containing a great amount of inside, invisible work. Because tailoring is work—let's accept that fact. It calls for more **preparation** than ordinary dressmaking, and more **fitting;** for considerable **hand-sewing** as you go along; for **accuracy;** for careful **pressing** every step of the way. All this is time-consuming, though not necessarily difficult. But a tailored garment is, or should be, a lasting garment. It is always designed along simple, classic lines, not according to some in-and-out fashion; its construction preserves its shape; and you will certainly have chosen durable fabric for such a project. Last but by no means least, your pride of achievement will be immense, and your pleasure in your garment will be with you a long time.

WHAT MAN-TAILORING MEANS

There seems to be considerable vagueness in the minds of even experienced sewers as to what exactly is the difference between man-tailoring and the dressmaker's tailoring that goes into any suit, dress, or coat with interfaced lapels, collar, etc.

In man-tailoring (which hereafter shall be referred to simply as tailoring) the garment is literally constructed on the interfacing, parts of which are shaped by pad-stitching. The aim is absolute firmness of shape. True tailoring is hand-tailoring, because only by doing the pad-stitching by hand can collar and lapels be shaped so that, when laid on a flat surface, they will not flatten out. Machine-tailoring (which we shall describe in its place for those who dislike hand sewing), takes less time, of course, but gives only firmness, not shape; moreover, because of its more conspicuous character, it cannot take care of lapels.

To return to what makes a tailored garment:

• The interfacing fabric is firmer. Hair-canvas, for instance, unless very lightweight, is used only in man-tailoring.

• The interfacing in a coat or jacket is cut for a larger area of the garment, often taking in the armholes.

• By means of seaming, stay-tapes, pad-stitching and pressing, the interfacing is given permanent shape (if it has been hand-tailored, it will not be possible to flatten out that part of the garment).

With the shape so firmly established, it follows that the fit must be perfect. Tailoring calls for considerable precision. We would not, therefore, suggest that you tackle this type of tailoring, unless you have had some successful experience with general sewing and with dressmaker's tailoring.

WHAT YOU WORK WITH

EQUIPMENT

The only extra equipment you will need is pressing equipment. Important as pressing is in dressmaking, it is twice as important in tailoring. We presume you already have most of the articles listed on page 67. If not, a sleeve-board, a pressing ham, a point-presser, all described and illustrated there, now become necessities. Other tailoring pressing aids are:

Pressing Mitt (1)—Can be used instead of a pressing ham. It goes over your hand for steaming curves or over end of sleeve board for pressing sleeve caps.

Clapper, also called a **Beater** or **Pounding Block** (2) —A wooden block about 9″ long, that, clapped down for a few seconds over a just-steamed edge or seam, will make a knife-sharp crease without causing a shine. While not an absolute necessity, it is extremely useful. Some point pressers have a bottom designed to be used as a clapper (p. 67).

Tailor Board (3)—A board with various different-shaped surfaces for pressing points, curves and flat parts. It allows any stitched part to be, not just pressed, but effectively shaped and molded. For pressing, it has a padded cover (3). Uncovered, it can be used with a clapper (4).

PATTERN

One or two of the pattern companies have designs meant for tailoring, with tailoring instructions; most, however, do not. With the help of the directions that follow, you can add tailoring to a garment, but only if the design lends itself to it; the collar of a "tailored-looking" dress, for instance, can be tailored by pad-stitching the undercollar as shown on p. 185. If the design of the dress in general is of a type to make this suitable, the pattern will usually call for interfacing and lining and often for a backing (underlining). For a jacket or coat that can be tailored, the fabrics indicated on the pattern envelope will be medium- to heavy-weight and will include woolens; often there will be a separate pattern for interfacing.

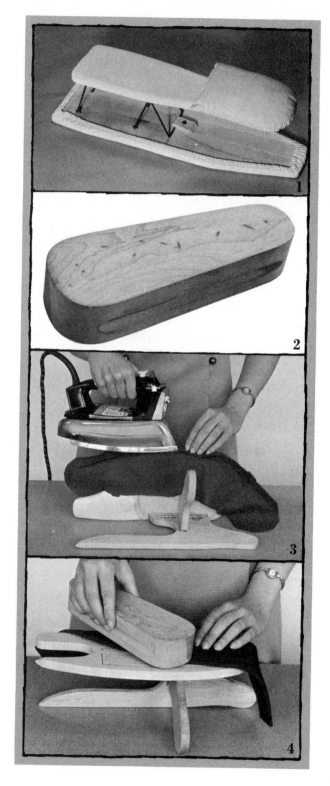

Check and adjust your pattern (pp. 132-144) even more carefully than usual, including length. If the style is one you have not worn before, you would be well-advised to make a trial muslin, especially if your fabric is expensive. Adapt the directions under MAKING A MUSLIN BASIC on p. 145 to making a muslin for your particular garment. Remember the extra thickness of backing, interfacing, lining, perhaps interlining, and be extra-careful not to "overfit". Making such a trial garment before buying your fabric may also save you some expensive yardage.

FABRIC

Buy fabric worthy of all the work you are about to put into it—in other words, the best you can afford. See BUYING FABRIC, p. 70. If the pattern envelope says that diagonal fabrics are not suitable for this design, remember that twill and gabardine (very tempting for tailoring) are diagonals, and avoid them. Firmly-woven fabrics are in general preferable, but tweeds, among other good fabrics, are often loosely woven and are still suitable—only they must be made firm with backing. Bonded fabrics do not shape well and should not be used for tailoring.

Consult PREPARING FABRIC FOR USE on p. 71. Make sure that the fabric grain is straight, that your fabric is preshrunk. If there is the slightest doubt in your mind on that score, it will do no harm to shrink it a second time. Just do not expose yourself to having the garment shrink after it is finished and you have it dry-cleaned.

BACKING (UNDERLINING)

Backing is necessary with any fabric that is soft or loosely woven. You will find useful information on backings in the chapter by that name, but the method of handling it is slightly different in tailoring, as you will see. Whether or not you use backing when the outer fabric does not absolutely demand it, is a matter of personal preference (for more or less body), of style and of cost. In selecting your backing, **consider the weight and thickness of outer fabric, backing and interfacing as a whole.**

Lightweight muslin, cheaper than special backing fabrics, makes an excellent backing. The number of threads per square inch (shown on bolt) indicates the quality—the higher the number the finer the muslin. If you prefer a backing that matches the color of your outer fabric—important when a loosely-woven fabric may let the color show through—choose one of the many special backing or underlining fabrics that are on the market.

If you add backing when the pattern does not specify it, use the same yardage indications as for outer fabric (taking fabric widths into account). If you back only part of the garment, you will of course need that much less.

It is of the utmost importance that backing fabrics will not shrink. Many of the backings on the market are preshrunk and are clearly marked as such (if in doubt, shrink the fabric). Muslin must always be shrunk (see p. 71).

Whether or not you use muslin as a regular backing, you will need 1 yard for reinforcing garment back (p. 183) and for interfacing hem edges (p. 191).

INTERFACING FABRIC

This essential of tailoring cannot be chosen with too much care. See the chapter on INTERFACING for general information. For tailoring, the fabric must have "give" to be shaped and manipulated, and therefore must be of a **woven** (not non-woven or iron-on) type. The most suitable is hair canvas. It comes in a variety of weights and qualities, depending on fiber content—the higher the hair content, (goat's hair) the better the quality. Interfacing must never be heavier than outer fabric. Regardless of what the label says, always preshrink interfacing by steaming, letting the steam penetrate well.

LINING

The inside of a tailored coat or jacket, with its various reinforcements, looks messy, and is always finished with a lining. Select a smooth, pliable fabric, light enough in weight so as not to interfere with the hang of the garment. Crepe, taffeta and satin of silk, rayon or synthetics, china silk, smooth cottons (for sports clothes), all make good linings. If you decide to line a winter garment with fleece or wool, you will still want a smooth fabric in the sleeves for easy slipping on and off. A smooth finish, plus warmth, are combined in quilted fabrics and in certain other fabrics which are satin-finished on one side and MILIUM®-coated for insulation on the other. These fabrics are handled like lining.

INTERLINING

Interlining is for warmth and warmth only. Usually made of loosely-woven wool, sometimes fleece (very expensive), it is generally added to the lining like a backing. Fabrics such as quilting, that combine lining and interlining, are handled like lining.

NOTIONS

The one notion that is special to tailoring is the stay-tape of cotton twill, ⅜″ wide, which prevents stretching and reduces bulk along front edges (p. 179). . . . Even if the tape is labelled pre-shrunk, shrink it before use. To do this, remove wrappings, but leave tape on card. Immerse the whole thing in water. Take out; bend card slightly as shown (5) and allow to dry. Some pattern directions suggest seam binding as stay-tape, to be stitched in the seams. This, however, is not a real tailoring technique.

For the **hand-sewing** to be done in tailoring, use a short needle (No. 7 or 8 Betweens). A short needle gives better control in picking up the tiny amounts of fabric required in pad-stitching and blind-stitching. And if you have not acquired the habit of wearing a thimble, this is the time to do so: sewing heavy or resistant materials without a thimble is terribly hard on the fingers.

HOW YOU WORK

A certain state of mind is necessary for successful and, especially, cheerful tailoring. It involves a readiness to take time and never rush a thing; to take pains, to be accurate. Try on the garment at various stages of construction to make sure that a step is right **before** it can no longer be corrected (see **Fitting,** p. 179). When you are not working on the garment, or on the separate garment parts, hang or pin them on a padded hanger. Avoid unnecessary pressing by avoiding unnecessary handling. After steam-pressing, let garment cool (dry) before handling it further.

CUTTING

Press out center crease; re-fold fabric on grain for cutting. If, through having been folded right-side-out on the bolt, the fabric has acquired a soiled or discolored crease line, avoid this line when laying out the pattern.

Cutting must be done with quite special accuracy.

If fabric is very thick or spongy . . .

• Trim off pattern margins, if any (**not** seam allowances) before laying out pieces.

• Make sure that pins go through both layers of fabric—you may have to use longer (glass head) pins.

• On folded fabric, cut top layer of fabric first, then bottom layer, following cut edge—this is easier than cutting pieces separately in a single thickness (6).

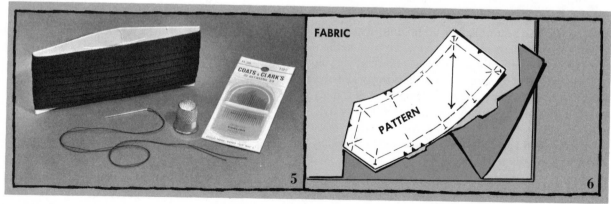

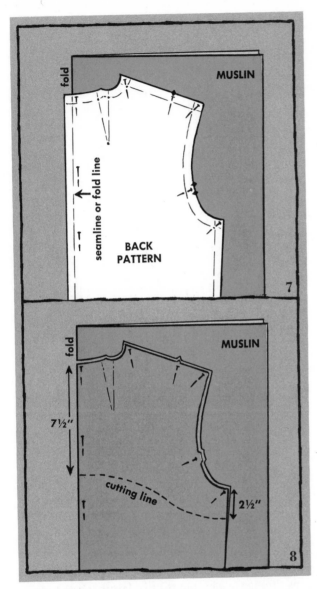

If there is no pattern for a **muslin reinforcement** for a coat or jacket back, cut one as follows: Use back pattern piece. Place on **folded muslin** even if garment has a **center back seam** (7). Cut around neck, shoulder and armhole edges and about 2½″ down along side seam. Remove pattern. On muslin, measure and mark 7½″ down from neck edge; measure and mark 2½″ down from bottom of armhole. Connect these marks with a curved line, as shown (8). Cut out.

Cut **backing** from garment pattern. Unless fabric weave is exceptionally loose, undercollar is not backed, and collar and facing only if interfacing would otherwise show through.

If your fabric is very bulky or loosely woven, you may use taffeta in matching color or lining fabric for undercollar and for cuff and pocket-flap facings.

BASTING

Two kinds of basting are special to tailoring. Use light-colored thread as usual (see p. 20).

Tailor-basting (9) is the diagonal basting shown on p. 21, but is used for attaching entire areas of fabric together. It is worked in up-and-down rows, with fabric flat on a table. Start with a short backstitch rather than a knot. Make diagonal stitches about 2″ long, right-to-left stitches short, and place rows 3″ to 4″ apart. Avoid putting a row directly over darts or buttonholes.

Tailor-basting is left in until the garment is finished except for the lining. It is removed before final pressing.

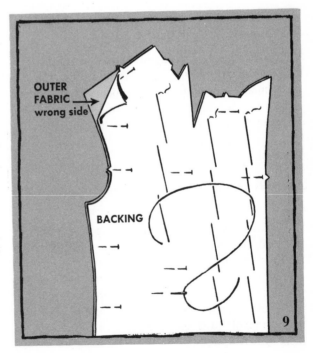

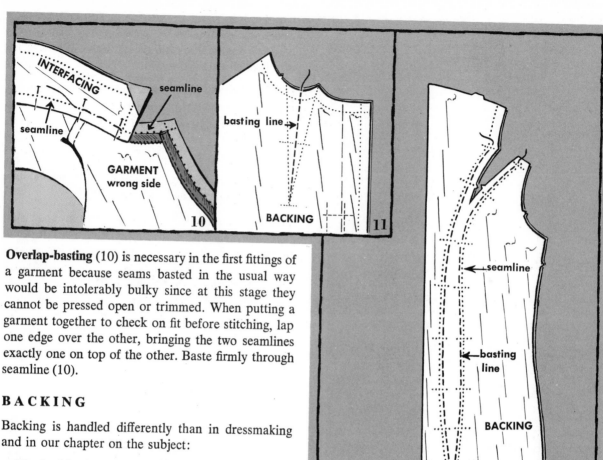

Overlap-basting (10) is necessary in the first fittings of a garment because seams basted in the usual way would be intolerably bulky since at this stage they cannot be pressed open or trimmed. When putting a garment together to check on fit before stitching, lap one edge over the other, bringing the two seamlines exactly one on top of the other. Baste firmly through seamline (10).

BACKING

Backing is handled differently than in dressmaking and in our chapter on the subject:

• The backing is marked only **after** it has been accurately lined up with the outer fabric section; if previously-marked backing were to be used, important markings such as buttonholes and pockets, might occur in the wrong place on the outer section.

• It is attached to the garment, not by stitching around, but by overall tailor-basting (see p. 175).

To apply backing, spread out garment section wrong side up:

. . . On front sections, match backing to garment at front edges (along fold line if there is an extended facing); pin edges together. Smooth out the two layers; pin together at notches, corners and various points over the entire area. Begin tailor-basting down the front edge and work across the section, but avoid the buttonhole area and, if possible, the place where there will be darts.

. . . On back and sleeve sections, where straight grain runs through center, pin the two layers together down the center, matching curved edges. Smooth out toward sides. Tailor-baste from center out. If there is a seam at center back, match side seam edges and work toward center back. Trim away any excess on backing fabric to make all edges even.

After backing is marked (see next paragraph) baste darts to outer fabric to hold the two layers of fabric together for further handling. Use hand- or machine-basting as shown: a straight dart is basted through center (11), a curved dart just inside seamline (12).

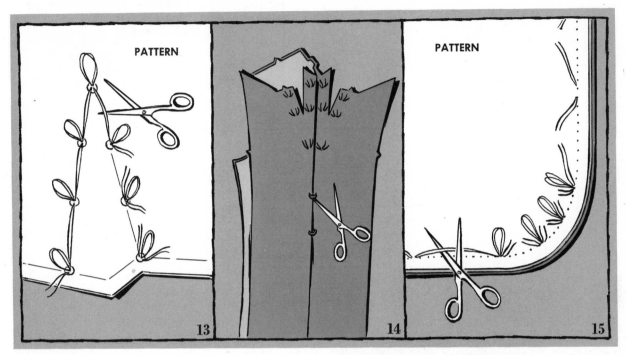

MARKING

As indicated in the chapter on MARKING, backing and lining can be marked with dressmaker's carbon paper; muslin and interfacing with carbon paper or blue pencil. An outer fabric used in a tailored garment, however, is almost always of a texture that requires thread-marking, mostly with tailor's tacks (see p. 122). To mark lines, use the following variations of tailor's tacks:

• **On short lines,** make a loop at beginning of line; take a 2″ to 3″ long stitch along line of marking and make another loop. (On darts, for instance, make loops at matching dots, 13.) Continue along line in same manner. Clip the long stitches between loops (13), then remove pattern. Separate the two thicknesses of fabric and cut through threads as shown (14).

• **On long lines,** the loops can be omitted. Make the stitches 3″ to 5″ long. Clip as shown (15) and remove pattern. When separating two thicknesses of fabric, be careful not to pull fabric off thread-ends.

• Sometimes the two methods can be used together. For instance, on a front section that ends in a curve, omit loops on straight edge, but make loops around curve, fairly close together (15).

If you have no backing, mark front sections as follows after cutting out:

... Darts, pockets and construction-markings with tailor's tacks.

... Front and neck seamline with tailor's tacks at one-inch intervals.

... Center front line and buttonholes with baste-marking: at center front put pins through both layers (see **Pins,** p. 123) at wide intervals. For buttonholes put pins through each end in right-hand side of garment only. With ruler, check straightness of center front line and straightness and intervals of buttonholes.

Baste-mark (by hand or machine) center front lines and buttonholes on right side.

If you have a backing, after cutting out and tailor-basting backing sections to garment sections, replace pattern over backing and mark all details, including front and neck seamlines. Baste-mark center front lines and buttonhole markings through to right side.

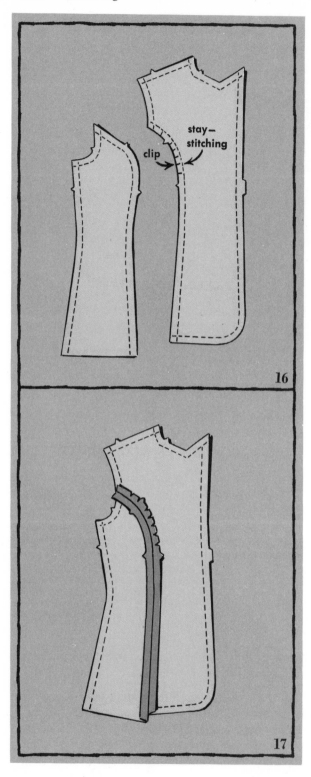

16

17

CURVED SEAMS

Before basting curved seams together, clip **concave curve** to stay-stitching (16). This will allow the seam allowance at curve to spread so that the seam can be basted and stitched (17).

PRESSING

Pressing is done as usual (see that chapter), but in tailoring takes on quite particular importance.

Press each part of garment as it is stitched, using the proper piece of equipment to give it the right curve and shape. Do not press too heavily. After steam-pressing, allow fabric to cool (dry) before handling. Handle fabric as little as possible.

All seams, even edge seams such as collar and front facing seams, should be pressed open (underpressed) over a point presser (18), to have a really sharp edge when they are pressed together afterwards.

18

When pressing on right side of fabric, always use a press cloth, even with a steam iron. When doing final outside pressing on wool, use a piece of garment fabric. If more steam is needed than the iron produces, put a damp press cloth over the woolen one.

FITTING

Fittings are more frequent than in dressmaking. Make sure darts are right before you slash them open. This is especially important in curved darts; also in curved seams that are stitched as darts (p. 176, ill. 12) before they are slashed open to form seams. Such checking can be done at the first fitting (p. 183), with garment-parts overlap-basted together. Wear whatever you plan to wear under the finished garment, or something similar. Pin garment opening closed to top buttonhole. If possible, use a full-length mirror.

THE FRONT INTERFACING

With the handling of the interfacing we come to the very crux of tailoring.

In order to avoid bulk, some patterns have the interfacing cut without seam allowance along front, neck and shoulder edges. Wherever there **is** a seam allowance, mark seamline. Mark darts, if any, and construction markings.

Darts—To avoid the bulkiness of a seam, cut along one side of dart to point (19). Lap cut edge over opposite side to seamline. Secure with two lines of stitching ⅛″ from cut edge. Trim close to stitching (20). If interfacing is very loosely woven, reinforce point with a piece of fabric stitched over it.

Front Edge—At front edge, if seam allowance is present, it should be cut away in order to reduce bulk. For reinforcement, stay-tape or a strip of lightweight fabric (organdy or backing) is then added. With stay-tape, which does not extend into seam allowance,

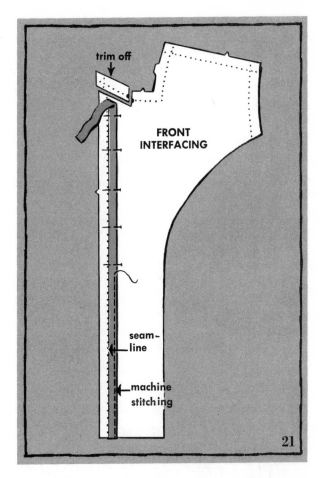

interfacing is attached to the garment by **hand;** with fabric strip, which extends to form a new, lighter seam allowance, interfacing is attached by **machine** when the facing is being applied.

When you are ready to stitch the facing in place, stitch on the **interfacing** side: Use the edge of the stay-tape or the edge of the **interfacing** (if fabric strip was used) as a guide for stitching.

TWILL-TAPE REINFORCEMENT
(interfacing prepared by machine, applied by hand)

Whether you have a **separate facing** or an **extended facing,** begin by trimming away top edge of interfacing (21) from corner to the mark for attaching collar, ¼″ below seamline (or cut edge if there is no seam allowance).

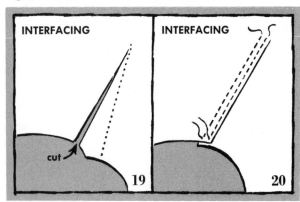

WITH SEPARATE FACING—Pin preshrunk tape along front edge of interfacing (21), keeping outer edge of tape just clear of seamline (or cut edge if there is no seam allowance) so that machine needle will stitch clear of it when facing is applied later on. At top, let tape extend an inch or so beyond trimmed edge.

If garment front ends in a curve, tape can be attached in two ways, depending on degree of curve:

. . . *Slight curve*—"Swirl," i.e., steam-press part of tape into a curve before applying (22).

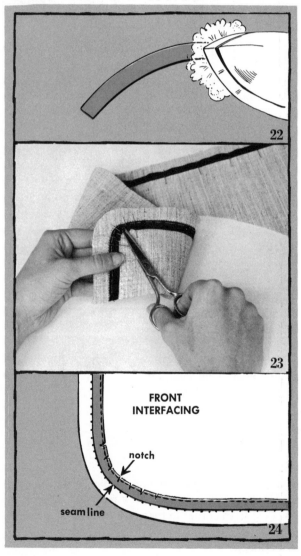

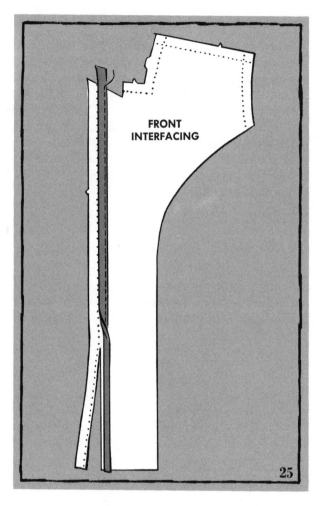

. . . *Sharp curve*—carefully baste outer edge of tape along line of application, then notch inner edge of tape around curve (23), i.e., remove excess fullness at the edge by cutting out little V's. Steam-press flat before machine-stitching (24).

Machine-stitch inner edge of tape to interfacing (25). Under tape, trim away interfacing edge ¼″ from seamline (or cut edge) as shown (25).

Pin interfacing to wrong side of front garment section, over backing if there is one, matching all notches, marks and edges at neck, shoulder and armhole; along front edge, keep tape just clear of seamline on outer fabric or backing. Starting along front edge, tailor-baste interfacing in place.

At top, trim end of tape to just clear of seamline on outer section. Add a short piece of tape as shown (26) from edge of long tape to the mark for attaching collar. Pin, keeping top edge of tape just clear of seamline. Blind-stitch lower edge to interfacing, being careful to pick up only interfacing, not outer fabric, with your needle.

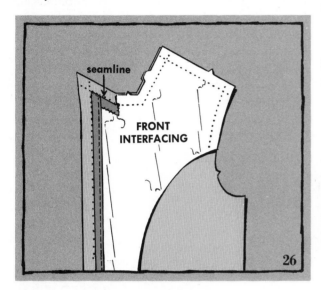

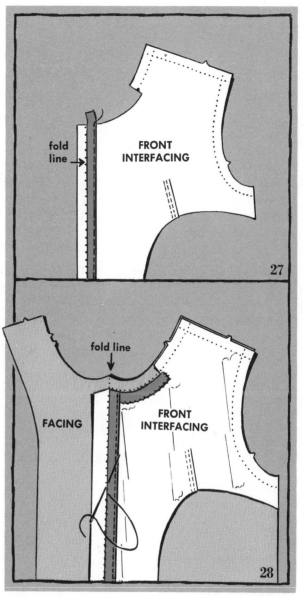

If there is no lapel (i.e., if the upper part of garment front is designed to be worn closed, or either open or closed). Blind-stitch all free tape edges to outer fabric or backing, using thread to match outer fabric. Always keep clear of seamlines. Pick up no more than one thread in outer fabric with each stitch.

If there is a lapel (i.e., if the upper part of garment front is designed to be worn open), leave tape edges unattached until after **roll line** on collar and lapels has been established (roll line may be printed on pattern, but this happens seldom) and taped, and lapels pad-stitched (p. 187).

WITH EXTENDED FACING—Interfacing may have an extra ⅝″. or so along front edge, meant to be folded to give body to the edge in the absence of seam allowances. Pin preshrunk tape along this fold line, outer edge even with it, or with cut edge if there is no such extension. At neck, let tape extend an inch or so beyond trimmed edge. Machine-stitch inner edge of tape to interfacing (27).

Pin and tailor-baste interfacing to front garment section as for separate facing (p. 180), matching tape edge exactly to fold line on outer fabric or backing. At top, trim end of tape just clear of seamline on outer fabric or backing. Blind-stitch free edge of tape to fold line, picking up no more than one thread in outer fabric with each stitch. Add a short piece of tape to neck edge as for separate facing (28).

FABRIC STRIP REINFORCEMENT
(all-machine application)

Use backing or any other firm, lightweight fabric.

If interfacing seam allowance is given—Pin front interfacing pattern to fabric, matching grain. Cut along front and neck edge, and for about 3″ along bottom and shoulder edges. Remove pattern; measure and mark 3″ back from cut edges; cut along this mark. Lay strip on interfacing, matching notches and outer edges. Be sure to make a right and a left side. Make two lines of stitching, one ¾″ inside front edge, the second the width of the presser foot in from first (29). (A line of multiple zigzag stitching can be done instead of the two lines of stitching.) Trim away ⅝″ of interfacing, as shown (29). On reverse side, trim fabric to ¼″ from second stitching line (30).

If interfacing seam allowance is not given—Pin interfacing pattern to fabric, and mark seamline along front, lapel and neck edges (31). Remove pattern. Make a mark ⅝″ **outside** seamline and another 2″ **inside** seamline (32). Cut out. Pin interfacing to fabric strip, matching front and neck edges of interfacing to seamline on strip. Be sure to make a right and a left side. Make two lines of stitching, one ⅛″ from interfacing edge, the second the width of the foot away. On reverse side, trim fabric to about ¼″ from second stitching line.

Pin interfacing to wrong side of garment section, outer edges even. Starting along front edge, tailor-baste interfacing in place.

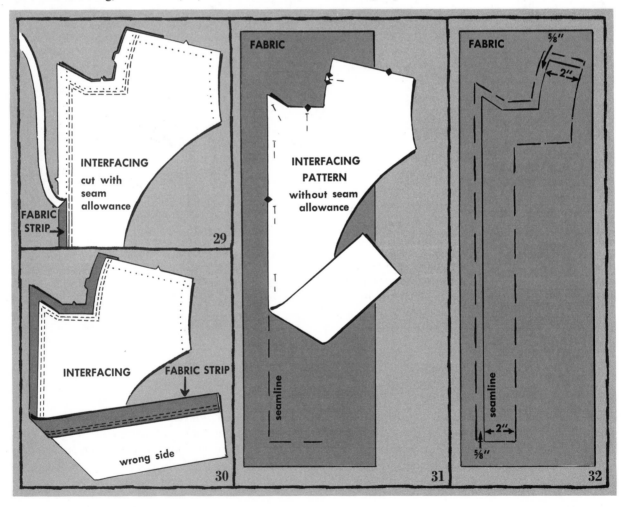

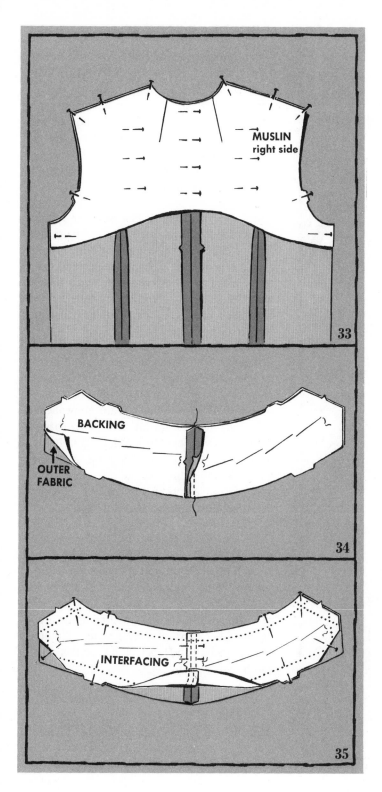

BACK REINFORCEMENT

You have cut this out of muslin according to instructions under Cutting (p. 168). After center-back seam (if any) and darts in outer fabric have been stitched and pressed, stitch darts in muslin and press in opposite direction. With wrong sides together, pin muslin to outer section, matching center-back lines. Pin to entire area from center out (33). Tailor-baste.

FIRST FITTING

Follow pattern instruction sheet for preparing sleeves. Prepare and shrink sleeve-cap as described in the chapter SLEEVES. Carefully overlap-baste garment seams together, putting in at least one sleeve. Have a thorough fitting and make whatever adjustments necessary before stitching, slashing, and pressing darts and seams. Mark sleeve length.

UNDERCOLLAR AND LAPEL

If backing is used on undercollar, tailor-baste backing to wrong side of outer section. If undercollar is in two sections, join center seam and press open; trim backing seam allowance close to stitching; trim fabric seam allowance to about ¼ ″ (34).

On interfacing mark seamlines. To join the two sections, avoid bulk by lapping one side over the other, matching seamlines. Make two lines of stitching ⅛ ″ apart. Trim close to stitching. Trim off outer corners ⅛ ″ inside seamline. Place over wrong side of undercollar, marked side out, matching notches, etc. Pin. Working from one end to the other, tailor-baste layers together through center with one row of 1″-long stitches (35).

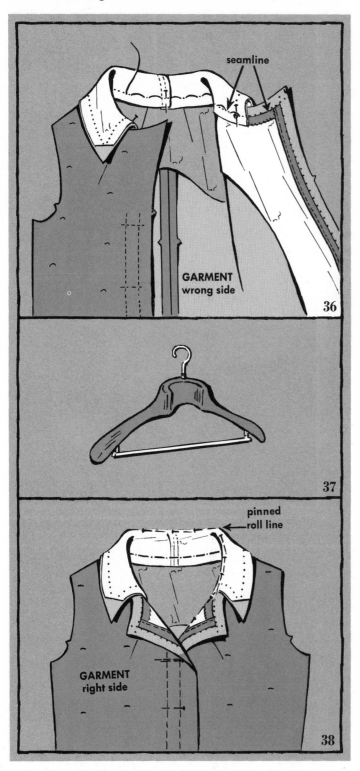

seamline

GARMENT
wrong side

36

37

pinned
roll line

GARMENT
right side

38

TO ESTABLISH ROLL LINE

Establishing the roll line is of the utmost importance. If line is not marked on pattern undercollar must be temporarily attached to garment. Starting at center back, lap right side of undercollar over wrong side of garment at neck edge, matching seamlines; pin with a vertical pin on inside; do the same at front points and shoulder seams. Overlap-baste on seamline, easing as necessary (36).

The roll is best established **on your person;** this necessitates having someone help you. The next best thing is a **dress form** in your size. In the absence of both helper and dress form, place garment on a **man's suit hanger** with fully-shaped shoulder and neck (37) and make very sure that shoulder seams are in correct position.

Pin garment front together to top buttonhole and let lapels (if any) and collar roll back. Now make sure that outer edge of collar—the **finished** edge, deduct seam allowance!—will cover neck seam (at present the basted seamline) by at least ½″. (Make doubly sure of this if you are working on a clothes hanger.) Depending on the style, the collar may of course spread way beyond ½″, but the **edge must not fall short of that.**

Once the roll is established, place a row of pins exactly along roll line (soft fold) of collar and lapel (if any) as shown (38). If you are working alone, try on garment and make sure that the roll is to your liking and the neck seam at back is well covered. Pad-stitching is the means of making sure that the finished collar (and lapel) will keep this shape and fit when worn.

Remove undercollar from garment. Since pins tend to fall out during work, replace them with a line of basting along roll line, making sure that the two halves of collar are symmetrical. Do the same on lapels.

PAD-STITCHING

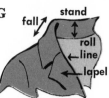

Pad-stitching is the next step. It can be done by hand or by machine.

Hand pad-stitching does by far the better job because it allows the section actually to be shaped, so that it does not flatten out when laid down. While working, hold section over your hand in the shape it will have when worn (39). The stitch, motion and direction are the same as in tailor-basting, but the padding stitch (40), much smaller and closer, stays in the finished garment. It must not show through on outside of fabric. Work on interfacing side. Use thread to match outer fabric and a shorter-than-usual needle (No. 7 or 8 Betweens). Start with a small backstitch, not a knot. Make the diagonal stitches about ⅜″ long and the right-to-left straight stitches very small, just catching a thread of outer fabric through interfacing. Make next row ⅜″ away. **Do not pad-stitch seam allowance**—stop stitches just short of seamline. Lapels can be pad-stitched only by hand. (Ideally these stitches will be invisible on the outer fabric. In lightweight fabrics, however, the stitch may be slightly perceptible and the padding as a whole will produce a surface impression on the outer fabric.)

. . . **Collar stand** (inner part of collar)—Make a row of pad-stitching along line of roll. Always holding collar in the shape it will have when worn, make next rows parallel to first until you reach neck seamline (41).

. . . **Collar fall** (outer part of collar)—Start at center back seam at roll line. Making stitches slightly larger and farther apart than on the stand, work toward outer seamline of collar, following grain-line of interfacing, as shown (42), and still keeping collar shaped over your hand. Cover entire area in this manner.

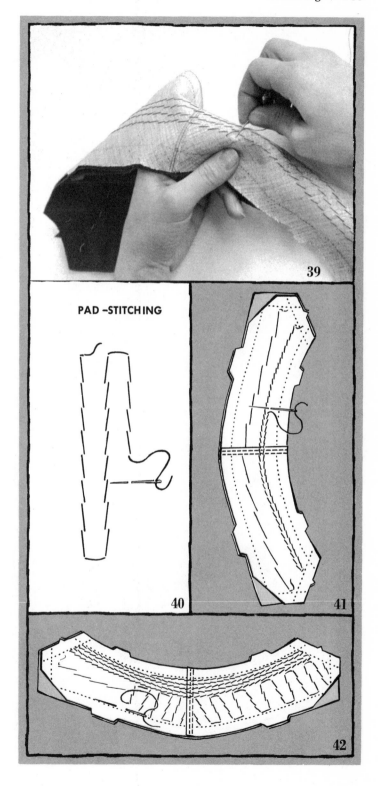

PAD-STITCHING

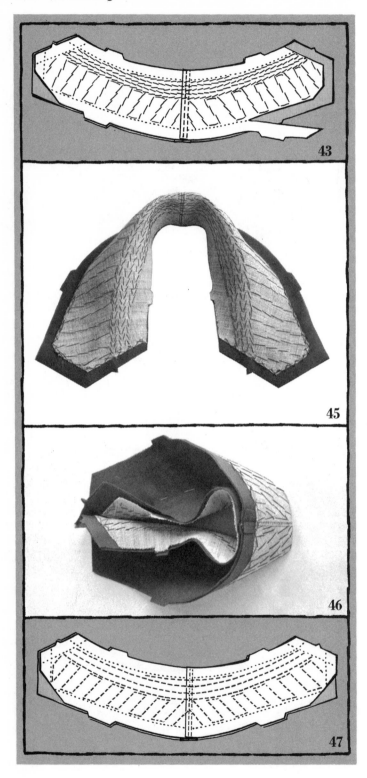

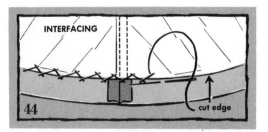

Trim away interfacing seam allowance close to seamline at ends and outer edge of collar, as shown (43). Catch-stitch cut edge to outer fabric (or backing if you have one). If there is no backing, be careful to pick up no more than a thread in outer fabric. Place stitches about ½″ apart and do not pull them up tight (44).

Press, using ham for shaping. Photograph (45) shows the collar completely finished and ready for the next stage in construction. Pin front edges together and keep pinned and upside down as shown (46) until you are ready to attach section to garment (after pad-stitching, collar should never lie open, which tends to flatten it; even if you are interrupted while pad-stitching, pin front together in the same way).

MACHINE PAD-STITCHING, or machine-tailoring, merely reinforces undercollar without shaping it. A lapel cannot be pad-stitched by machine. If machine-tailoring (which of course is quicker) is used, it is omitted on lapels.

. . . **Collar stand** (inner part of collar)—make first row of stitching along roll line, and succeeding rows the width of presser foot apart, working toward neck seamline (47).

. . . **Collar fall** (outer part of collar)—Start at center back seam at roll line. Following grain of interfacing stitch to outer seamline, then along seamline for ½″ to ¾″; pivot and repeat in the other direction. Continue as shown to front of collar, always following grain. Then repeat on other half of collar, starting again at center (47).

TAPING AND PAD-STITCHING LAPEL

Taping and pad-stitching lapel has been referred to under "If there is a lapel" on p. 181. You were instructed to leave the stay-tape unattached to garment along front and top edges.

Taping roll line (fold) of a lapel is done to prevent stretching. Place tape as shown (48), with one edge along basted roll line. Blind-stitch edges to interfacing, being careful not to stitch through garment fabric. Cut tape-ends diagonally as shown, just short of neck seamline (48) and even with edge of front tape.

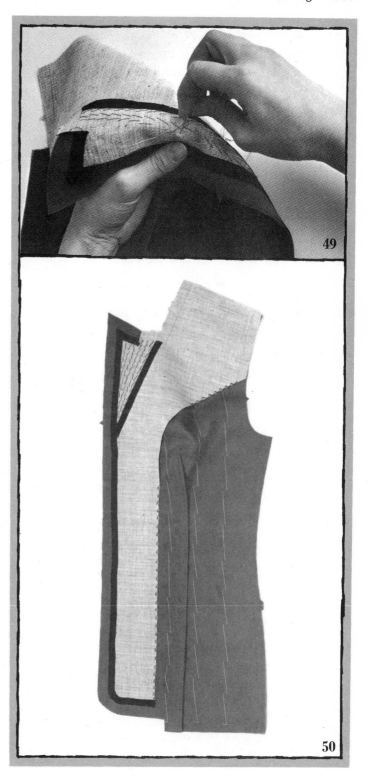

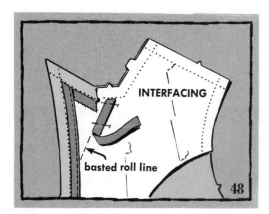

Pad-stitching in this area can be done by hand only; if you are machine-tailoring, omit it. Start at roll line and fill in lapel with parallel lines, holding it over your hand to the shape it will have when worn (49). Press carefully, using ham to maintain shape.

Blind-stitch free edges of stay-tape to outer fabric or backing along front and top, being careful to pick up no more than one thread in garment fabric with each stitch.

Catch-stitch free edge of interfacing loosely to backing or outer fabric, leaving curved part around bust area unattached, as shown (50). Be sure your thread matches outer fabric.

BUTTONHOLES

Tailored garments practically always take a bound buttonhole—see BUTTONHOLES. For heavy fabrics, the patch method (pp. 36-37, **Patch Buttonhole**) is best because the wider seam allowance makes handling easier.

BUTTONHOLES IN HEAVY INTERFACING

The heavier interfacing fabrics used in tailoring are often too bulky to be included in the buttonholes. In such a case, the buttonholes are made **before** the interfacing is applied, and openings are then cut in the interfacing to accommodate the buttonhole patches.

If there is a backing, it is sufficient interfacing. Otherwise, each buttonhole is individually interfaced with a patch of light interfacing fabric, such as organdy; or with lightweight iron-on interfacing if garment fabric allows it.

• For each buttonhole, cut a piece of lightweight interfacing 1″ wide and 1″ longer than buttonhole. Baste or iron to wrong side of each buttonhole location.

• Make buttonholes.

• Apply interfacing as instructed on pp. 180, 181.

• Put a pin through each end of buttonhole from right side through to interfacing. With pencil and ruler, measure about ⅜″ out from pins on all four sides, and mark out a rectangle as shown (51).

• Cut out rectangle, slightly rounding corners. Slip buttonhole patch through opening (52) and catch-stitch edges loosely to interfacing all around.

FINISH FACED WITH LIGHTWEIGHT FABRIC

In tailoring heavy fabrics, we especially recommend this finish on the under or facing side of the buttonhole. It is suitable in all cases, but if you prefer another method, see page 38.

Finishing is done after the facing has been attached along front seam (if facing is separate), but **before** stitching lapel and collar. You may, here, have to depart from pattern instructions if they call for as-

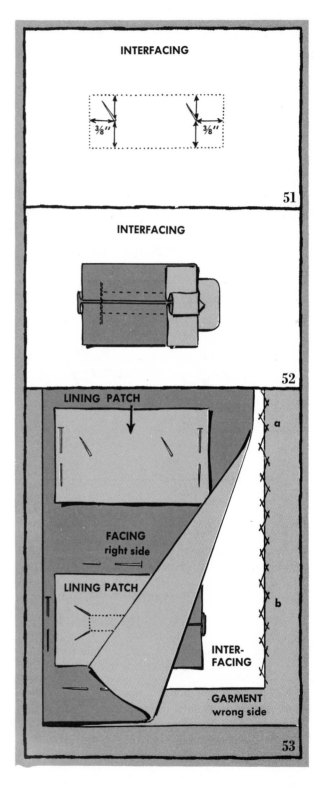

sembling upper collar and frontfacings and then attaching them in one operation.

Use very lightweight fabric in matching color. Organdy is excellent; your backing or lining fabric may be right if it does not fray.

• Stitch facing to garment along **front edge only.** Press seam open, then fold facing to wrong side. Hold in place with pins, especially near sides and ends of buttonholes. For each buttonhole, cut a rectangular patch 1½″ wide and 1″ longer than buttonhole, of the lightweight fabric.

• In order to locate position of patch on facing, put a pin through each end of a buttonhole from front through to facing. Center patch over pins and pin to facing only (53a). Remove marking pins. In order to mark exact outline of buttonhole put a pin through **each corner** of buttonhole from front through to facing (53b). On patch, mark location of these pins with a dot in contrasting pencil. Remove pins. Open out facing, keeping patch firmly pinned in place. Using pencil and ruler, connect corner dots in an even rectangle.

• Set machine to 16 to 18 sts. per inch. Stitch around, keeping **inside** the rectangle on long edges (it should be slightly narrower than buttonhole). Pivot at corners to make them sharp and square (54).

• Slash through center and cut diagonally into each corner as for actual buttonhole (55). Push patch through opening (56) and smooth out to form a perfect rectangular opening. Press flat. (57).

• Assemble collar and facings as instructed in pattern primer; stitch. After the seams have been processed (see below), and the facing turned, slip-stitch edges of openings over buttonholes. Press lightly.

POCKETS

The pattern primer always gives instructions for making the pockets in your garment. Like buttonholes, they have to be made with great care. **Always interface the opening edge** of a pocket in a tailored garment. Once a slashed pocket has been made, close it with diagonal basting until garment is finished. See chapter on POCKETS for useful hints.

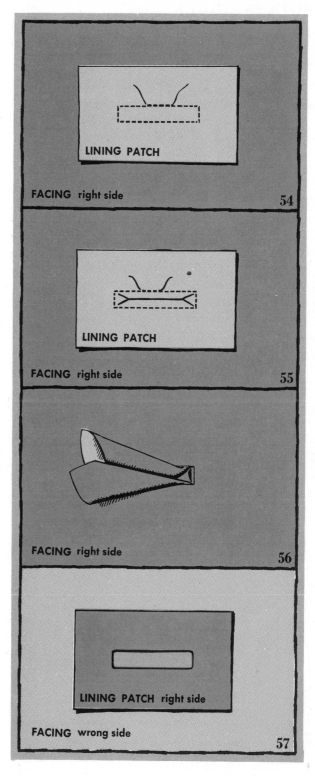

LINING PATCH

FACING right side 54

LINING PATCH

FACING right side 55

FACING right side 56

LINING PATCH right side

FACING wrong side 57

REDUCING BULK

In tailoring, where so much of the final effect depends on general smoothness and sharply-defined edges, and fabrics tend to be heavier, it is particularly necessary to reduce bulk wherever possible.

Edge-seams along facings and collar are the most important. Before trimming their seam allowances (except for interfacing), underpress them, i.e., press them open over a point presser (18, p. 178) in order that they may have a really sharp edge when they are pressed together afterward. Then trim and grade them as directed under **Processing the Seam** in FACINGS, pp. 82 and 83. (Do not, however, understitch as directed on page 84.) Where there is a lapel, reverse the order of widths at the point where lapel is folded back (58)—i.e., if along front edge you have trimmed outer fabric to ¼″ (slightly more if fabric is heavy) and facing to ⅛″, along lapel, trim outer fabric to ⅛″ and facing to ¼″.

Interfacing, when it is caught in a seam, is always trimmed as close to stitching as possible.

Ends of darts caught in seams are trimmed diagonally with the scissors held at an angle, as shown, to grade the layers of fabric (59).

Seam-ends caught in another seam are trimmed diagonally like darts (60).

In **hems,** at garment bottom or sleeves, trim seam allowances to ¼″ from raw edge to marked hemline, as shown (61).

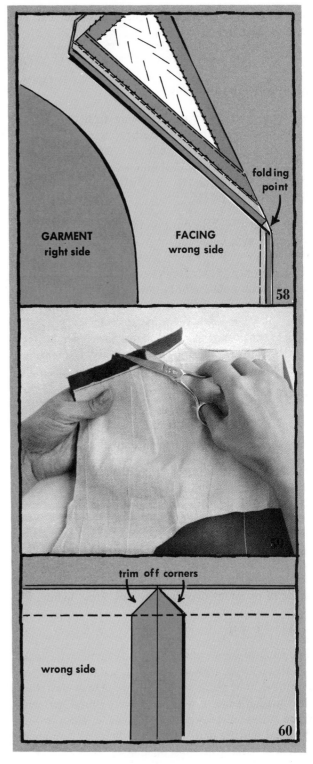

GARMENT right side

FACING wrong side

folding point

58

trim off corners

wrong side

60

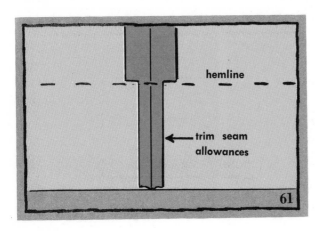

hemline

← trim seam allowances

61

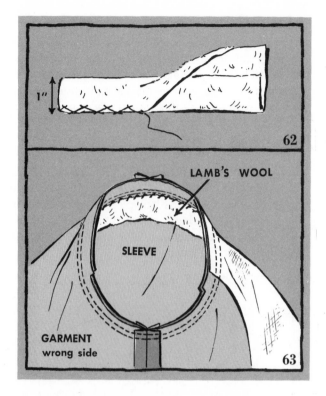

SLEEVE CAPS

A tailored sleeve cap should be slightly padded out. Cut two strips of lamb's wool, each 3″ by 6½″. Fold the two edges in 1″, making a 1″ strip; catch-stitch edges together as shown (62). Place strip inside sleeve cap, centered at shoulder seam. Slipstitch one folded edge to armhole seamline (63).

HEMS

On jackets, coats, and cuffless sleeves, hems are given body by means of a strip of muslin. Cut strips on the true bias, 2″ wide. Fold one long edge ¼″ over and press.

On **garment,** if front interfacing extends beyond marked hemline, trim it even with hemline, as shown (64). Pin muslin strip along hemline with fold toward you (not against garment) and folded edge exactly even with marked hemline (64). At front, cut ends even with edge of interfacing. Slipstitch folded edge to hemline, as shown, picking up no more than a thread in outer fabric with each stitch. To join strips, just let ends overlap (fold within fold at bottom edge). Catch front ends loosely to interfacing and upper edge to vertical seam allowances, as shown (64).

For **sleeves,** cut ends of strip straight and overlap at underarm seam. Slipstitch folded edge in place as on garment.

FINAL PRESSING

When garment is finished except for lining, loosely tack front facing to interfacing, taking long running stitches and using a strong thread. Remove all tailor-basting and thread marks. Carefully press garment, or better, have it pressed by a tailor, with attention paid to each detail. This will give your garment a professional finish that will be out of your reach once the lining is in.

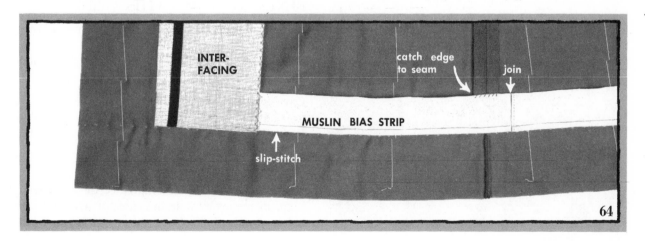

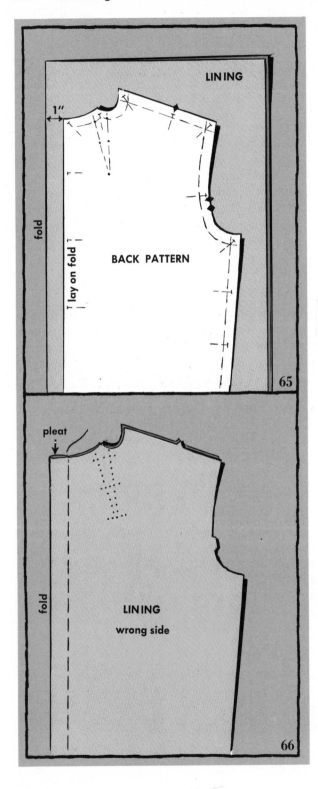

LINING

Before lining goes in, catch facing loosely to backing or outer fabric, making sure that no stitch shows on the right side. Lining in a tailored jacket or coat should have extra ease in the back. If you have no separate pattern piece for lining, place back pattern as shown when cutting out lining (65), i.e., allow an extra 1″ pleat at center back. Baste up pleat (66) and press it to one side. Before putting in lining, fasten down upper end of pleat with a few catch stitches (67), then turn pleat-end under at neck, together with seam allowance. Catch-stitch pleat at waist level in the same way. If lining is attached at hem, turn pleat under as at neck, otherwise let it hang free. Remove basting.

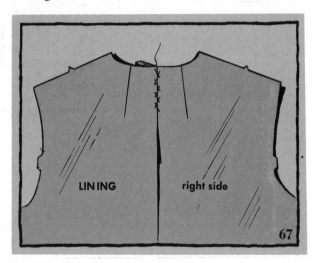

FINISHING DETAILS

Seam allowances in areas that are to be covered with a lining need not be finished unless fabric is extremely ravelly—in that case make a line of machine-stitching along edges.

Covered snap (68)—A large snap is sometimes used to fasten the upper edge of front facing under collar. It should be covered with fabric, but garment fabric is always too thick. Use lightweight fabric, preferably a dull silk, as close to garment color as possible.

• Cut two circles of material twice the diameter of snap. Pierce a tiny hole in center of one circle and pull circle over ball of snap. Run a gathering thread around edge of circle, draw up tightly and secure (69). If desired, the same thread may be used to sew on the snap-half, putting needle through fabric at the usual four holes.

• To cover socket half of snap, gather circle as before and secure it over snap. Then rub a little chalk on tip of ball and snap the two halves closed. Open, and pierce hole at chalk mark.

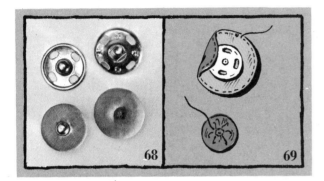

The Arrowhead Tack, used as a "stop" and a decoration at the top of single pleats or at pocket-corners (it may also serve to camouflage a mishap in cutting or sewing!) is the one outward touch of handwork in tailoring. It is really a handsome bit of tailored embroidery, done with buttonhole twist or embroidery floss. The three sides of the tack are equal in size, seldom more than ¾" and sometimes as small as ⅜". At the top of a kick-pleat, the tack is centered over pleat line (70), so that it can be stitched both through seam allowances and through pleat. At pocket-opening ends (71), it should span the two lips of the opening.

• Mark out triangle with basting thread. Bring out needle at left-hand corner as shown (72a) and fill in area, proceeding as shown (72b,c). Keep threads very close together.

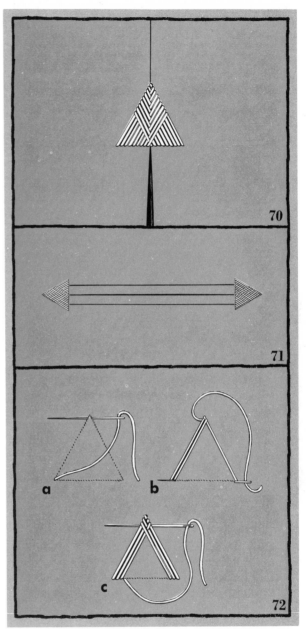

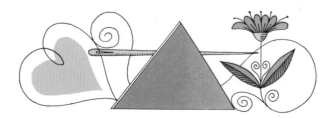

THREAD AND NEEDLES

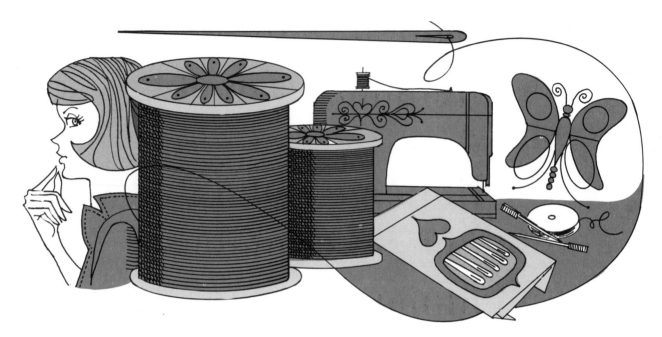

Thread and needle, without which no sewing could be done, are practically a unit. Not only is one useless without the other, but, to do a proper job, they must be suited to each other. And, above all, to the fabric you want them to stitch.

THREAD

Thread may be made of cotton, synthetic fiber, silk, or a combination of fibers. Cotton thread comes in a variety of sizes (thicknesses), usually indicated by a size number on the spool—the higher the number, the finer the thread, with 50 as a general-purpose medium size. In colored thread, the number on the other end of the spool is the color number. Threads, like fabrics, are often treated with finishes to impart special qualities and improve performance. Mercerization and Glacé finishes are the oldest of these; Silicone finishes are new. Cotton threads are mercerized for much the same reasons cotton fabrics are: strength, smoothness, luster, and better affinity for dyes. Glacé finish produces a hard, smooth surface, as waxing does; and Silicone finish lubricates, to ease the thread through the fabric smoothly.

COTTON THREAD

Mercerized Sewing—For light and medium-weight fabrics of every kind. Size 50 only. In over 175 colors that vary with fashion trends. Regular spool and large spool.

"Heavy Duty" Mercerized Sewing—A heavier thread, suitable for draperies, slipcovers, heavier coat and suit fabrics, etc. In 50 colors, featuring decorator shades. Large spool.

"Dressmaker Spool" Mercerized Sewing—Large spool in white and black only; sizes 40, 50, 60.

Mercerized "Best Cord"—White and black only, in 10 sizes, from coarsest, size 8, to finest, size 100 in white and 70 in black. For white and black cottons and linens. Also used with colored cottons too heavy for matching colored thread. Small spool, regular spool, large spool.

Button and Carpet—Extra-heavy, extra-strong, glacé-finished thread. Can only be used by hand. In 10 basic colors. Large spool.

Quilting—Fine, strong glacé-finished thread for hand- and machine-quilting. In 14 colors (no black). Large spool.

SYNTHETIC THREAD

Dual Duty—Cotton-covered polyester thread with a silicone finish for smoother stitching. Particularly good for permanent press, stretch and knit fabrics. Can be safely pressed and handled like cotton thread, but has the durability and "give" of synthetic fiber. Size 60, but with the strength of size 40. In 90 colors. Regular spool.

Dual Duty Plus—The thread on the Golden Spool. Basically the same as Dual Duty with the added feature of mercerization. Suitable for every fabric, from fine tricot to sailcloth. In about 185 colors. Regular spool and large spool.

Dual Duty Plus Extra Strong—For buttons and hand sewing on very heavy fabrics. 6 basic colors.

SILK THREAD

Silk Sewing—For use with silk and lighter wool fabrics. It handles differently from cotton thread—test the tension on your machine when you start using it. Comes in one size (A), in about 100 colors.

Buttonhole Twist—A strong twist specially designed for hand-worked buttonholes and decorative stitching by hand or machine. 30 colors.

NEEDLES

Needles are made in different types, to suit the type of work they are used for; and in different sizes, so they may draw thread of different sizes easily through fabrics of different weights.

Sewing Machine Needles—The make and model of your sewing machine will determine the type of needle you buy. Some needles, such as Coats & Clark's, will fit several popular makes of sewing machines (see package). Size of needle is determined by weight of fabric to be sewn (see chart, p. 196). Size numbers vary with brands—to be safe, ask for fine, medium, coarse, etc. (see chart). Buy quality

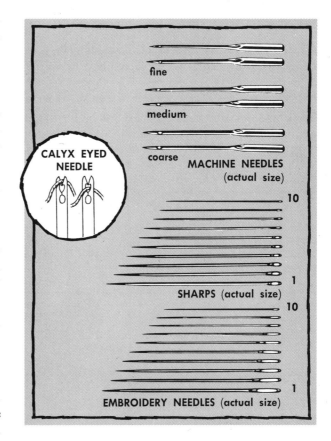

needles—poorly-made needles may have rough spots that will cause thread to break.

Hand-Sewing Needles—Buy good quality needles—an inferior needle may have a blunt point or a rough eye which may fray the thread. Needles come in ten sizes, from No. 1, very coarse, to No. 10, very fine. *Sharps* are needles of medium length, most commonly used. Other sewing needles differ from them only in length: *Betweens,* shorter, good for fine stitching on heavy fabric; *Milliners,* longer, best for millinery and basting. Packaged assortments of needles, size 3 to 9 and 5 to 10, are practical. *Calyx Eyed Sharps,* size 4 to 8, are open at the top for easy threading.

Embroidery Needles are often preferred for sewing because of their long eye, which makes for easy threading. Otherwise they are like sharps. They are also called Crewel Needles.

HOW TO CHOOSE THE CORRECT THREAD AND NEEDLE

Choose your thread and needle according to your fabric—the chart below will show you how to coordinate the essentials in your sewing—fabric, thread, needle, and the machine stitch-size best suited to them.

Knits and permanent press fabrics—use the finest needle the fabric will take and the longest stitch which will still look good (this is to avoid splitting the fabric threads).

Buttons—depending on your fabric use any of the threads below; for very heavy fabrics use Button & Carpet thread or Dual Duty Plus Extra Strong.

FABRICS		COATS & CLARK'S O.N.T.® or J. & P. COATS THREADS			NEEDLES	
The fabrics listed below can be of any fiber—cotton, linen, wool, silk, rayon, synthetic, or blends; they are listed only as an example of weight.		For any fabric except for stretch	For wash-and-wear, stretch fabrics, rayons, silks, wools, knits	For cottons and linens in white and black	COATS & CLARK'S or MILWARDS For hand-sewing	COATS & CLARK'S for machine-sewing
Sheer	chiffon, dotted Swiss, marquisette, net, ninon, nylon tricot, organdy, sheer crepe, voile	MERCERIZED SEWING thread—over 175 colors plus white and black use thread one shade darker than fabric	DUAL DUTY® cotton-covered polyester thread—over 90 colors	MERCERIZED BEST CORD® thread sizes 70, 100	sizes 9, 10	finest needle 16 stitches per inch
Medium Light	challis, gingham, jersey, knits, percale, satin, sheer wool crepe, surah, taffeta			sizes 60, 70	sizes 8, 9	finest needle 12 stitches per inch
Medium	broadcloth, chintz, corduroy, faille, flannel, knits, linen, pique, sateen, satin, seersucker, shantung, velveteen		"DUAL DUTY PLUS" cotton-covered polyester thread, mercerized—about 185 colors use thread one shade darker than fabric	sizes 50, 60	sizes 7, 8	medium needle 12 stitches per inch
Medium Heavy	burlap, coating, denim, drapery fabric, felt, fleece, gabardine, knits, leather, quilted fabric, suiting, terry cloth, tweed, vinyl	"HEAVY DUTY" MERCERIZED SEWING thread—over 50 colors plus white and black use thread one shade darker than fabric		size 40	size 6	medium coarse needle 10 stitches per inch
Heavy	coating, sailcloth, ticking, upholstery fabric			sizes 24, 30	sizes 4, 5	coarse needle 8 stitches per inch
Very Heavy	awning cloth, canvas, duck	MERCERIZED "BEST CORD" thread in white and black —sizes 8, 16, 20		sizes 8, 16, 20	sizes 1, 2, 3	coarsest needle 6 stitches per inch

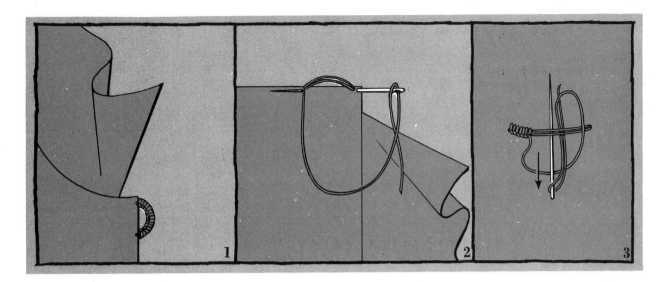

THREAD LOOPS

Thread loops consist of a core of a few threads covered with blanket stitch. Used in slightly different form for various purposes, they vary, especially in the degree in which they "loop." The Bar Tack and the French Tack (p. 198) are not really loops at all, but are made the same way.

Blanket Stitch on a loop differs from blanket stitch in embroidery in that needle is used eye-first, as shown above (3). When length of central threads is entirely covered with blanket stitch, worked close together but not too tight, fasten thread securely (on wrong side when possible) and cut off.

Button Loop

An inconspicuous loop usually placed at the neck corner of an opening (1), often for use with a small button concealed under a collar.

• Use thread single; bring out at one end of loop-position in a manner that will conceal knot. Across loop-position, take three or four stitches (2), loose enough to form loop of desired size. Then cover with blanket stitch (3).

Thread Eye

Used in place of a metal eye in a hook-and-eye closure (4). About ¼″ long.

• Follow instructions for Button Loop, but draw thread up so "eye" is straight and there is practically no slack.

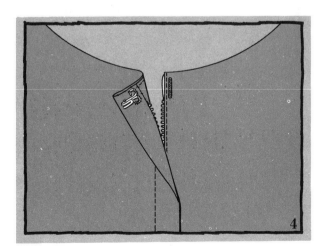

Belt Carrier

Used on side seams of dresses to keep belt in place (5).

• Mark placement (width of belt, one half above and one half below center of belt line). Cut 48″ of thread matched to fabric; use doubled, with ends knotted together. At bottom mark of position, put needle and thread through from inside of garment to outside. Take a small horizontal stitch at top mark (6) and draw thread up, leaving necessary slack in loop. Repeat down and up three or four times, as shown. Take an extra stitch to fasten thread; cover with blanket stitch (3).

Bar Tack

An inconspicuous reinforcement, generally placed on wrong side of garment, at points of strain such as end of a slit at hem or neck. Hardly more than ⅛″ long (7).

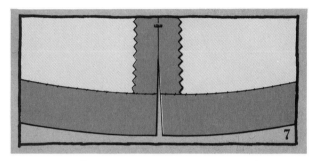

• Follow instructions for Button Loop, but draw thread up completely, leaving no slack.

French Tack

Used to hold two parts of a garment, such as lining and outer part of a coat, loosely together at hem, usually at side seams (8).

• Bring needle out in one of the two garment parts, then take a small stitch in the other, holding the two apart the desired amount (probably an inch or so). Take three or four stitches back and forth in the same manner, then anchor thread with another small stitch. Cover with blanket stitch (3).

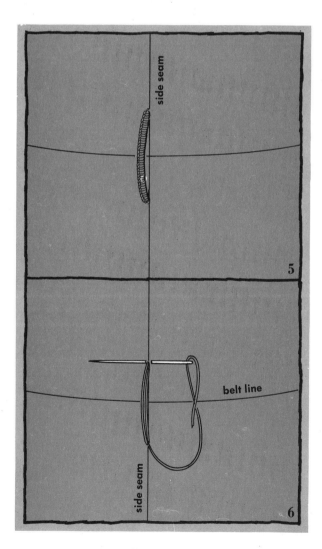

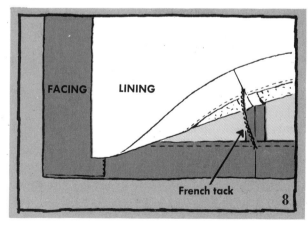

TUCKS

A tuck is a fold of fabric, usually not very deep, that is stitched along all or part of its length. A tuck stitched in its entire length serves as decoration only. A tuck stitched only to a certain point furnishes fullness and contributes to fit, and may or may not be decorative as well (e.g., the Pin Tucks below serve both design and fit, while the Dart Tucks are for fit only).

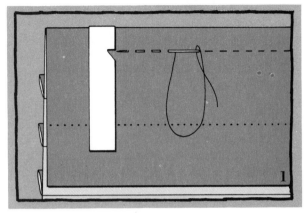

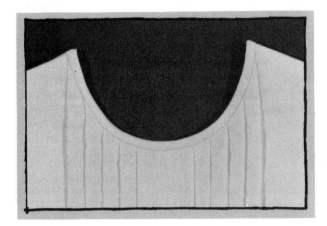

Pin Tucks are very narrow tucks stitched close to fold. They are often stitched on wrong side of garment (2).

Dart Tucks serve the purpose of darts, but without coming to a point, and release fullness at one or both ends (3, 4).

Where there is a series of decorative tucks (as in some blouses) stitched in their entire length, the tucks are usually made before pattern is cut out. As a general rule, stitching on decorative tucks is done on the outside and is very visible—almost a part of the design. It can be done by machine with carefully selected thread and a very small stitch (20 to the inch). It can also be done by hand, with a small running stitch. If you are fond of tucks, you would do well to learn to use the "tucker" sewing machine attachment, which will help to make equally-spaced tucks (see your sewing machine manual).

When making tucks, transfer tuck markings carefully from pattern to fabric. In some fabrics a thread can be drawn if tucks are on straight grain. Crease or press on marked line and stitch at distance from fold indicated; use a gauge (self-made or other) to keep depth even (1).

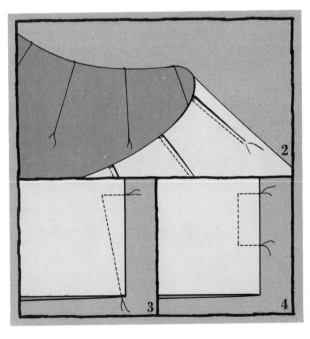

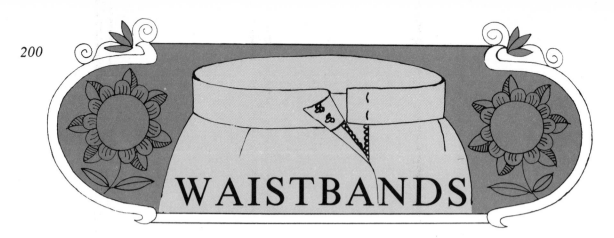

WAISTBANDS

A waistband, the doubled, straight-grain strip of fabric, stitched to the top of a skirt or pants to make it fit the waist, may be as narrow as ⅝″ or as wide as 2″. Its ends overlap in the usual direction for female clothes: right over left on a front or side closure, left over right on a back closure. The top end, which has the buttonhole or the hooks, is made even with opening edge (sometimes it is extended just enough to have the end rounded or pointed). The other end, which has the button or the hook-eyes, extends about 1½″ underneath.

The raw top edge of the skirt or pants (unless skirt is gathered) is usually ½″ to 1″ wider than the finished waistline (waist measurement), and is eased to the waistband.

Patterns generally include a piece for the waistband and instructions for its application. You may, however, wish to vary the width and the method according to your preference and your fabric. The methods of

application that follow have been found most practical from every standpoint.

The narrowest waistband width (⅝″) is automatically reinforced by the width of the seam allowances. To keep a wider band from rolling, it must be reinforced either with interfacing or with grosgrain belting.

Regular Waistband—suitable for any fabric. A waistband should, if possible, be cut on the lengthwise grain, preferably on a selvage. Length: waist measurement plus 2¾″. Width: on a selvage, twice desired width plus ⅝″ (1). If there is no selvage, add ¼″ to this width, turn under and topstitch. Use this edge as "selvage edge."

• Cut interfacing (if any) to match above strip. Stitch to wrong side of strip along both long edges. Measuring across width from selvage (or finished) edge, mark width of finished waistband less ⅛″. At this point, make a line of stitching along length of band to hold interfacing in place, as shown (2).

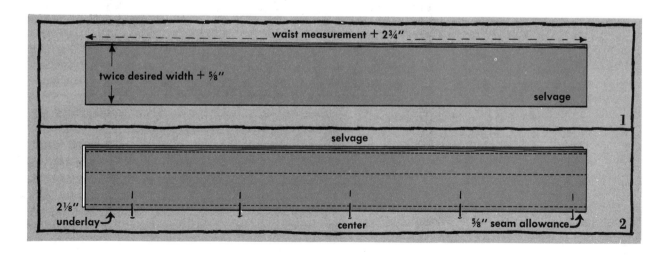

• Measure and pin-mark raw edge as shown (2): 2⅛″ at underlying end, ⅝″ at overlap; divide space between into four equal parts. Divide raw edge of garment into four equal parts, starting at the zipper opening (3).

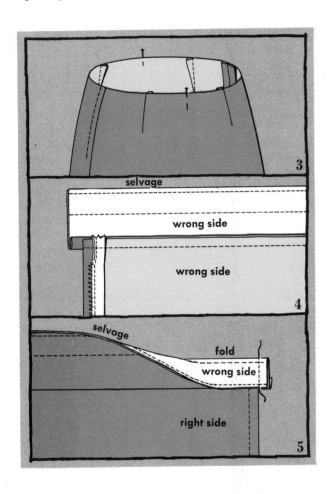

• To attach loose edge, either a) slipstitch to seamline; or b) baste in place with edge ⅛″ below stitched line, then machine-stitch from the *outside*, either on waistband close to seamline (topstitching), or in seamline (invisible stitching).

• Press. Sew on hooks and eyes, or make worked buttonhole and sew on button.

Waistband Backed with Grosgrain Belting—For bulky or pile fabrics, leather and suede.

Use grosgrain ⅝″ to 1″ wide and 2¾″ longer than waist measurement. Cut waistband of fabric to same length as grosgrain and ⅞″ wider. Lap one edge of grosgrain ¼″ over one edge of waistband (right side) and topstitch (6). Then follow directions in third paragraph under **Regular Waistband**.

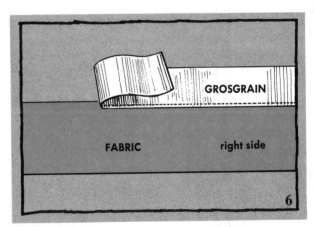

• Pin garment edge to raw edge of waistband, right sides together, matching at pin marks, edges even. Baste, easing garment edge. Stitch. Press waistband and seam up (4).

• Fold waistband in half wrong side out. If you plan to hand-sew loose edge down, match edge to seamline; if you plan to machine-stitch, bring edge ⅛″ below seamline. Pin ends; stitch across ⅝″ from edges (5). Trim and grade the two end-seams. Turn waistband right side out and press.

Self-Interfaced Waistband—For light- to medium-weight, firmly-woven washable fabrics only. Eliminates need for separate interfacing.

• Cut waistband to waist measurement plus 2¾″, and four times desired finished width plus 1¼″ for seam allowance.

• Fold waistband in half lengthwise and stitch raw edges together. Measuring across width from folded edge, mark width of finished waistband less ⅛″. At this point make a line of stitching along length of band to hold the two layers together. From here on follow directions in third paragraph under **Regular Waistband**.

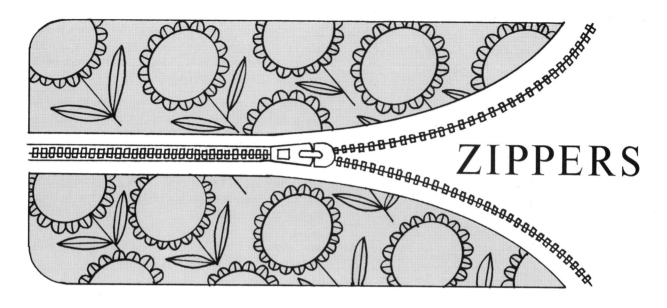

ZIPPERS

Zippers are another of those things that scare a home-sewer. Yet inserting a zipper takes no particular skill or practice. There's a trick to it, of course, but it is by no means a difficult trick once you know what the motions are (i.e., once you have *followed through* on them). What's more, the job is done in a few minutes.

The motions are simple—if the instructions seem lengthy, it is because we do not want to leave you with questions on your mind. Do not try to understand the procedure by reading the directions all at once. For a regular (non-separating or hidden) zipper, first read and follow through on **Preparation—Half the Job,** on p. 204. Then turn to the page that applies to your placket and type of application (lapped or centered). Follow the directions *one step at a time,* consulting the related illustrations. The zipper will be in before you know it.

There are three ways of inserting a zipper:

. . . **The Lapped Application** (1), in which one edge of opening forms a lap that completely conceals the zipper. It has only one line of visible stitching, and is neat and smart. It is suitable in any garment, provided fabric (not too bulky) and design lend themselves to it.

. . . **The Centered Application** (2), in which the two edges of opening meet over the zipper which is centered underneath. It has two lines of visible stitching. It is suitable in any garment, but is particularly good for bulky fabrics.

. . . **The Hidden Zipper Application** (3) is a centered application with no stitching on the outside. The zipper placket looks exactly like a continuation of the seam. This application can be made only with a specially constructed zipper, on the market under the name of "Hidden Zipper" or "Invisible Zipper". It may be inserted with a special or a regular zipper foot.

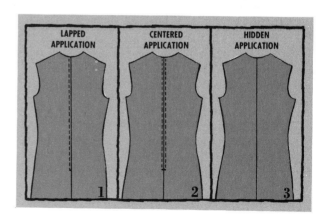

ABOUT THE ZIPPERS THEMSELVES

Zippers consist of either synthetic coils or metal teeth (referred to as a chain when closed), fastened to tapes, and locked together by means of a slider. The back of some coil zippers is covered with tape to protect the coils when pressing. Guidelines, woven into tape, are a help for straight stitching. For description of the different zippers available, see NOTIONS.

Care of Zippers

• When pressing a synthetic zipper, never allow your iron to come into contact with the coils. Whenever possible, keep zipper closed when pressing. If zipper must be open, cover coils well with a press cloth.
• When putting on or taking off a garment, open zipper all the way to prevent strain and breakage.
• Be sure to close zipper for washing or dry-cleaning a garment. This prevents possible distortion which may result in a malfunctioning of the zipper.

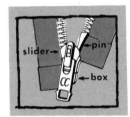

• When closing a separating zipper, be sure to have the slider all the way down and to insert the pin **through** the slider and **firmly down** into the "box".

• If zipper has become stiff after washing or dry-cleaning, run a piece of candlewax, beeswax, or soap over teeth or coils.

Length of Zipper

The length of a zipper, whether mentioned in this book or on a pattern envelope, **never** includes the tape-ends. Measurement is from lower edge of bottom stop to top of slider (or to bar tack, if any). Zipper length for a garment is always given on the pattern envelope. If —for wearing convenience or because of your figure proportions— you should prefer a different length, adjust opening as instructed on the following page.

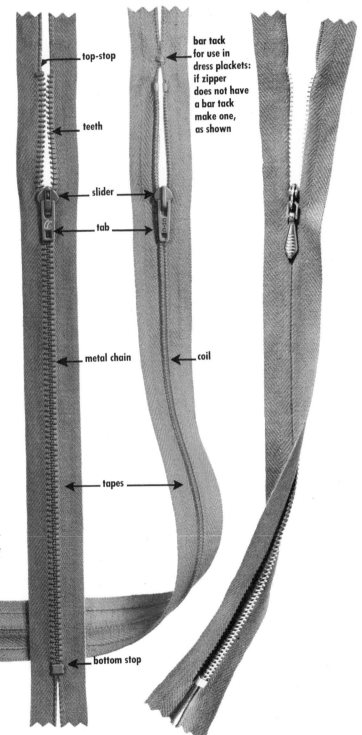

METAL ZIPPER   FLEXIBLE COIL ZIPPER   HIDDEN ZIPPER

top-stop

teeth

bar tack for use in dress plackets: if zipper does not have a bar tack make one, as shown

slider

tab

metal chain

coil

tapes

bottom stop

bottom stop   guide line

PREPARATION—HALF THE JOB

With a regular zipper, the preparation is the same for a Lapped Application or for a Centered Application. If you have a separating zipper, see p. 209; for a hidden zipper see p. 212.

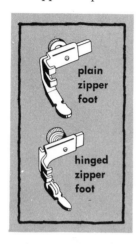

A zipper foot must be on hand before starting—without one you cannot stitch close enough to coil or teeth. A plain zipper foot does the job but a hinged foot is easier to manage. Changing to zipper foot, when directions call for it, doesn't take a minute by the clock. Be careful to have needle exactly centered in notch of foot. For a hidden zipper there is a special zipper foot (see p. 212).

If zipper placket crosses a seam trim ends of seam allowances, as shown (4).

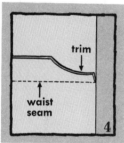

When stitching the seam containing zipper placket, stop at marks (usually notches) that indicate opening, but do not tie off threads.

Length of opening is adjusted, if necessary, when you are ready to insert zipper. A little extra space is needed if zipper is to close properly. Match opening to zipper as follows:

. . . *On a skirt placket:* length of zipper with tab turned up, plus waist seam allowance.

. . . *On a dress side placket:* length of zipper with tab turned up or to just above bar tack.

. . . *On a neck placket:* length of zipper plus ½″ (for hook and eye). Add seam allowance if neck is unfinished.

Mark bottom point of opening with pin. At stitched seam-end(s), pull out or add a few stitches as needed (to add, thread one thread-end into a hand-needle). Then tie off thread securely.

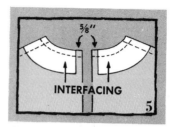

Any interfacing extending to a zipper placket must be trimmed as shown (5), i.e., you cut away width of seam allowance along placket edge.

All work is done with opening basted together.

Machine-baste (longest stitch) opening together on seamline, as shown (6). Press basted seam open. In a neck placket, if facing has already been applied, extend it out, lining up neck seam, and continue stitching to edge of facing as shown in insert. Keep facing extended for rest of application.

Contrasting bobbin thread will make it easier to remove basting after finishing a lapped application, especially in fabrics where thread may blend in.

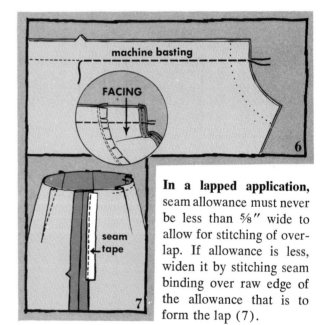

In a lapped application, seam allowance must never be less than ⅝″ wide to allow for stitching of overlap. If allowance is less, widen it by stitching seam binding over raw edge of the allowance that is to form the lap (7).

Pinning or hand-basting are not specified in any of these directions. While they can be dispensed with, there is no reason why you should not pin or hand-baste if, for instance, your fabric is hard to handle, or if you just feel safer doing so.

Never stretch zipper during application.

LAPPED APPLICATION IN A SKIRT PLACKET

You have, of course, carefully gone over **Preparation —Half the Job,** on the preceding page. The opening is basted together and the seam pressed open.

Throughout this application
- Stitch on inside of garment.
- Stitch from **bottom** to **top** of placket—otherwise the lap will face the wrong way.
- Keep slider tab turned **up.**
- Position of zipper is determined by Step 1. Do this step very carefully.

Step 1—*Continue using regular presser foot and longest stitch* (as you used for basting the opening together). With bottom of placket away from you, extend the right-hand seam allowance by itself, as shown. Place closed zipper on it face-down, with bottom stop at bottom-of-opening mark. Hold zipper so that coil or chain lies with its **full width** on the extended seam allowance and its edge exactly against seamline, *not on it.* Stitch along edge of tape, checking position of coil or chain as shown, every inch or two. Stitching may curve out around slider.

Step 2—*Change to zipper foot and regular stitch.* Turn (flip) zipper face-up, forming a fold in seam allowance (not in tape). Bring fold close to coil or chain but not close enough to touch, and topstitch fold to zipper tape, as shown, the full length of tape.

Step 3—Spread garment out flat, as shown, and turn zipper face-down over free seam allowance (a pleat will form at each end of placket; this is as it should be). At bottom of zipper, stitch across tapes and pleat, through all thicknesses; stop at guideline or at about center of tape. Then pivot on needle and stitch along zipper (it is helpful to hold fingers lightly over zipper while stitching). As you approach the top, make sure a) that the pleat in seam allowance is maintained; and b) that tape lies straight. Stitch to end of tape.

Finish

At bottom of placket bring thread-ends to inside (if necessary, take out a stitch or two so that, on outside, stitching does not cross garment seam). On inside, clip machine-basting that holds opening together and pull out threads. Press finished placket first on wrong side, then on right side, carefully pressing out crease under lap (on a coil zipper, use press cloth).

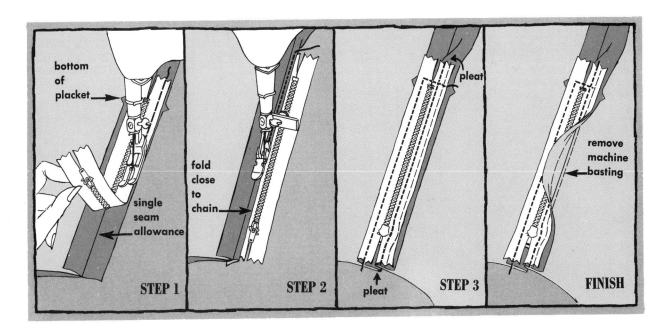

bottom of placket

single seam allowance

STEP 1

fold close to chain

STEP 2

pleat

pleat

STEP 3

remove machine basting

FINISH

LAPPED APPLICATION IN A DRESS SIDE PLACKET

You have, of course, carefully gone over **Preparation—Half the Job,** on p. 204. The opening is basted together and the seam pressed open. If your zipper does not have a bar tack at the top, make one as shown on p. 203 to protect the dress seam.

Throughout this application

• Stitch on inside of garment.
• Stitch from **bottom** to **top** of placket—otherwise the lap will face the wrong way.
• Keep slider tab turned **down.**
• Position of zipper is determined by Step 1. Do this step very carefully.

Step 1—*Continue using regular presser foot and longest stitch* (as you used for basting the opening together). With bottom of placket away from you, extend the right-hand seam allowance by itself, as shown. Place closed zipper on it face-down, with bottom stop at bottom-of-opening mark. Hold zipper so that coil or chain lies with its **full width** on the extended seam allowance and its edge exactly against seamline, *not on it.* Stitch along edge of tape, checking position of coil or chain as shown, every inch or two. Stitching may curve out around slider.

Step 2—*Change to zipper foot and regular stitch.* Turn (flip) zipper face-up, forming a fold in seam allowance (not in tape). Bring fold close to coil or chain but not close enough to touch, and topstitch fold to zipper tape, as shown, the full length of tape.

Step 3—Spread garment out flat, as shown, and turn zipper face-down over free seam allowance (a pleat will form at each end of placket; this is as it should be). At bottom of zipper, stitch across tapes and pleat, through all thicknesses; stop at guideline or at about center of tape. Then pivot on needle and stitch along zipper (it is helpful to hold fingers lightly over zipper while stitching). As you approach the top, make sure a) that the pleat in seam allowance is maintained; and b) that slider tab is down. Above bar tack, pivot again on needle and stitch across.

Finish—At bottom of placket bring thread-ends to inside (if necessary, take out a stitch or two so that, on outside, stitching stops at garment seam). On inside, clip machine-basting that holds opening together and pull out threads. Press finished placket first on wrong side, then on right side, carefully pressing out crease under lap (on a coil zipper, use press cloth).

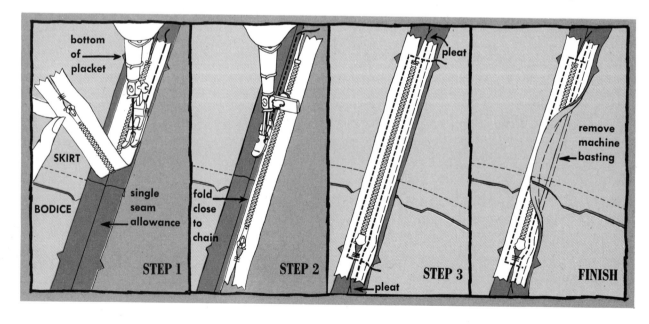

STEP 1   STEP 2   STEP 3   FINISH

LAPPED APPLICATION IN A NECK PLACKET

You have, of course, carefully gone over **Preparation—Half the Job,** on p. 204. The opening is basted together and the seam pressed open.

Throughout this application
- Stitch on inside of garment.
- Stitch from **bottom** to **top** of placket—otherwise the lap will face the wrong way.
- Keep slider tab turned **up.**
- Position of zipper is determined by Step 1. Do this step very carefully.

Step 1—*Continue using regular presser foot and longest stitch* (as you used for basting the opening together). With bottom of placket away from you, extend the right-hand seam allowance by itself, as shown. Place closed zipper on it face-down, with bottom stop at bottom-of-opening mark. Hold zipper so that coil or chain lies with its **full width** on the extended seam allowance and its edge exactly against seamline, *not on it.* Stitch along edge of tape, checking position of coil or chain as shown, every inch or two. Stitching may curve out around slider.

Step 2—*Change to zipper foot and regular stitch.* Turn (flip) zipper face-up, forming a fold in seam allowance (not in tape). Bring fold close to coil or chain but not close enough to touch, and topstitch fold to zipper tape, as shown, the full length of tape.

Step 3—Spread garment out flat, as shown, and turn zipper face-down over free seam allowance (a pleat will form at each end of placket; this is as it should be). At bottom of zipper, stitch across tapes and pleat, through all thicknesses; stop at guideline or at about center of tape. Then pivot on needle and stitch along zipper (it is helpful to hold fingers lightly over zipper while stitching). As you approach the top, make sure that the pleat in seam allowance is maintained. Stop about an inch from neck seamline and cut off end of zipper tape at seamline, as shown. Then continue stitching to neck edge.

Finish—At bottom of placket bring thread-ends to inside (if necessary, take out a stitch or two so that, on outside, stitching stops at garment seam). On inside, clip machine-basting that holds opening together and pull out threads. Press finished placket first on wrong side, then on right side, carefully pressing out crease under lap (on a coil zipper, use press cloth). For finishing facing, see next page.

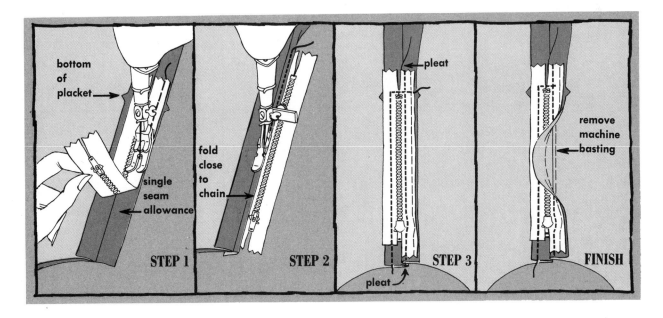

STEP 1 — bottom of placket / single seam allowance

STEP 2 — fold close to chain

STEP 3 — pleat / pleat

FINISH — remove machine basting

FINISHING A NECK FACING IN A LAPPED APPLICATION

REGULAR FINISH

Facing is applied either before or after zipper.

Trim, clip, turn in and sew down raw edges as shown (8). Add hook and eye at top (9).

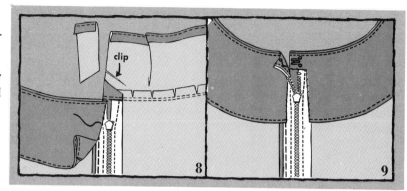

SPECIAL FINISH

Facing must be applied before zipper.

This facing finish is excellent for any neckline, with or without collar, regardless of fabric. Bulk is minimal and handling easy; finished corners lie flat and smooth. It is equally good at other zipper openings, wherever there is a facing. It requires only that, *regardless of pattern primer instructions,* facing be applied before zipper, as directed here.

• As you pin facing in place, turn back 1″ of facing at the left-hand side (lapped edge of zipper placket). Trim this folded end to ½″ (10).

• Stitch facing to garment. Trim, grade, and clip seam, *except* for the 1″ of unfaced neck seam allowance (11). Understitch facing.

• Turn folded end of facing and the 1″ of unfaced seam allowance to inside of garment (12).

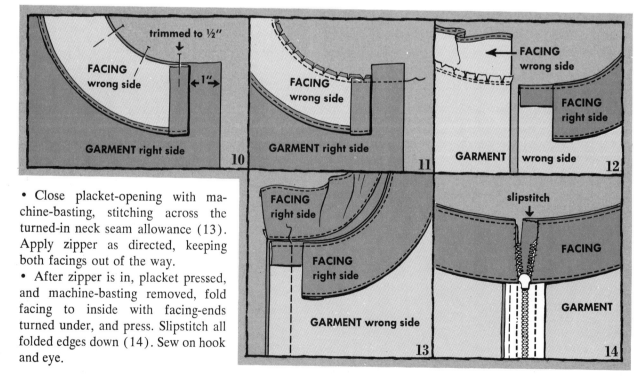

• Close placket-opening with machine-basting, stitching across the turned-in neck seam allowance (13). Apply zipper as directed, keeping both facings out of the way.

• After zipper is in, placket pressed, and machine-basting removed, fold facing to inside with facing-ends turned under, and press. Slipstitch all folded edges down (14). Sew on hook and eye.

IN CASE OF ZIPPER STRAIN IN A DRESS—Waistline Stay

A snug fit at the waist, in a dress, can put quite a strain on the zipper. This can be eased by a sturdy waistline stay.

Use ½" or ¼" twill tape or ⅝" grosgrain ribbon; or cut a 1" strip along the selvage of your dress fabric and press it folded through center so that selvage edge extends just beyond raw edge. Cut stay 1" longer than body waist measurement.

Turn ends of strip ½" under. Sew on a hook and eye, placed so that ends of strip meet. With dress wrong side out, place stay around waist, hooking ends at zipper, as shown. Pin stay to waist seam allowance on either side of zipper, with garment *looser than* stay at this point—this is essential if strain on zipper is to be removed. Pin rest of stay to seam allowance, easing seam to stay as needed.

Starting and stopping 2" from either side of hook and eye, as shown (a), stitch stay to seam allowance,

either by machine or by hand (for hand-sewing, use "Heavy Duty" thread, or Mercerized Sewing thread doubled).

On a dress without a waist seam (princess style), tack stay to seams and darts.

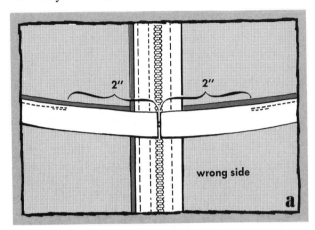

LAPPED APPLICATION FOR A SEPARATING ZIPPER

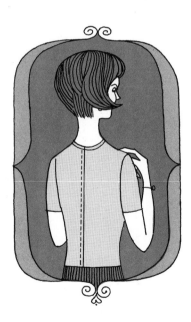

This is good in back closures in blouses that. open all the way down, and in the (left) side seam of sleeveless blouses. If your pattern does not specify a separating zipper, you may wish to use one to replace either buttons or a closed-end zipper. In both cases this application is recommended.

Zipper foot—Have one on hand before starting.

Length of Zipper must be at least 1" less than finished length of blouse opening edges—½" for a hook and eye both at top and at bottom.

Prepare opening: Zipper may be applied before or after neck or armhole facing. If facing is already in, extend it out of the way. Hem should also be extended. Machine-baste opening together on seamline; press basted seam open. To determine position of *bottom of zipper,* match zipper to seam with top ½" below finished top edge (neck or armhole seamline); place pin at bottom.

(continued on next page)

(continued from preceding page)

Throughout this application

- Stitch on inside of garment.
- Stitch from **bottom** to **top** of placket—otherwise the lap will face the wrong way.
- Keep slider tab turned **up.**
- Position of zipper is determined by Step 1. Do this step very carefully.

Step 1—*Continue using regular presser foot and longest stitch* (as you used for basting the opening together). With bottom of placket away from you, extend the right-hand seam allowance by itself, as shown. Place closed zipper on it face-down, with bottom stop at bottom-of-opening mark. Hold zipper so that coil or chain lies with its **full width** on the extended seam allowance and its edge exactly against seamline, *not on it.* Stitch along edge of tape, checking position of coil or chain as shown, every inch or two. Stitching may curve out around slider.

Step 2—*Change to zipper foot and regular stitch.* Turn (flip) zipper face-up, forming a fold in seam allowance (not in tape). Bring fold close to coil or chain but not close enough to touch, and topstitch fold to zipper tape, as shown, the full length of garment.

Step 3—Spread garment out flat, as shown, and turn zipper face-down over free seam allowance (a pleat will form at each end of placket; this is as it should be). Start stitching at bottom of garment, in line with guideline or center of tape; stitch through all thicknesses along zipper. (It is helpful to hold fingers lightly over zipper while stitching.) As you approach top, make sure that pleat in seam allowance is maintained. Stop about an inch from seamline and cut off end of zipper tape at seamline, as shown. Then continue stitching to fabric edge.

Finish

On inside, clip machine-basting that holds opening together (a) and pull out threads. Press finished placket first on wrong side, then on right side, carefully pressing out crease under lap (on a coil zipper, use press cloth). Finish hem. For finishing facing, see page 208. Sew on hook and eye at top and at bottom.

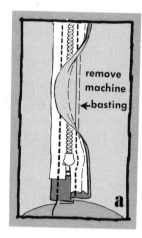

remove machine ←basting

a

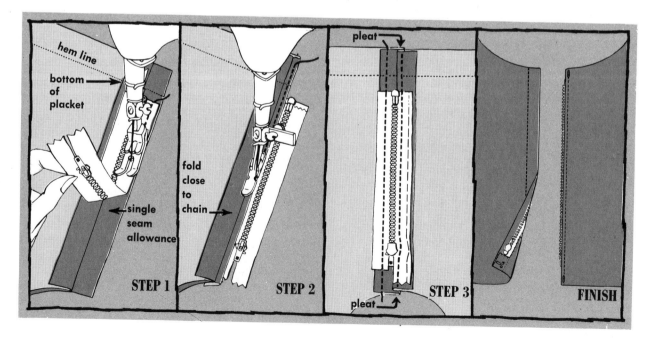

hem line

bottom of placket

←single seam allowance

STEP 1

fold close to chain →

STEP 2

pleat

pleat ↑

STEP 3

FINISH

CENTERED APPLICATION

Suitable for most openings, but is used most often in a neck placket, as shown below. The same directions are good for a skirt, a dress placket, or a long, fitted sleeve. For a separating zipper first follow directions on p. 209 for preparation of opening, then adapt the directions below as necessary.

You have, of course, carefully gone over **Preparation—Half the Job,** on p. 204. After machine-basting opening together as instructed, clip basting at 2″ intervals for easier removal later.

For Steps 1 and 2 that follow below, use *regular presser foot and longest stitch,* as in basting opening. Keep tab turned **up** for skirt or neck, **down** for dress.

Step 1—Work on inside of garment. Open zipper. With *bottom of placket* away from you, extend right-hand seam allowance by itself, as shown. Place one tape on it face-down, as shown, with bottom stop at bottom-of-opening mark and coil or teeth against seamline. Starting below slider, machine-baste along edge of tape (15), until you are about an inch from neck seamline. Stop and trim off tape-end at seamline. Then continue stitching to edge of garment, as

shown (15-a). On a *skirt* or a *dress* placket, tape is not trimmed.

Step 2—Close zipper. On a neck placket, trim off second tape-end even with first. With *top of placket* away from you, place extended unstitched seam allowance and tape under presser foot. Machine-baste along edge of tape (16).

Step 3—*Change to zipper foot and regular stitch.* Work on outside, with garment spread flat, as shown. Mark bottom of zipper with pin. Starting at top of placket, stitch down along one side of zipper, a scant ¼″ from seamline, to just past the pin, which you remove. Pivot on needle. Stitch slowly across bottom, counting stitches to seamline. Count same number of stitches on other side of seamline, pivot again, and stitch along other side of zipper (17) to top of placket. (On a dress placket, pivot and stitch across top above bar tack.) NOTE: If your fabric is loose-woven or has cross-lines that must match: after stitching across bottom, stop, break off thread, and stitch other side by starting again at top of placket.

Finish—Working from outside, take out machine-basting. Press placket, first on wrong side, then on right. Finish neck facing and add hook and eye (17-a).

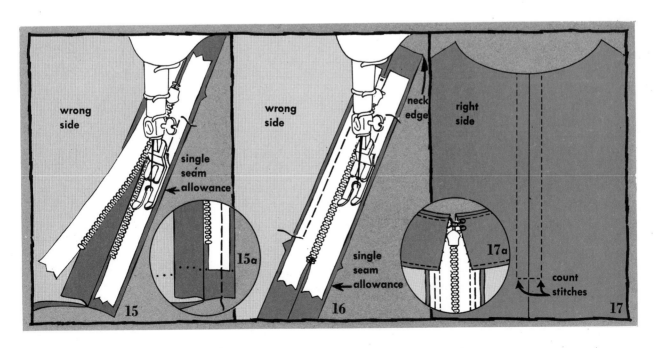

HIDDEN ZIPPER APPLICATIONS

The Hidden Zipper is most easily applied with a SPECIAL ZIPPER FOOT: One stitching line along each side attaches the zipper; then the seam is closed. However, if your fabric is very heavy or if the special zipper foot does not work on your sewing machine, the zipper may be applied with a REGULAR ZIPPER FOOT: You will then need two stitching lines along each side, one of basting to hold the tape in place and one of stitching close to teeth; then the seam is closed. The end-result in both methods is exactly the same and both applications are very simple.

BEFORE YOU BEGIN:

• Do not stitch any part of the seam: The Hidden Zipper is attached to the two sides of opening before ANY PART of the seam is stitched.

• On both sides of opening, mark location for top of zipper teeth below cut edge of waist or neck: ¾″ on a skirt, 1⅛″ on a neck.

• Place right sides of fabric together at zipper seam. Hold together temporarily by placing a pin approximately 2″ below point where zipper will end.

APPLICATION WITH SPECIAL ZIPPER FOOT

Step 1—Working on the opening-edge shown below, place open zipper face-down on right side of fabric: top of teeth at mark, edge of tape a scant ¼″ from cut edge. Turn zipper teeth up and place right-hand groove of Hidden Zipper Foot over teeth so that needle hole is over tape. Stitch slowly, until foot comes up against slider. Backstitch.

Step 2—Attach second tape to other side of opening in the same manner, using the other groove in zipper foot. Close zipper. About an inch of zipper will remain unattached at bottom. Below zipper, pin seam together all the way down.

Step 3—*Change to regular zipper foot.* Keep zipper-end out of the way as shown. Moving fly-wheel of machine by hand, lower needle exactly into end of last stitch. Take three stitches forward, then three stitches back for reinforcement. Then stitch forward, completing the seam.

Finish—See next page.

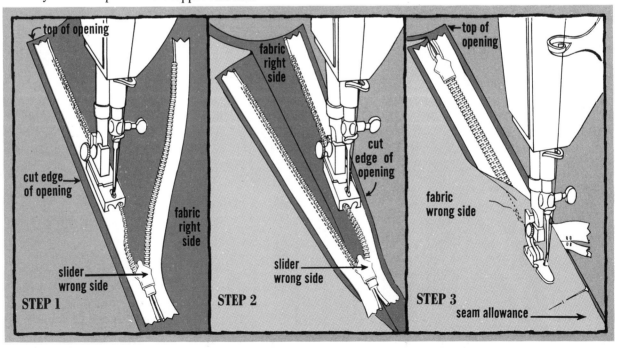

STEP 1 — top of opening, cut edge of opening, fabric right side, slider wrong side

STEP 2 — fabric right side, cut edge of opening, slider wrong side

STEP 3 — top of opening, fabric wrong side, seam allowance

APPLICATION WITH REGULAR ZIPPER FOOT

Step 1—Working on the opening-edge shown below, place open zipper face-down on right side of fabric: top of teeth at mark, edge of tape a scant ¼″ from cut edge. Machine-baste zipper through center of tape; stop at slider.

Turn zipper teeth up and place zipper foot as close to teeth as possible. Stitch slowly, keeping teeth up and foot close to teeth until foot comes up against slider. Backstitch.

Step 2—*Reverse position of needle.* Attach second tape to other side of opening in same manner as before, using other side of zipper foot. Close zipper. Notice that about an inch of zipper will remain un-attached at bottom. Below zipper, pin seam together all the way down.

Step 3—Keep zipper end out of the way as shown. Moving fly-wheel of machine by hand, lower needle exactly into end of last stitch. Take three stiches forward, then three stitches back for reinforcement. Then stitch forward, completing seam.

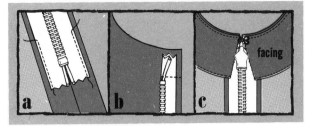

Finish—Press seam open. Press zipper placket on right side. Lay zipper flat and pin tape-ends to seam allowances (not to garment!). Stitch, remov-ing each pin after bringing down needle (a). Tie thread-ends.

Open zipper. To assure that top of zipper will lie flat for easy sliding, fold tape-ends back as shown. Stitch across tapes through seam allowances (not garment!) about ¼″ above zipper top (b). Tie thread-ends. On a neck opening, cut tapes at neck seamline.

A neck facing may be applied before or after zipper. Finish as shown (c).

See HELPFUL HINTS on next page.

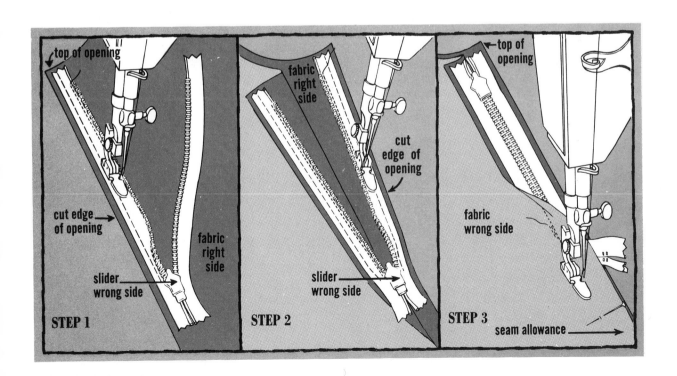

HELPFUL HINTS FOR
HIDDEN ZIPPERS

• SHORTENING ZIPPER—bring slider down to desired length of opening. Using strong thread doubled, whip-stitch over teeth **a full inch below slider.** Cut through teeth and tape ½" below stitches.

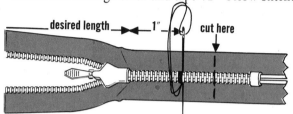

• STITCHING ON SLIPPERY AND NAPPED FABRICS—Baste the zipper in place by hand before machine stitching. For **velvet** place a strip of tissue paper between fabric and zipper before stitching. Tear away paper after stitching. This prevents the foot from marking the fabric.

• MATCHING CROSSWISE SEAMS OR LINES—After stitching first tape, close zipper. On second tape, mark where matching must occur as shown below. Open zipper; following directions for STEP 2 on p. 212 or 213 pin tape to garment with the mark **exactly** at seam or line to be matched. (If this is some distance down the garment, continue pinning upward to the top.) Finish application.

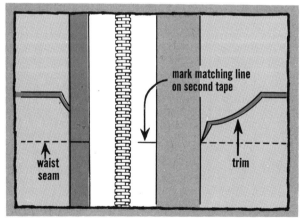

• REPLACING A ZIPPER—When a Hidden Zipper is used as a replacement, remove old zipper and open the **entire seam** below the opening; press out. Then follow directions on pp. 212 or 213.

THE ELEGANT HAND-FINISH

In these mechanical times, one way of achieving an expensive custom-look is through hand-work—which is noticeable by its very inconspicuousness. In a zipper application, this would be the last step, visible from the outside. With some fabrics, however, it is recommended that the application be done by hand throughout (see **Handling the Different Fabrics,** p. 72).

• When substituting hand- for machine-stitching in any step, simply hand-baste where you are instructed to machine-baste, and use a prick-stitch where you are instructed to stitch with regular stitch (see below for exact procedure in the **Lapped Application).**

• For **prick-stitch,** use buttonhole twist or "Heavy Duty" thread (or regular thread doubled). Work from right side. Take tiny backstitches over just one or two threads on outside, not too close together (18).

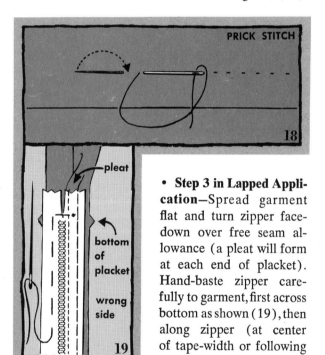

• **Step 3 in Lapped Application**—Spread garment flat and turn zipper facedown over free seam allowance (a pleat will form at each end of placket). Hand-baste zipper carefully to garment, first across bottom as shown (19), then along zipper (at center of tape-width or following guideline). On a dress placket, baste across top. Remove basting at opening and open zipper. Starting at garment seam, use basted line as a guide to stitch zipper in place with prick-stitch, going through all thicknesses. Press placket inside and outside.

SIMULATED HAND-FINISH

You can fake a hand-finish with machine blind-stitching (this is also described in HEMS). If you are unfamiliar with the technique, be sure to *try it out* first! Once the knack is acquired, the method is quick and easy. It may be done on a straight-stitch or a zigzag machine, or with an attachment. Be sure to follow instructions exactly.

Lapped Application (20)—Complete the application through **Preparation—Half the Job,** p. 204, and Steps 1 and 2.

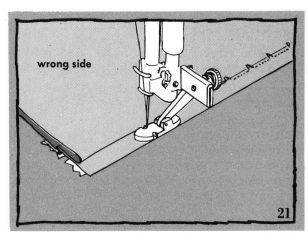

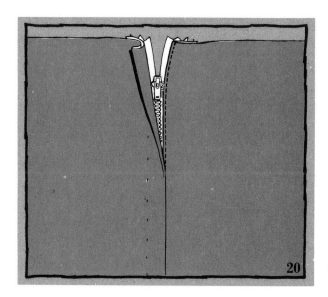

Step 3—As usual, spread garment flat (still wrong side out) and turn zipper face-down over free seam allowance, letting a pleat form at each end of stitched seam allowance. Baste free zipper tape to garment through all thicknesses, carefully maintaining pleats: baste along center of tape or follow guideline. Be very careful to keep basted line straight.

Fold garment back on basted line as shown (21). Place on machine with bottom of placket away from you and zipper tape underneath, as shown, stitching from bottom to top.

... On a straight-stitch machine—Adjust zipper foot so it is on right side of needle. Set stitch length at 12 per inch. Place zipper foot on seam allowance and needle close to garment fold. Go slowly. Take five stitches through seam allowance, very close to fold, ending with needle up. Lifting and lowering presser foot as needed, pivot fabric slightly, let needle down through about a thread of fabric in fold, take one stitch, ending with needle up, and pivot fabric back for another five stitches in seam allowance. Continue in same manner for full length of placket.

... On a zigzag machine—If automatic, consult machine manual and set stitch accordingly; if non-automatic, manipulate lever to take one sideward stitch in garment fold every sixth stitch. Stitch from bottom to top of placket.

... With a blind-stitcher attachment—Follow attachment instructions, stitching from bottom to top of placket and taking blind-stitch in fold of garment.

NOTE: Only the length of placket is blind-stitched. Stitching across bottom (and top in a dress placket) is omitted or done by hand.

Finishing—Remove basting, press and finish placket as usual.

REPLACING A ZIPPER IN A SKIRT, DRESS OR NECK PLACKET

To replace a zipper in a skirt, dress or neck placket, use either Method I or Method II (below). When fabric has been permanently marked by original stitching or folds, or when zipper has been only partially removed, only Method II is suitable. Before removing old zipper, always examine your garment to see how zipper was put in. Since you must follow the lines of old folds and stitching, you may have to adapt directions to variations in construction.

Method I

Preparation—Remove old zipper; in a dress placket, no extra ripping is necessary; in a skirt or neck placket, remove enough stitching on waistband or neck facing so that the parts of garment attached to zipper can be opened out. Press out folds of seam allowances. Close opening with machine-basting along old seamline.

Application—Follow instructions for **Lapped Application,** or **Centered Application.**

Method II

Preparation—Remove old zipper; in a skirt waistband or neck facing, remove the stitching that holds tape in place.

Application—Use zipper foot on machine. Work from outside of garment. For a lapped application, pin or baste the underlap of opening to zipper close to chain or coil, and topstitch. Baste overlap to zipper tape just outside of old stitching line; make sure that edge covers stitching on underlap and is in line with garment seam. Stitch, following old stitching line. For a centered application, pin and baste each side of opening to zipper so that the edges meet in center of chain or coil. Stitch around, following old stitching line. For both applications, bring thread-ends to inside and tie off. Press.

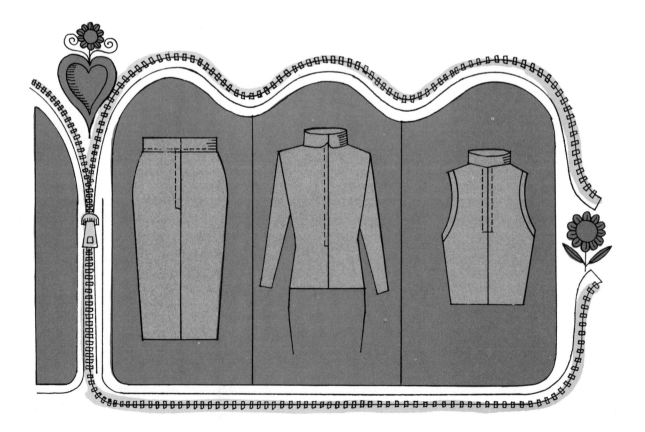

INDEX

SMALL CAPITALS refer to chapter titles. **Bold face** page numbers indicate most comprehensive treatment of specific subject.

A

Accordion pleats, 150
Adjustable zipper foot, 204
ALTERATIONS ON FINISHED
  GARMENTS, 11
  darts, 12
  hemline, 12
  letting out, 13
  taking in, 13
  waistline, 12
Alterations on patterns, 134
Anchoring facing, 84, 86
Appliqué, 57
  bias strip, 57
  hand, 57
  iron-on, 57
  machine, 57
Armhole (Armscye), 11,
  144, 145, 162
Arranging pattern pieces
  for cutting, 53
Arrowhead tack, 193
ASSEMBLING A GARMENT, 15
  unit construction, 15-17

Attaching buttons, 43

B

Back reinforcement, 183
BACKING, 18, 173, 176
  darts, **19,** 56
  fabrics, 18
  garment, 18
  pre-shrinking, 18
  See also: FABRICS,
    Handling different, 72
Backstitch, 97
Backstitching, 117, 156
Balance, **116,** 77, 79
Balanced stitch, 116
Bar tack, 198
  buttonholes, 39
  plackets, 148
  zippers, 203, 206
Basic pattern, 127, 145
Basic weaves, 68
Baste-marking, **123,** 35
  position marks, 120
  uneven basting, 20
  See also:
    BUTTONHOLES, 34
BASTING, 19, 175
  baste-marking, **123,** 35
  centered zipper
    application, 211

BASTING *(cont.)*
  hand-basting, 20, 21
  machine-basting, 21
  overlap-basting, **176,** 183
  pin-basting, 19
  removal of, 20. See
    also: ZIPPERS
  tailor-basting, **175,** 181,
    183
  thread-basting, 20
  See also: BUTTONHOLES
    FABRICS
    HEMS
    TAILORING
Beads, 58
  sewed on in a group, 58
  sewed on singly, 58
Beater, 172, 67
Beeswax, 58, 203
BELT BUCKLES, 21
  covered buckle, 21
  recover an old buckle, 21
  sewing on, 21
Belt carriers, see
  BELT LOOPS, 22
Belting, **124,** 23, 200
BELT LOOPS, 22
  fabric loops, 22
  thread loops, 197
BELTS, 23
  corded, 25
  fabric covered, 23

BELTS *(cont.)*
  stiffened with iron-on
    fabric, 24
Bent trimmers, 65
Best Cord thread, **194,** 43,
  196
Betweens, needles, **195,**
  174, 185
Beveling, see Grading, 83
BIAS, 25
  bias binding, 28, 124
    concealed machine-
      finished, 29
    French binding, 28
    inside corners, 29
    machine-finished, 28
    outside corners, 29
    quick-topstitched, 28
    sewing machine
      attachment, 29
    topstitched, 29
  bias facing, 80, 85
    on a hem, 104
  bias, locating, 26
  bias seam, 25
  bias strips, 26
    appliqué, 57
    hand-cut, 26
    joining, 27
    packaged, 26, 124
    stretching and
      swirling, 27

bias tape, **124,** 26
    gusset, 95
    hem, 98, 102
    kimono sleeve, 163
bias tubing, 30
facing, 80, 85
garments cut on bias, 25
piping, 31, 124
    See also: GRAIN, 92
Bias strip appliqué, 57
Bight, 57
Binding, see Bias, 28, 124
Blanket stitch, **58,** 39, 197, 198
Blind-stitch, 101, 187
Blind stitcher attachment, 103, 215
Blue jean zipper, 126
Bobbin-stitched dart, 56
Bobbins, 66
Bobbin thread, contrasting for easy removal, 204
Bodice alterations, 137, 139, 140, 141, 142
Bodkin, 30, 31, 46, 67
Body measurements, 130, 132
Bonded fabrics, 72, 173
Boning, 125
Bound edge
    bias binding, 28
    concealed machine-finished, 29
    corners, 29
    French binding, 28
    machine-finished, 28
    quick-topstitched, 28
    seam finish, 160
    topstitched, 29
Bow, tailored, 58
Box pleats, 149
Brocade, 112
Bulk reducing
    facing seam, **82, 83,** 47, 48, 86, 87
    hem, 99, 106
    seam crossed by zipper, 204
Button and Carpet thread, **194,** 43, 196
BUTTONHOLES, 32, 164, 188
    bar tack, 39
    bound buttonhole, **34,** 32
        corded, 35, 36, 37
        facing the, 38

one-piece folded, 35
    patch, 36
buttonhole attachment, 32, 39
buttonhole stitch, 39
buttonholes in heavy interfacing, 188
facing finish, 38, 188
length, 33
marking for, 33, 177
re-spacing, 33
test buttonhole, 33
worked buttonhole, **38,** 32
    hand, 38
    machine, 39, 166
    See also: FABRICS, Handling the different, 72
Buttonhole twist, **195,** 38, 60, 214
BUTTON LOOPS, 40
    concealed, 42
        fabric loop, 42
        thread loop, 42, 197
    decorative, 40
        frogs, 41
        on a finished edge, 41
        row of loops, 40
        single loops, 41
BUTTONS, 42, 125
    making fabric buttons, 44
        Chinese ball, 44
        covered, 44
    pierced buttons, 42, 43
    position of, 42
    reinforcing button position, 43, 164, 165
    sewing on, 43
    shank buttons, 42, 43
    types of, 42

C

Cable cord, **125,** 30
Calyx-eyed needles, 195
Care of zippers, 203
CASINGS, 45
    applied casings, 45
    casing in a bias-faced hem, 45
    casing in a turned-up hem, 45
    casing with a heading, 45
Catch-stitch, 101, 187

Centered zipper application, 202, 211
Chain stitch, 58
Chainstitched hem, removal of, 12
Chalk, 65, 123
Chalk-marking, 123
Chalk pencil, 65
Chart of patterns, 130
Chart of threads and needles, 196
Check-list for trouble spots, 117
    irregular or skipped stitches, 117
    machine stuck, 117
    needle breakage, 117
    thread breakage, 117
China silk, 18, 112
Chinese ball buttons, 44
Circular hemline, 98, 99, 100
Clapper, 172, 67
Clay chalk, 65
Clean finish, 81
Clip-marking, **55,** 46
Clipping seams, 83
    collars, 47
    corners, 83
    curves, 83
    facings, 83, 85
    scalloped facing, 86
Coil zipper, 203
Collar fall, 185, 186
COLLARS, 46
    attaching, 48
    detachable, 48
    interfacing, 46, 185, 186
    making a perfect collar, 46
    one-piece collar, 48
    tailored, 185, 186
    two-piece collar with corners, 47
    two-piece collar with rounded edge, 47
Collar stand, 185, 186
Construction details, pattern markings, 120
Construction stitching, 118
Continuous lapped placket, 146, 147
Cord, **125,** 30, 35
Corded belt, 25
Corded buttonholes, 35, 36, 37
Corded frogs, 41
Corded loops, 40, 41

Corded piping, 31, 124
Corded seam, 31
Corded tubing, **30,** 25, 40, 41, 44
Cording, 31
    corded belt, 25
    corded buttonhole, 35, 36, 37
Cording foot, 31, 103
Corduroy, 75
CORNERS, 49
    bound, 29
    clipping, 83
    mitered, 155
    reinforcing, 82
    tapering, 83
    See also: GUSSETS, 93
Cotton thread, 194
Cottons, 68, 109, 150, 158
Covered buttons, 44
Covered snaps, 192
Crepe, 112, 158
Crewel or embroidery needles, 195
Cross stitch, 58
Crosswise grain, **92,** 69, 79
CUFFS, 49
Curved dart, 56, 176
Curved hemline, 99
Curved seams, 178
CUTTING, 50
    folding the fabric for, 52
    grain in, 53
    heavy fabrics, 174
    large printed designs, 54
    layouts for, 52
    notches, 54
    pinning pattern to fabric, 53
    plaids and stripes, 54
    preparation for, 50
    single thickness, 55
    trial layout, 54
    See also: EQUIPMENT, 64
        FABRICS, Handling the different, 72
Cutting board, 65
Cutting line, 54
Cutting surface, 65

D

Darned-in patch, 169
Darning, 167
Darning cotton, 122, 167

Dart tucks, 56, 199
DARTS, 55
  alterations in, **134,** 12
  bobbin stitched, 56
  dart finishes, 56
  dart tucks, 56
  in backed garments, 19,
    56, 176
  in heavy interfacing, 179
  marking, 55, 121
  trimming ends, 190
  See also: FABRICS,
    Handling the different,
    72
DECORATION, 57
  appliqué, 57
    bias strip, 57
    hand, 57
    iron-on, 57
    machine, 57
  beads, 58
  bow, tailored, 58
  embroidery, 58
  fringe, 59
    knotted fringe, 59
    ready-made fringe, 59
    self-fringe, 59
  lace, 59
  machine appliqué, 57
  machine embroidery, 58
  machine-quilting, 60
  machine-stitching, 60
  pompons, 60
  rick rack, 60
  sequins, 61
  smocking, 61
  tassels, 60
Decorative facing, 85
Deep dart, 56
Depth of hem, 98, 99
Detachable collar, 48
Diagonal basting, 21
  See also: BUTTONHOLES, 37
    PLEATS, 151
Directional stitching, 118
Double cutting line, 54
Double-fold bias tape, **124,**
  28, 160
Double knits, 74
Double-pointed dart, 56
Double-stitched seam,
  160, 75
Dress form, 67
Dressmaker's carbon, **121,** 65
Dressmaker's spool, 194

Dressmaker's tracing paper,
  121, 65
Dress zipper, **206,** 126, 211
Drip-dry, see Wash-and-
  wear, 78
Dual Duty thread, 195, 196

E

Ease
  in a hem, 100
  in a pattern, 127, 132, 133
  in sleeve cap, 162
Ease-stitching, **118,** 63,
  100, 162
EASING, 63, 100, 162
Edge-stitched hem, 104
Edge-stitched pleats, 151
Edge-stitching, 118
Elastic, 125
  in a casing, 45, 46
Embroidery, 58
Embroidery floss, 58, 62, 122
Embroidery needles, 195
Embroidery scissors, 65
Emery bag, 66
English smocking, 61
EQUIPMENT, **64,** 50, 172
  cutting, **65,** 50
    cutting surface, 65
    scissors, 65
      bent trimmers, 65
      light trimmers, 65
      pinking or scalloping
        shears, 65
      sewing and
        embroidery, 65
  marking, 65, 120
    chalk, 65
    dressmaker's carbon
      paper, 65
    tracing wheel, 65
  measuring, 64
    hem gauge, 64
    ruler, 64
    skirt marker, 65
    tape measure, 64
    yardstick, 64
  miscellaneous, 67
    beater, 172
    bodkin, 67
    clapper, 172
    dress form, 67
    loop-turner, 67

    needle-threader, 67
    point-presser, 67
    pounding block, 172
  pressing, 67, 157
    ham, 67
    iron, 67
    ironing board, 67
    press cloth, 67
    pressing mitt, 172
    sleeve-board, 67
    tailor board, 172
    velvet board, 75
  sewing, 66
    emery bag, 66
    needles, 66, 195, 196
      betweens, 195, 174,
        185
      calyx-eyed sharps,
        195
      crewel or embroidery,
        195
      machine, 195, 196
      milliners, 195
      sharps, 195
    pincushion, 66
    pins, 66
    sewing machine, 66, 114
      straight stitch, 66
      zigzag stitch, 66
    thimble, 66, 97
Even basting, 20
Extended facing, 80, 81, 108,
  110, 111, 181
Eyelets, 22, 46

F

Fabric finishes, 69, 93
Fabric loops, 22, 40
  belt carrier, 22
  concealed button loops,
    42
  decorative button loops,
    40, 41
FABRICS, 68
  bonded fabrics, 72
  brocade, 112
  buying, 70
  China silk, 18, 112
  cotton, 68, 150, 158
  crepe, 112
  drip-dry, see Wash-and-
    wear, 78
  fabric construction, 68

  knitted fabrics, 69
  lace and net, 69
  non-woven fabrics, 69
  woven fabrics, 68
  fake fur, 72
  finishes, 69, 93
  handling the different,
    72
  interfacing fabrics, 108,
    109
  knits, 73
  labels, 70
  lace, 74
  lawn, 18, 109
  linen, 68, 157, 158
  muslin, 109
  napped fabrics, 51, 70
  organdy, 109
  organza, 18
  pile fabrics, 75
  plaids and stripes, 54
  preparing for use, 71
    shrinking, 71
    straightening, 71
  rayon, 70, 150, 158
  satin, 70, 112
  sheer fabrics, 76
  silk, 68, 112, 150, 158
  stretch fabrics, 76
  synthetics, 68, 150, 157
  taffeta, 18, 112
  vinyl, 77
  wash-and-wear, 78
  wool, 68, 150, 158
  See also: CUTTING, 50
    GRAIN, 92
    MACHINE-STITCHING, 114
    MARKING, 120
    PRESSING, 157
    THREAD AND
      NEEDLES, 194
Faced hem, **104,** 98, 102
Faced placket, 148
FACINGS, 80
  bias, 80, 85
  buttonholes, 38
  extended, 80, 81, 108, 110,
    111, 181
  fake fur, 73
  fastening the facing, 84
  fitted, 80, 81, 180
  in washable garments, 111
  lace, 75
  neck facing at zipper
    placket, 208

processing the seams, 82
scalloped edge facing, 86
separate, 80, 81, 180
shaped, 80, 81, 180
step-by-step demonstration
    of shaped neck
    facing, 86
turned to right side, 85
understitching, 84
vinyl, 78
Fake fur, 72
FASTENERS, 88
    buttonholes, 32
    button loops, 40
    buttons, 42
    corded frogs, 41
    corded loops, 40
    fabric loops, 22, 42
    hooks and eyes, 88
    lingerie strap holders, 125
    snaps, 88
    thread loops, 197
    zippers, 202, 126
Fastening facing, 84
Feather stitch, 58
Fibers, 68
Figure types and sizes,
    127-131
Filling, 92
Final pressing, 158
Finishing off thread ends
    hand-sewing, 97
    machine-sewing, 117
Fitted facing, 80, 81, 180
FITTING A GARMENT, 89, 179,
    183
Flared hemline, 98, 99, 100
Flat felled seam, 161
Flat hemming, 101
Flat tubing, 30
Folding fabric for cutting, 52
French binding, 28
French knot, 58
French seam, 161
French tacks, 198
Fringe, 59
Frogs, 41

G

Gaping neckline, 90, 144
GATHERS, 91
    by hand, 91, 97
    by machine, 91

pressing, 91
Glacé finish, 194
Gloves, repairing, 166
Gold chain weight, 126
Gored hemline, 98, 99, 100
Grading seams, **83**, 47, 48,
    85
GRAIN IN FABRIC, 92
    bias, 25
    crosswise grain, 92
    cutting, 53
    effects of fabric finishes,
        70, 93
    grain and the human
        figure, 92
    knits, 69
    lace and net, 69
    lengthwise grain, 92
    non-woven fabrics, 69
Grain line, 50, 53, 135
Grain-perfection, 69
Grosgrain ribbon, 209
Grosgrain belting, 200, 201
GUSSETS, 93
    gusset pattern, 94
    reinforcing point of slash,
        94

H

Hair canvas, 109, 171
Half backstitch, 97
Ham, **67**, 56, 163
Hand embroidery, 58
    appliqué, 57
    blanket stitch, 58
    chain stitch, 58
    cross stitch, 58
    feather stitch, 58
    French knot, 58
    herringbone stitch, 58
    lazy daisy stitch, 58
    outline stitch, 58
    satin stitch, 58
    stem stitch, 58
Handling the different
    fabrics, 72
Hand pad-stitching, 185
HAND-SEWING, 96
    backstitch, 97
    bar tacks, 198
    basting, 19
    belt carriers, 198
    blind-stitch, 101

catch-stitch, 101
diagonal basting, 21
even basting, 20
finishing off, 96, 97
French tacks, 198
half backstitch, 97
hand-worked buttonhole,
    38
hems, 101
motions of hand-sewing,
    97
overcasting, 160
prick-stitch, 214
running stitch, 97
securing thread ends, 96,
    97
sewing on buttons, 43
slip-basting, 20
slipstitch, 101
thread and needles, 195,
    196
thread eye, 197
thread loops, 197
zipper application, 214
Hand-sewing needles, **195,**
    174, 185
Hand-tailoring, 171, 185
Heading at a casing, 45
Heavy Duty mercerized
    sewing thread, **194,** 43 196
Hem gauge, 64
Hemline, **99,** 12
Hemmed patch, 169
Hem marker, 99
HEMS, 98
    chainstitched, removal
        of, 12
    edge-stitched hem, 98, 104
    faced hem, 98, 104
    flat hemming, 101
    hand-rolled hem, 98, 104
    hem in a coat, 106, 190,
        191
    hem in a pleat, 106
    hem with seam binding,
        98, 102
    horsehair braid, 105
    inside hemming, 101
    interfacing, 173, 191
    machine-finished hem, 103
    marking the hemline, 99
    pressing, 99, 100
    reducing fullness in a
        curved hem, 100
    removal of, 12

repairing, 166
rolled hem, 104
simplified rolled hem, 104
stitches used, 101
    blind-stitch, 101
    catch-stitch, 101
    slipstitch, 101
    tailor's hem, 98, 102
    turned-and-stitched hem,
        98, 103
See also: FABRICS,
    Handling the different,
    72
Herringbone stitch, 58
Hidden zipper, **212, 213,** 126,
    202, 203, 214
    application with special
        zipper foot, 212
    Application with regular
        zipper foot, 213
Hinged zipper foot, 204
Hooks and Eyes, **125,** 88
Horsehair braid, 105, 125

I

Imaginative mending, 165
Inserting sleeve in garment,
    162
INTERFACING, 108, 171, 173,
    179
    applying interfacing, 110,
        111, 180, 181, 182, 183
    buttonhole reinforcement,
        33
    collar, 47, 48
    cuffs, 50
    cutting, 110
    extended facing, 111, 181
    fitted facing, shaped facing,
        110, 180
    interfacing fabrics, 108,
        109, 173
    marking, 110
    pockets, 155
    separate facing, 110, 180
    shaped facing, 110, 180
    trimming, 110, 190
    washable garments, 111
    See also: FABRICS,
        Handling the different,
        72
Interfacing without a
    pattern, 110

Interfacing in hems, 173, 191
Interlining, 174
Inverted pleats, 149
Invisible zipper, see Hidden zipper
Iron, 67
Ironing board, 67
Iron-on interfacing, 109
Iron-on mending, 165
Irregular designs, 70
Irregular or skipped stitches, 117

J

Jersey, **74,** 69
Joining bias strips, 27

K

Kick pleat, **152,** 106
Kimono sleeve, 162
  with gusset, 93
  with reinforced seam, 163, 165
Knife pleats, 149
Knits, **73,** 69
Knotted fringe, 59

L

Lace edging or insertion, 59
Lace fabric, 69, 74
Lamb's wool, **191**
Lapel, 80, 181, 183, 187
Lapped zipper application, 202, 205, 206, 207, 209
Large printed designs, 54
Lawn, 18, 109
Layering, see Grading, 83
Laying out the pattern, 51
  circle pattern layout, 51
  pinning pattern to fabric, 53
  position grainline, 53
  pressing the pattern, 50
  trial layout, 54
Layouts of fabric for cutting, 52
Lazy daisy stitch, 58

Lead weight by the yard, 126
Lengthening a garment
  finished garment, 12
  pattern, 137, 138, 139
Length of zipper, 203
Lengthwise grain, **92,** 69, 72, 93
Letting out a garment
  finished garment, 13
  pattern, 140, 141, 143
Light trimmers, 65
Linens, 68, 157, 158
Lingerie strap holders, 125
LINING, 112, 173, 192
  See also: FABRICS, Handling the different, 72
Lining a garment without pattern, 112
Loop-turner, 30, 67

M

Machine appliqué, 57
Machine-basting, 21
Machine-finished bias binding, 28
Machine-finished hem, 103
Machine needles, 195, 196
Machine pad-stitching, 186
Machine-quilting, 60
MACHINE-STITCHING, 114
  balanced stitch, 116
  basting, 118
  check-list for trouble spots, 117
  directional stitching, 118
  ease-stitch, 118
  edge-stitching, 118
  gathering, **118,** 91
  plain stitching, 118
  pressure, 115
  ripping out stitches, 119
  starting and ending stitching, 117
  stay-stitching, 118, 119
  tension, 116
  test seam, 116
  thread and needle to suit fabric, 166
  topstitching, **118,** 60
  understitching, 84
  See also: DECORATION, 60
  FABRICS, Handling *the*

different, 72
SEAMS AND SEAM FINISHES, 158
Machine stuck, 117
Machine-tailoring, 171, 182, 186
Man-tailoring, 171
MARKING, 120, 177
  how to mark, 121
    baste-mark, **123,** 35, 177
    chalk, 123
    clip mark, **46,** 55
    pin marking, 123
    tailor's tacks, 122, 177
    tracing paper and wheel, 121
  marking hems, 99
  tools, 65
  what to mark, 120
  See also: FABRICS, Handling the different, 72
Measuring
  equipment, 64
  personal measurements, how to take, 132
  your pattern, 133
Mending, 164
Mercerization, 194
Mercerized Best Cord, **194,** 43, 196
Mercerized Sewing Thread, **194,** 43, 196
Metal teeth, 126, 203
Metal zippers, 126, 203
Milliners needles, 195
Mitering corners, **155,** 29
Muslin, 109, 173
Muslin basic, 145, 173

N

Nap, 69, 70
  purchasing fabric yardage, 70
  selecting your layout, 51
    with nap, 51
    without nap, 51
Natural fibers, 68
Neckline alterations, 90, 144, 145
Neck facing
  step-by-step demonstration, 86

zipper placket, 208
Neck zipper, **207,** 126, 211
Needle and thread chart, 196
Needle breakage, 117
Needles, **195,** 66, 196
  betweens, **195,** 174, 185
  calyx-eyed sharps, 195
  crewel or embroidery, 195
  machine, 195, 196
  milliners, 195
  sharps, 195
Needle-threader, 67
Non-woven fabrics, 69
Non-woven interfacing fabrics, 109
Notches in cutting, 54
  matching plaids and stripes, 54
NOTIONS, 124
  belt buckles, **124,** 21
  belting, **124,** 23, 200
  bias hem facing, **124,** 104
  bias tape, **124,** 26
  boning, 125
  buttons, 42, 125
  cable cord, 125
  corded piping, **124,** 31
  elastic, **125,** 45, 46
  for Wash-and-wear, 79
  hooks and eyes, **125,** 88
  horsehair braid, **125,** 105
  lingerie strap holders, 125
  seam binding, **125,** 98, 102
  shoulder pads, **125,** 79
  snaps
    hammer-on, 126
    sew-on, **126,** 88
  stays, 125
  twill tape, 126, 174
  weights, 126
  wide bias tape, **124,** 26
  zippers, **202,** 126
Nylon jersey, 74

O

Off-grain, 78, 93, 118, 119
One-piece collar, 48
One-way design, 70
Opening in a casing, 46
Organdy, 109
Organza, 18

Outline stitch, 58
Overcast, 81, 160

P

Packaged bias tape, 26, 124
  double fold, **124,** 28
  single fold **124,** 28
Packaged corded piping,
  31, 124
Pad-stitching, 171, 185
  by hand, 185
  by machine, 186
  lapel, 187
Patch buttonhole, 36
Patches, 168, 169, 170
Pattern brands, 127
Pattern markings, 120
  construction details, 120
  position marks, 120
Pattern primer, **51,** 15
PATTERNS, 127
  alterations, 134
    basic how-to's, 135
    darts, lowering and
      raising
        bust, 139
        sleeve, 140
    length, shortening and
      lengthening
        bodice, 137
        skirt, 138
        sleeve, 138
    neckline, 144, 145
    sleeveless armhole, 144
    width, reducing and
      increasing
        bust, 141
        hip, 140
        sleeve, 143
        waist, 140
  arranging pattern pieces
    for cutting, 53
  chart of types and sizes,
    130
  envelope, 8, 70, 203
  figure type, 128
  measuring your pattern,
    133
  muslin basic, 145
  personal measurements,
    how to take, 132
  size, 129, 130, 131
  See also: FABRICS, and

TAILORING
Permanent finishes, 93
Personal measurements,
  how to take, 132
Pierced buttons, 42, 43
Pile fabric, 75
Pin-basting, 19
Pincushion, 66
Pinked edge, **159,** 81, 102
Pinking shears, 65
Pin-marking, 123
Pinning for fitting, 19
Pinning pattern to fabric, 53
Pinning seams, 19
Pins, 66
Pin tucks, 199
Piped seam, 31
Piping, 31, 124
  corded, 31, 124
PLACKETS, 146
  continuous lap, 146
    in a seam, 146
    in a slash, 147
    faced placket in a slash,
      148
  See also: ZIPPERS, 202
Plaids, 54
  even, 54
  uneven, 54
Plain seam, 159
Plain stitching, 118
Plain weave, 68
Pleat with seam, **106,** 152
PLEATS, 149
  accordion, 150
  alteration in width, 150,
    151
  basting, 151
  box, 149
  commercial pleating, 152
  cutting, 150
  edge-stitched, 151
  inverted, 149
  kick pleat, 164
  knife, 149
  made from patterns, 150
  marking, 150
  pressing, 151
  side, 149
  simulated kick pleat, 152
  stitched-down, 151
POCKETS, 154
  bound, 155
  flap, 155
  hip, 155

  in a seam, 155
  patch, 155
    lined, 156
    unlined, 155
  repairing, 167
  welt, 155
Pointed collar, 47, 48
Point of dart, 55, 121
Point-presser, 67, 82, 178
Pompons, 60
Position marks, 120
Pounding block, 67, 172
Preparation for zipper
  application, 204
Preparation of fabric for
  cutting, 50
Press cloth, 67
  See also: FABRICS, Han-
    dling the different, 72
Presser foot, 115
PRESSING, 157, 178
  darts, 56
  eased seam, 63
  equipment, 67, 172
  faced edges, 84
  final pressing, 157, 158,
    191
  gathers, 91
  general rules, 157
  hems, 100
  pleats, 151
  seams, 159
  shirring, 91
  sleeve cap, 163
  standard fabrics, 158
  stitch-and-press, 157
  tissue pattern, 50
  underpressing, 82
  See also: FABRICS,
    Handling the different,
    72
  ZIPPERS, 202
Pressing ham, **67,** 56, 163,
  172
Pressing mitt, 172
Pressure, **115,** 77, 79
Preventive mending, 164
Prick-stitch, **214,** 97
Puckered seams, **117,** 78

Q

Quick rolled hem, see Simplified rolled hem, 104

Quick-topstitched binding,
  29
Quilting thread, 195, 60

R

Raglan sleeve, 162, 163, 165
Raveling, 159
Ravelly fabrics, 32, 81, 102,
  110, 160
Rayon, 70, 150, 158
Rayon bias seam binding,
  125, 28
  gussets, 95
  hem, 98, 102
  kimono sleeve, 163
Ready-made fringe, 59
Reducing bulk in seams, 80,
  82, 83, 190
Reducing fullness in curved
  hem, 100
Reinforced seam
  in kimono sleeve, 163,
    165
  in placket, 146
Reinforcing corners, 82
Reinforcing point of slash,
  94, 147
Released tucks, see Dart
  tucks, 199
Removal of basting, 20
  See also: ZIPPERS, 204
Replacing a zipper, 216
Reversible jacket zipper, 126
Rick rack, 60
Ripping out stitches, 119
Roll line, 184
Rolled hem, 104
Round collar, 47
Round lead weights, 126
Ruler, 64
Running stitch, 97

S

Saddle stitch, 60, 97
Sag in hemline, 99
Satin, 70, 112
Satin stitch, 58
Satin weave, 68
Scalloped edge, 86
Scalloping shears, 65
Scissors, 65

Seam allowances, 158
Seam binding, 125
  gusset, 95
  hem, 98, 102
  kimono sleeve, 163
SEAM FINISHES, 158
  bound edges, 160
  double stitched seam,
    160, 75
  overcast edges, 160
  pinked edges, 159
  stitched-and-pinked
    edge, 159
  stitched-and-turned
    edge, 160
  zigzagged edge, 160
Seam guide, 159
Seamlines, 158
Seam puckering, **117,** 78
SEAMS, 158
  clipping, 83
  corded, 31
  curved, 178
  fell or felled, 161
  flat felled, 161
  French, 161
  grading, 83
  pinning, 19
  piped, 31
  plain, 159
  pressing, 159
  stitching over tissue,
    74, 76, 77
  strengthening, 164
  topstitched, 160
  trimming, 83, 190
  welted, 161
  See also: FABRICS, Han-
    dling the different, 72
Securing thread-ends
  hand-sewing, 96, 97
  machine-sewing, 117
Self-filled tubing, **30,**
  40, 41, 44.
Self-fringe, 59
Selvage, **68,** 23, 52, 53,
  200, 209
Separate facing, 80, 81, 180
Separating zippers, **209,** 126
Sequins, 61
Set-in patch, 169
Set-in sleeve, 162
Sewing equipment, 64
Sewing guide, 159
Sewing machine, 66, 114

a clean machine,115
balanced stitch, 116
cabinet model, 66
check-list for trouble
  spots, 117
  irregular or skipped
    stitches, 117
  machine stuck, 117
  needle breakage, 117
  thread breakage, 117
portable model, 66
pressure, 115
straight stitch machine, 66
tension, 116
zigzag machine, 66
Sewing scissors, 65
Shank, 43
Shank buttons, 42, 43
Shaped facing, 80, 81, 180
Sharps (needles), 195
Shears, **65,** 54
Sheer fabric, 76
Shirring, 91
  by hand, 97
  by machine, 91
Shortening a garment
  finished garment, 12
  pattern, 137, 138, 139
Shoulder pads, **125,** 79
Shrinking, 71
Shrink-resistance, 70, 93
Side pleats, 149
Silicone finish, 194
Silk, 68, 112, 150, 158
Silk thread, 195
Simplified rolled hem, 104
Simulated kick pleat, 152
Single cutting line, 54
Single-fold bias tape, 124
Sizes, pattern, 129, 130, 131
Skirt alterations, 138, 140
Skirt lining, 112
Skirt marker, **65,** 99
Skirt with pleats, 149
Skirt zipper, **205,** 126, 211
Slash, 94, 147
Sleeve alterations, 138, 140,
  143
Sleeve board, 67
Sleeve cap, 162
SLEEVES, 162
  kimono, 163
  raglan, 163
  set-in, 162
  in a coat, 190, 191

Slip-basting, 20
Slip cover zipper, 126
Slipstitch, **101,** 57
Smocking, 61
  general rules, 62
  surface honeycomb
    stitch, 62
  trellis stitch, 62
Snaps
  covered, 192
  hammer-on, 126
  sew-on, **126,** 88
Standard body
  measurements, 130
Starting and ending
  stitching, 117
Stay-button, 43
Stays, 125
Stay-stitching, 118, 119
Stay-tape, **179,** 171, 174, 187
Stem stitch, 58
Stitch-and-press, 157
STITCH IN TIME, 164
Stitched-and-pinked edges,
  159
Stitched-and-turned edges,
  160
Stitched-down pleats, 151
Stitches used in hems, 101
  blind-stitch, 101
  catch-stitch, 101
  slipstitch, 101
Stitching, see MACHINE-
  STITCHING, 114
Stitching pace, 117
Stitching seams over tissue,
  74, 76, 77
Stitch length, 159, 196
Straight grain
  fabric, 71, 74, 78, 79
  pattern marking, 93
Straight of goods, 72, 74, 93
Straight stitching, 118
Straight stitch machine, 66
Straightening fabric, 71
Stretch fabric, 76
Stretching bias, 27
Stretch Lace, **125,** 102
Stripes, 54
  even, 54
  uneven, 54
Surface honeycomb stitch, 62
Swirling bias, 27
Synthetic thread, 195

Synthetic coils, 126, 203
Synthetics, 68, 150, 157
Synthetic zipper, 126, 203

T

Tacks
  arrowhead, 193
  bar tack, 198
  French tack, 198
  tailor's tacks, 122
Taffeta, 18, 112
Tailor basting, **175,** 181, 183
Tailor board, 172
Tailor's chalk, 65
TAILORING, 171
  hand-tailoring, 171, 179,
    185
  machine-tailoring, 171,
    179, 182, 186
Tailor's ham, see Pressing
  ham, 67
Tailor's hem, **102,** 98
Tailor's tacks, 122, 177
Taking in a garment
  finished garment, 13
  pattern, 140, 141, 142,
    143
Tape measure, 64
Tapering
  corners, 83
  darts, 55
Taping interfacing, 179, 187
Tassels, 60
Temporary finishes, 93
Tension, **116,** 77, 79
Test seam, 116
Thimble, 66, 97
THREAD, 194
  Best Cord thread, **194,**
    43, 196
  Button and Carpet thread,
    194, 43, 196
  buttonhole twist, **195,** 38
    60, 214
  chart, 196
  dressmaker's spool, 194
  Dual Duty thread, 195,
    196
  glacé finish, 194
  Heavy Duty mercerized
    sewing thread, **194,** 43,
    196
  mercerization, 194
  Mercerized Best Cord

thread, **194,** 43, 196
Mercerized Sewing thread, **194,** 43, 196
Quilting thread, **195,** 60
silicone finish, 194
silk thread, 195
synthetic thread, 195
Thread basting, 20
Thread breakage, 117
Thread eye, 197
THREAD LOOPS, 197
  bar tack, **198,** 39, 148
  belt carrier, 198
  button loop, 197
  French tack, **198,** 107
  thread eye, 197
Topstitching, 118
  binding, 28, 29
  decoration, 60
  gussets, 95
  patches, 169
  pockets, 156
  seams, 160
Tracing paper, 121
Tracing wheel, 121
Trellis stitch, 62
Trial layout for cutting, 54
Tricot, 69
  as lining, 77
Trimming seams, 83
  waist seam, 204
Trouser zipper, 126
True bias, 25, 26
  See also: GRAIN IN FABRIC, 92
Tubing, 30, 58
  corded, 30
  flat, 30
  self-filled, 30
TUCKS, 199
  dart tucks, 199
  pin tucks, 199

Turned-and-stitched edges, 160
Turned-and-stitched hem, 103
Twill tape, 126, 174, 179, 187, 209
Twill weave, 68, 70, 92
Two-piece collar, 47
  with corners, 47
  with rounded edge, 47

U

Undercollar, 46, 47, 183
Underlining, 18
Underpressing, 82
Understitching, 84, 86
  facing turned to right side, 85
  facing turned to wrong side, 84
Uneven basting, 20, 123
Unit construction, 15

V

Velvet, 75
Velvet board, 75
Velveteen, 75
Vinyl, 77

W

WAISTBAND, 200
  grosgrain backed, 201
  regular, 200
  self-interfaced, 201
Waistline alterations
  finished garment, 12
  pattern, 140

Waistline seam, trimming, 204
Waistline stay, 209
Warp, 92
Washable garments, interfacing in, 111
Wash-in-wear fabric, 78
Weft, 92
Weights, 126
  gold chain weight, 126
  lead weight by the yard, 126
  round lead weights, 126
Welted seam, 161
Whipstitch, 46, 59, 106, 166
Wide bias tape, **124,** 28
With nap, 51, 54, 70
  See also: FABRICS, Handling the different, 72
Without nap, 51, 70
Woof, 92
Woolens, 68, 150, 158
Worked buttonholes, **38,** 32
  by hand, 38
  by machine, 39, 166
Woven fabrics, 68
Woven-in patch, 170
Woven interfacing fabrics, 109

Y

Yardage, **70,** 54
Yardstick, 64

Z

Zigzag machine, 66, 215
Zigzag stitch, 39, 57, 74, 160
Zipper applications, 202
  centered applications, 202, 211

hand finished, 214
hidden zipper, 212, 213, 214
invisible zipper, (see above)
lapped applications, 202
  dress side placket, 206
  neck placket, 207
  neck facing finishes, 208
  separating zipper, 209
  skirt placket, 205
preparation for, 204
replacing a zipper, 216
simulated hand finish, 215
zipper strain, eliminating, 209
Zipper chain, 203
Zipper foot, **204,** 66, 103
ZIPPERS, 202, 164
  blue jean zipper, 126
  care of zippers, 203
  dress zipper, 126, 206
  hidden zipper, **212, 213,** 126, 202, 203, 214
  invisible zipper, (see above)
  length of zipper, 203
  metal zippers, 126, 203
  neck zipper, 126, 207
  reversible jacket zipper, 126
  separating zippers, 126, 209
  skirt zipper, 126, 205
  slip cover zipper, 126
  synthetic zipper, **203,** 126
  trouser zipper, 126